James L. Watkins

The cost of cotton production

James L. Watkins

The cost of cotton production

ISBN/EAN: 9783337775315

Printed in Europe, USA, Canada, Australia, Japan

Cover: Foto ©ninafisch / pixelio.de

More available books at **www.hansebooks.com**

Miscellaneous Series.—Bulletin No. 16.

U. S. DEPARTMENT OF AGRICULTURE.

DIVISION OF STATISTICS.

THE COST OF COTTON PRODUCTION.

PREPARED UNDER THE DIRECTION OF

JOHN HYDE,

STATISTICIAN,

BY

JAMES L. WATKINS,

DIVISION OF STATISTICS.

WASHINGTON:
GOVERNMENT PRINTING OFFICE.
1899.

LETTER OF TRANSMITTAL.

U. S. DEPARTMENT OF AGRICULTURE,
OFFICE OF THE STATISTICIAN,
Washington, D. C., December 31, 1898.

SIR: I have the honor to transmit herewith a report on the cost of cotton production in the United States, prepared by Mr. James L. Watkins, of this Division, and respectfully recommend its publication as Bulletin No. 16, Miscellaneous Series, Division of Statistics.

Respectfully,

JOHN HYDE, *Statistician.*

Hon. JAMES WILSON,
Secretary of Agriculture.

CONTENTS.

THE COST OF COTTON PRODUCTION.

INTRODUCTION.

So much depends upon many elements difficult to calculate—upon the quality of the soil cultivated, the thrift of the planter, the efficiency of the labor, the character of the seasons, and the condition of the market—that any investigation into the cost of cotton production, even when confined within the narrowest limits, must be conducted with the utmost care.

The rich alluvial bottoms of the Mississippi and the fresh black prairie lands of Texas, with an expenditure of less labor than that given to the arid uplands of the Carolinas and Georgia, will yield more abundant crops. The planter practicing the most prudent economy in the conduct of his plantation and the laborer giving the most unremitting toil to the cultivation of his crop must surely enjoy greater returns than the planter who is extravagant or the laborer who is slothful. And yet, however economical the planter or industrious the laborer, he can not successfully combat a long continued drought or the swarm of insects that may ravage his fields. So that it may be fairly contended that the cost of cotton production will differ one year with another, contingent as it must be upon such varying conditions. Moreover, the law of supply and demand, when the crop is most abundant, may set so low a price upon his product as to cut off all profit, if not result in actual loss.

There are three classes of planters engaged in cotton cultivation, namely: owners of the land, renters, who pay a money rental, and share-croppers, who cultivate the land for a share of the crop. In the ten principal cotton States, according to the census of 1890, there were 57 per cent of the first class, 15 per cent of the second, and 28 per cent of the third. Although more than half the plantations are cultivated by their owners, it appears that but a small proportion of them are in the habit of keeping accounts, and of the renters and share croppers who do so the number must be insignificant. Therefore one of the chief difficulties encountered in investigating the cost of cotton production has been to obtain sufficient information from all three classes so that each may be fairly represented.

During the summer of 1897 several thousand circulars were sent by this Department to planters living in counties producing 400 or more bales of cotton, the names being selected at random from a list on file in the Department, and as far as possible from different sections of each county. Estimates were received from 3,846 planters in 717 counties, and of this number 400 were rejected either on account of incompleteness, manifest errors, or dependence of the estimates upon experiments with 1 or 2 acres. None was rejected on account of high or low cost of cultivation, or high or low price of cotton. The returns show that the estimates were made by owners of the land, renters, and share croppers.

The circular sent out by the Department requested the planter to make an estimate of what it cost him, per acre, in 1896 to cultivate and market his cotton, basing that estimate upon the cost of his entire acreage planted in cotton.

The items of cost embraced in the circular were: Rent of land, cost of plowing, seed for planting, planting seed, fertilizers, distributing fertilizers, chopping (to stand), hoeing, picking, ginning and pressing, bagging and ties, marketing, repairing implements, and incidental expenses not described.

The items relating to the yield from 1 acre were: Number of pounds of lint produced, the price per pound realized, the number of bushels of seed produced, and the price per bushel realized.

AVERAGE COST OF PRODUCTION IN EACH STATE AND TERRITORY.

Table 1 is an exhibit of the average itemized cost of production, the ret rns, and net profit, in each State and Territory, upon 3,335 upland plantations, 2,659 of which reported a profit and 676 a loss, and upon 111 plantations producing sea-island cotton, 85 of which reported a profit and 26 a loss.

Included in the table is the average cost of picking cotton per 100 pounds, the cost of producing lint per pound in each State and Territory, and the averages of the same for all States and Territories; the number and per cent of plantations reporting profit and loss and the number of counties in each State and Territory from which reports were received. The small number of estimates from sea-island plantations is due to the comparatively small production of this variety of cotton.

The results of this investigation show that the average total cost of cultivation per acre on the 3,335 upland plantations is $15.42 and the average total return $19.03, the average net profit being $3.61 per acre. The average yield is 255.6 pounds of lint and 16 bushels of seed per acre, and the average price of lint 6.7 cents per pound and of seed 11.9 cents per bushel. The average cost of picking per 100 pounds is 44 cents and the average cost of producing lint cotton in all States and Territories is 5.27 cents per pound. Of the 3,335 plantations reporting from 705 counties, 80 per cent show a profit and 20 per cent a loss. The average total cost of cultivation on 111 sea-island plantations reporting is $21.95 and the average total return $28.65, the average net profit being $6.70 per acre. The average yield is 168.2 pounds of lint and 10.3 bushels of seed per acre, and the average price of lint

15.57 cents per pound and of seed 23.9 cents per bushel. The average cost of picking per 100 pounds is $1.03 and the average cost of producing lint cotton (sea-island) in South Carolina, Georgia, and Florida is 11.59 cents per pound. Of the 111 plantations reporting from 37 counties, 77 per cent show a profit and 23 per cent a loss.

TABLE 1.—*Average cost of producing an acre of cotton in 1896, by States and Territories.*

States and Territories.	Rent.	Plowing.	Seed.	Planting seed.	Fertilizers.	Distributing fertilizers.	Chopping and hoeing.	Picking.	Ginning and pressing.	Bagging and ties.	Marketing.	Repairing implements.	Other expenses.	TOTAL COST.
Upland.														
Alabama	$2.30	$2.90	$0.22	$0.25	$1.87	$0.24	$1.28	$2.90	$1.00	$0.54	$0.56	$0.39	$0.39	$14.93
Arkansas	3.00	2.88	.20	.29	.30	.08	1.54	3.24	1.13	.55	.67	.39	.29	14.56
Florida	1.55	2.73	.27	.40	1.99	.35	1.10	3.05	.98	.56	.57	.33	.39	14.27
Georgia	2.44	2.83	.23	.25	2.30	.23	1.21	2.91	.82	.54	.18	.40	.53	15.17
Indian Ter.	2.64	2.36	.16	.25	.01	(*a*)	1.58	4.08	1.49	.65	.68	.41	.28	14.59
Louisiana	3.17	3.01	.23	.28	.85	.13	1.72	4.36	1.38	.71	1.22	.52	.47	18.05
Mississippi	2.93	2.94	.22	.26	1.12	.18	1.42	3.57	1.16	.59	.74	.44	.45	16.02
Missouri	3.00	2.23	.20	.47	.66	.09	1.66	4.70	1.30	.84	.87	.33	.25	16.60
N. Carolina	3.76	3.00	.27	.31	2.77	.27	1.29	3.24	1.09	.63	.57	.37	.34	17.91
Oklahoma	1.84	1.38	.12	.27	.03	(*a*)	1.45	3.31	1.20	.60	.74	.25	.31	11.50
S. Carolina	2.88	2.74	.25	.24	3.05	.22	1.05	3.51	.99	.61	.53	.42	.47	16.96
Tennessee	3.09	2.83	.25	.31	.33	.11	1.42	3.53	1.13	.61	.53	.39	.45	14.98
Texas	3.03	2.56	.16	.30	.16	.05	1.10	3.37	1.11	.49	.52	.36	.39	13.60
Virginia	2.56	3.16	.27	.41	2.31	.22	.89	2.80	1.10	.60	1.01	.20	.34	16.05
Average	2.88	2.81	.21	.28	1.30	.16	1.31	3.37	1.08	.57	.64	.40	.41	15.42
Sea-island.														
Florida	2.10	3.68	.36	.48	2.62	.44	1.31	4.31	1.36	.62	.71	.42	.31	18.72
Georgia	2.68	4.17	.35	.37	3.14	.31	1.27	5.88	1.95	.60	.84	.35	.21	22.12
S. Carolina	3.09	2.58	.55	.51	7.48	.33	4.70	8.35	5.30	.62	2.08	.53	2.08	38.22
Average	2.36	3.65	.38	.46	3.35	.40	1.73	5.17	1.99	.62	.91	.42	.51	21.95

States and Territories.	Pounds of lint.	Price per pound.	Bushels of seed.	Price per bushel.	TOTAL RETURN.	Net profit.	Cost of picking per 100 pounds.	Cost of producing lint, per pound.	Number of plantations reporting. Profit.	Number of plantations reporting. Loss.	Number of plantations reporting. Total.	Per cent of plantations reporting. Profit.	Per cent of plantations reporting. Loss.	Number of counties reporting.
Upland.		*Cents.*		*Cents.*				*Cents.*						
Alabama	242.0	6.69	15.0	12.6	$18.08	$3.15	$0.40	5.38	270	80	350	77	23	64
Arkansas	231.6	6.46	14.6	10.8	16.54	1.98	.47	5.61	220	117	337	65	35	73
Florida	230.7	6.70	14.8	13.0	17.38	3.11	.44	5.35	40	13	53	75	25	27
Georgia	252.0	6.73	15.7	12.8	19.42	4.25	.39	5.23	473	72	545	87	13	123
Indian Ter.	255.2	6.45	16.1	10.6	18.17	3.58	.53	5.05	43	15	58	74	26	5
Louisiana	316.6	6.67	20.0	11.0	23.32	5.27	.46	5.01	251	77	328	77	23	47
Mississippi	266.0	6.74	16.9	10.2	19.65	3.63	.45	5.36	267	55	322	83	17	72
Missouri	285.3	6.42	18.3	11.9	20.49	3.89	.55	5.06	8	3	11	73	27	8
N. Carolina	289.4	6.96	18.1	12.8	22.46	4.55	.37	5.39	265	39	304	87	13	59
Oklahoma	208.8	6.72	13.2	12.4	15.67	4.17	.53	4.72	28	6	34	82	18	11
S. Carolina	294.5	6.94	18.2	14.4	23.06	6.10	.40	4.87	173	8	181	96	4	37
Tennessee	251.6	6.63	16.4	10.7	18.44	3.46	.47	5.26	95	16	111	86	14	33
Texas	222.1	6.63	13.9	11.9	16.38	2.78	.51	5.38	512	171	683	75	25	141
Virginia	259.3	6.90	16.2	12.7	19.95	3.90	.36	5.40	14	4	18	78	22	5
Average	255.6	6.70	16.0	11.9	19.03	3.61	.44	5.27	2,659	676	3,335	80	20	705
Sea island.														
Florida	148.0	14.28	9.2	24.0	23.34	4.62	.97	11.13	51	21	72	71	29	19
Georgia	199.9	12.72	10.7	20.1	27.58	5.46	.98	9.99	20	5	25	80	20	15
S. Carolina	213.6	27.29	15.0	30.1	63.32	25.10	1.30	15.78	14	0	14	100	0	3
Average	168.2	15.57	10.3	23.9	28.65	6.70	1.03	11.59	85	26	111	77	23	37

a No fertilizers used.

PLANTATIONS SHOWING A PROFIT.

Table 2 shows the average itemized cost of production, returns, and profit, in each State and Territory on 2,659 upland and 85 sea-island plantations reporting a profit only.

Included in the table is the cost of picking cotton per 100 pounds, the cost of producing lint per pound in each State and Territory, and the averages of the same for all States and Territories; also the number of plantations reporting.

The average total cost of cultivation on the 2,659 upland plantations showing a profit is $15.60, and the average total return $20.80, leaving an average profit of $5.20 per acre. The average yield is 275.9 pounds of lint and 17.3 bushels of seed per acre, and the average price of lint 6.78 cents per pound and of seed 12 cents per bushel. The average cost of picking per 100 pounds is 43 cents, and the average cost of producing lint in all States and Territories 4.90 cents per pound.

The average total cost of cultivation on all sea-island plantations reporting a profit is $23.02, and the average total return $33.97, leaving an average profit of $10.95 per acre. The average yield is 186 pounds of lint and 11.3 bushels of seed per acre, and the average price of lint 16.41 cents per pound and of seed 24.8 cents per bushel. The average cost of picking sea-island cotton per 100 pounds in the States producing it is 99 cents, and the average cost of producing lint 10.87 cents per pound.

TABLE 2.—*Average cost of producing an acre of cotton in 1896 on farms showing a profit, by States and Territories.*

States and Territories.	Rent.	Plowing.	Seed.	Planting seed.	Fertilizers.	Distributing fertilizers.	Chopping and hoeing.	Picking.	Ginning and pressing.	Bagging and ties.	Marketing.	Repairing implements.	Other expenses.	TOTAL COST.
Upland.														
Alabama	$2.32	$2.84	$0.22	$0.25	$1.82	$0.23	$1.24	$3.04	$1.05	$0.56	$0.57	$0.37	$0.37	$14.88
Arkansas	3.06	2.53	.20	.29	.29	.07	1.48	3.64	1.23	.59	.73	.38	.30	14.79
Florida	1.55	2.58	.30	.42	2.03	.38	1.11	3.35	1.06	.60	.52	.30	.35	14.59
Georgia	2.44	2.72	.22	.25	2.33	.23	1.19	2.99	.84	.55	.49	.39	.51	15.15
Indian Territory	2.03	2.26	.15	.22	(a)	(a)	1.58	4.03	1.64	.71	.73	.42	.29	15.26
Louisiana	3.35	2.91	.24	.28	.81	.12	1.75	4.85	1.52	.77	1.30	.55	.52	18.97
Mississippi	2.98	2.87	.21	.26	1.08	.17	1.40	3.70	1.20	.61	.73	.42	.44	16.07
Missouri	3.12	1.91	.22	.43	.66	.06	1.59	5.15	1.38	.82	.76	.32	.29	16.71
North Carolina	3.75	2.96	.26	.31	2.77	.26	1.24	3.30	1.12	.64	.57	.37	.35	17.90
Oklahoma	1.80	1.14	.12	.26	.04	(b)	1.34	3.42	1.22	.57	.75	.21	.30	11.17
South Carolina	2.87	2.68	.25	.23	3.05	.21	1.04	3.57	1.00	.63	.53	.43	.48	16.97
Tennessee	3.15	2.68	.23	.31	.30	.11	1.40	3.61	1.17	.64	.50	.37	.46	14.93
Texas	3.09	2.34	.16	.29	.12	.04	1.03	3.61	1.20	.53	.50	.33	.42	13.66
Virginia	2.46	2.82	.26	.43	2.16	.19	.76	2.88	.72	1.10	1.21	.34	.41	15.74
Average	2.91	2.67	.21	.28	1.36	.16	1.27	3.55	1.13	.60	.64	.39	.43	15.60
Sea-island.														
Florida	2.23	3.68	.36	.49	2.81	.45	1.25	4.58	1.51	.66	.56	.36	.26	19.20
Georgia	2.80	4.06	.30	.36	3.13	.32	1.30	5.99	1.96	.60	.83	.31	.18	22.14
South Carolina	3.09	2.58	.55	.51	7.48	.33	4.70	8.35	5.30	.63	2.09	.53	2.08	28.22
Average	2.50	3.59	.38	.46	3.66	.40	1.83	5.53	2.24	.64	.88	.37	.54	23.02

a No fertilizers used. *b* Cost trifling.

TABLE 2.—*Average cost of producing an acre of cotton in 1896 on farms showing a profit, by States and Territories*—Continued.

States and Territories.	Pounds of lint.	Price per pound.	Bushels of seed.	Price per bushel.	TOTAL RETURN.	PROFIT.	Number of farms reporting.	Cost of picking per 100 pounds.	Cost of production per pound.
Upland.		*Cents.*		*Cents*				*Cents.*	*Cents.*
Alabama	261.1	6.72	16.2	12.6	$19.63	$4.75	270	.39	4.92
Arkansas	266.0	6.52	16.6	10.9	19.22	4.43	220	.46	4.88
Florida	252 7	6.80	16.3	13.1	19.39	4.80	40	.44	4.93
Georgia	262.1	6.93	16.3	12.8	20.24	5.09	473	.38	4.98
Indian Territory	291.3	6.51	18.1	10.4	20.82	5.56	43	.53	4.59
Louisiana	358.6	6.75	22.7	10.7	26.80	7.83	251	.45	4.61
Mississippi	281.1	6.79	17.9	10.2	20.96	4.89	207	.44	5.07
Missouri	318.5	6.26	20.1	12 2	22.45	5.74	8	.54	4.48
North Carolina	300.6	6.98	18.8	12.8	23.42	5.52	265	.37	5.15
Oklahoma	220.5	6.75	14.0	12.7	16.61	5.44	28	.52	4.26
South Carolina	298.9	6.95	18.5	14.4	23.40	6.43	173	.40	4.79
Tennessee	262.8	6.63	17.0	10.7	19.30	4.37	95	.46	4.99
Texas	242.1	6.67	15.1	12.1	17.94	4.28	512	.50	4.89
Virginia	281.4	6.88	17.3	13.0	21.57	5.83	14	.34	4.79
Average	275.9	6.78	17.3	12.0	20.80	5.20	2,659	.43	4.90
Sea-island.									
Florida	168.9	14.74	10.2	25.1	27.60	8.40	51	.90	9.85
Georgia	210.3	13.05	11.4	20.5	29.68	7.54	20	.95	9.42
South Carolina	213.6	27.29	15.0	30.1	62.81	25.10	14	1.30	15.78
Average	186.0	16.41	11.3	24.8	33.97	10.95	85	.99	10.87

a No fertilizers used. *b* Cost trifling.

PLANTATIONS SHOWING A LOSS.

Table 3 shows the average itemized cost of production, returns, and loss, in each State and Territory on 676 upland and 26 sea-island producing plantations reporting a loss only.

Included in the table is the cost of picking cotton per 100 pounds, the cost of producing lint per pound in each State and Territory, and the averages of the same for all States and Territories; also, the number of plantations reporting.

The average total cost of cultivation on the 676 upland plantations showing a loss is $14.68 and the average total return, $12.70, leaving an average loss of $1.98 per acre. The average yield is 176 pounds of lint and 11.1 bushels of seed per acre, and the average price of lint 6.52 cents per pound and of seed 11.4 cents per bushel. The average cost of picking per 100 pounds is 49 cents, and the average cost of producing lint in all States and Territories 7.62 cents per pound. The average total cost of cultivation on the 26 sea-island plantations is $18.44 and the average total return $15.44, leaving an average loss of $3 per acre. The average yield is 110.1 pounds of lint and 7 bushels of seed per acre, and the average price of lint 12.85 cents per pound and of seed 20.9 cents per bushel. The average cost of picking sea-island cotton per 100 pounds in the States producing it is $1.21, and the average cost of producing lint 15.42 cents per pound.

TABLE 3.—*Average cost of producing an acre of cotton in 1896 on farms showing a loss, by States and Territories.*

States and Territories.	Rent.	Plowing.	Seed.	Planting seed.	Fertilizers.	Distributing fertilizers.	Chopping and hoeing.	Picking.	Ginning and pressing.	Bagging and ties.	Marketing.	Repairing implements.	Other expenses.	TOTAL COST.
Upland.														
Alabama	$2.23	$3.48	$0.23	$0.25	$2.07	$0.26	$1.40	$2.41	$0.87	$0.47	$0.52	$0.45	$0.47	$15.11
Arkansas	2.87	3.55	.20	.31	.31	.09	1.64	2.49	.95	.46	.56	.43	.25	14.13
Florida	1.54	3.19	.16	.32	1.87	.28	1.06	2.14	.74	.44	.73	.40	.40	13.27
Georgia	2.48	3.53	.24	.28	2.09	.23	1.36	2.40	.71	.47	.43	.51	.65	15.38
Indian Territory	2.67	2.67	.19	.33	.00	.00	1.56	2.49	1.04	.50	.56	.39	.24	12.64
Louisiana	2.59	3.31	.21	.28	.99	.18	1.60	2.76	.94	.51	.92	.44	.30	15.03
Mississippi	2.64	3.30	.25	.29	1.35	.22	1.53	2.92	.94	.53	.77	.57	.45	15.76
Missouri	2.67	3.08	.17	.58	.67	.17	1.83	3.50	1.12	.87	1.15	.36	.13	16.30
North Carolina	3.84	3.31	.28	.30	2.77	.32	1.62	2.81	.92	.59	.58	.39	.27	18.00
Oklahoma	2.00	2.50	.13	.32	.00	.00	1.94	2.82	1.09	.70	.70	.46	.38	13.04
South Carolina	3.20	4.04	.27	.28	3.07	.33	1.14	2.34	.63	.31	.47	.45	.26	16.79
Tennessee	2.72	3.75	.31	.29	.51	.13	1.56	3.07	.89	.47	.68	.45	.41	15.24
Texas	2.86	3.23	.18	.32	.25	.09	1.30	2.67	.38	.84	.56	.45	.30	13.43
Virginia	2.88	4.38	.31	.38	2.81	.34	1.31	2.50	1.09	.59	.31	.15	.10	17.15
Average	2.72	3.38	.21	.30	1.07	.16	1.46	2.61	.88	.46	.61	.46	.36	14.68
Sea-island.														
Florida	1.80	3.69	.36	.48	2.13	.41	1.45	3.65	.50	1.00	1.08	.59	.44	17.58
Georgia	2.20	4.60	.54	.42	3.18	.30	1.12	5.45	1.93	.60	.86	.50	.34	22.04
Average	1.88	3.87	.39	.46	2.33	.39	1.30	4.00	1.18	.52	1.04	.57	.42	18.44

States and Territories.	Pounds of lint.	Price per pound.	Bushels of seed.	Price per bushel.	TOTAL RETURN.	Loss.	Number of farms reporting.	Cost of picking per 100 pounds.	Cost of production per pound.
Upland.		*Cents.*		*Cents.*				*Cents.*	*Cents.*
Alabama	177.5	6.62	11.2	12.6	$13.10	$2.00	80	.45	7.72
Arkansas	166.8	6.35	10.6	10.6	11.66	2.47	117	.50	7.80
Florida	163.1	6.43	10.1	12.0	11.69	1.58	13	.44	7.39
Georgia	186.0	6.78	11.5	12.9	14.05	1.33	72	.43	7.47
Indian Territory	151.7	6.27	16.2	11.1	10.60	2.04	15	.55	7.59
Louisiana	179.6	6.38	11.7	10.3	12.58	2.45	77	.51	7.70
Mississippi	194.6	6.48	12.2	10.3	13.81	1.95	55	.50	7.45
Missouri	196.7	6.83	13.7	10.8	14.62	1.68	3	.59	7.53
North Carolina	213.3	6.80	13.1	12.7	16.04	1.96	39	.44	7.66
Oklahoma	154.1	6.58	9.8	10.8	11.26	1.78	6	.61	7.78
South Carolina	199.5	6.71	12.6	14.8	15.27	1.52	8	.39	7.48
Tennessee	184.9	6.64	12.4	10.3	13.47	1.77	16	.55	7.55
Texas	162.5	6.50	10.2	11.3	11.66	1.77	171	.55	7.56
Virginia	181.8	7.00	12.0	11.5	14.15	3.00	4	.46	8.67
Average	176.0	6.52	11.1	11.4	12.70	1.98	676	.49	7.62
Sea-island.									
Florida	98.6	13.19	6.8	21.5	14.50	3.08	21	1.23	16.35
Georgia	158.6	11.40	8.0	18.4	19.37	2.67	5	1.15	12.97
Average	110.1	12.85	7.0	20.9	15.44	3.00	26	1.21	15.42

COMPARISON OF ITEMS OF COST ON PROFIT AND LOSS PLANTATIONS.

Of the 3,335 estimates of the cost of cotton production on upland plantations 676, or 20 per cent, and of the 111 on sea-island plantations 26, or 23 per cent, show a loss. The average profit and loss estimates are separated (in Tables 2 and 3) for the purpose of ascertaining as nearly as possible the causes of the losses.

Table 4 presents a comparison of each item of average cost on the profit and loss plantations, and shows the difference in cost, whether on the one side or the other, the sum of these differences, and the excesses expended in each State and Territory.

TABLE 4.—*Difference in each item of average cost of cultivation.*

States and Territories.	Plantations.	Rent.	Plowing.	Seed.	Planting seed.	Fertilizers.	Distributing fertilizers.	Chopping and hoeing.	Picking.
Upland.									
Alabama	Profit	$0.09			$0.00				$0.63
	Loss		$0.64	$0.01	.00	$0.25	$0.03	$0.16	
Arkansas	Profit	.19		.00					1.15
	Loss		1.02	.00	.02	.02	.02	.16	
Florida	Profit	.01		.14	.10	.16	.10	.05	1.21
	Loss		.61						
Georgia	Profit					.24	.00		.59
	Loss	.04	.81	.02	.03		.00	.17	
Indian Territory	Profit					.00	.00	.02	2.14
	Loss	.04	.41	.04	.11	.00	.00		
Louisiana	Profit	.76		.03	.00			.15	2.09
	Loss		.40		.00	.18	.06		
Mississippi	Profit	.34							.78
	Loss		.43	.04	.03	.27	.05	.13	
Missouri	Profit	.45		.05					1.65
	Loss		1.17		.15	.01	.11	.24	
North Carolina	Profit				.01	.00			.49
	Loss	.09	.35	.02		.00	.06	.38	
Oklahoma	Profit					.04	.00		.60
	Loss	.20	1.36	.01	.06		.00	.60	
South Carolina	Profit								1.23
	Loss	.33	1.36	.02	.05	.02	.12	.10	
Tennessee	Profit	.43			.02				.54
	Loss		1.07	.08		.21	.02	.16	
Texas	Profit	.23							.94
	Loss		.89	.02	.03	.13	.05	.27	
Virginia	Profit				.05				.38
	Loss	.42	1.56	.05		.65	.15	.55	
Average	Profit	.19		.00		.29	.00		.94
	Loss		.71	.00	.02		.00	.19	
Sea-island.									
Florida	Profit	.43		.00	.01	.68	.04		.93
	Loss		.01	.00				.20	
Georgia	Profit	.60					.02	.18	.54
	Loss		.54	.24	.06	.05			
Average	Profit	.62			.00	.33	.01	.44	1.53
	Loss		.28	.01	.00				
States and Territories.	**Plantations.**	**Ginning and pressing.**	**Bagging and ties.**	**Marketing.**	**Repairing implements.**	**Other expenses.**	**TOTAL.**	**Excess on profit plantations.**	**Excess on loss plantations.**
Upland.									
Alabama	Profit	$0.18	$0.09	$0.05			$0.09		
	Loss				$0.08	$0.10	1.27		$1.18
Arkansas	Profit	.28	.13	.17		.05	.24		
	Loss				.05		1.29		1.05
Florida	Profit	.32	.16				.56		
	Loss			.21	.10	.02	.73		.17
Georgia	Profit	.13	.08	.06			.24		
	Loss				.12	.14	1.33		1.09
Indian Territory	Profit	.60	.21	.17	.03	.05	.10		
	Loss						.60		.50
Louisiana	Profit	.58	.26	.38	.11	.22	1.27	$0.63	
	Loss						.64		
Mississippi	Profit	.26	.08				.34		
	Loss			.04	.15	.01	1.11		.77
Missouri	Profit	.26				.16	.66		
	Less		.05	.39	.04		1.72		1.06
North Carolina	Profit	.20	.05			.08	.09		
	Loss			.01	.02		.92		.83

TABLE 4.—*Difference in each item of average cost of cultivation*—Continued.

States and Territories.	Plantations.	Ginning and pressing.	Bagging and ties.	Marketing.	Repairing implements.	Other expenses.	TOTAL.	Excess on profit plantations.	Excess on loss plantations.
Upland—Continued.									
Oklahoma	Profit	$0.13		$0.05			$0.04		
	Loss		$0.13		$0.25	$0.08	2.56		$2.52
South Carolina	Profit	.37	.32	.06		.22	.22		
	Loss				.02		2.02		1.80
Tennessee	Profit	.28	.17			.05	.50		
	Loss			.18	.08		1.62		1.12
Texas	Profit	.82				.12	.35		
	Loss		.31	.06	.12		1.51		1.16
Virginia	Profit		.51	.90	.19	.31	.55		
	Loss	.37					3.38		2.83
Average	Profit	.25	.14	.03		.07	.55		
	Loss				.07		.99		.44
Sea-island.									
Florida	Profit	1.01					1.16	.54	
	Loss		.34	.52	.23	.18	.62		
Georgia	Profit	.03	.00				.80		
	Loss		.00	.03	.19	.16	1.24		.44
Average	Profit	1.06	.12			.12	1.52	1.03	
	Loss			.16	.20		.49		

It will be noticed that in some of the items there is quite a marked difference, and that this is especially true with reference to the cost of plowing, chopping, and hoeing, the difference, except in the case of upland plantations in Louisiana and sea-island in Florida, being on the side of plantations showing a loss. The difference in the cost of plowing ranges all the way from 35 cents in North Carolina to $1.56 in Virginia, and in chopping and hoeing from 15 cents in favor of the profit plantations in Louisiana to 60 cents on the loss side in Oklahoma, showing three cases of difference in the former to eleven in the latter.

On the other hand, the difference in the cost of picking, ginning, and pressing, bagging and ties, and marketing is still more marked, except in a few instances, on the side of plantations showing a profit. But this excess is not only naturally greater, because of the greater yield, but for the most part is greater in proportion to the yield. The difference in all other items of cost is comparatively small and in some instances inappreciable. The averages of profit plantations for sea-island cotton include South Carolina, where there are no losses reported, as well as Georgia and Florida.

If the cost of picking, ginning and pressing, bagging and ties, and marketing be left out, as they should be for the reasons above mentioned, the difference in the total cost of cultivation, with the exception of Louisiana, is on the side of plantations showing a loss, and ranges from 17 cents in Florida to $2.83 in Virginia, this difference, as already stated, being due mainly to the higher cost of plowing, chopping, and hoeing. In Louisiana the excess of 63 cents on the side of plantations showing a profit appears to be due to the higher cost of rent, chopping, and hoeing and incidental expenses.

The general average on all upland plantations shows a difference of 44 cents on the side of plantations sustaining a loss, due to the higher cost of plowing, chopping, and hoeing.

In the case of sea-island cotton, if the cost of picking, ginning and pressing, bagging and ties be left out, the total difference in the cost of all other items is 54 cents on the side of profit plantations in Florida, and 44 cents on the side of loss plantations in Georgia. In Florida the difference is due to the higher cost of rent and fertilizers, and in Georgia chiefly to the higher cost of plowing and seeding. The general average on all sea-island plantations, including South Carolina, which reported no losses, shows a difference of $1.03 on the side of profit plantations, due to higher cost of rent, fertilizers, chopping, and hoeing.

CAUSES OF LOSSES.

The cause of the losses sustained on the 676 upland and 26 sea-island plantations is due mainly to the smaller yield, and only in part to the higher cost of cultivation; for, notwithstanding the higher cost, if the yield on the loss plantations were as great as on the profit plantations there would still be a profit in each State and Territory, as shown in Table 5. Take the State of Alabama, for instance. The yield on the profit plantations is 83.6 pounds greater than on the loss plantations and its value is $5.59. If the excess in cost of cultivation on the loss plantations, which is $1.18, is deducted from this value there would be a profit of $4.41.

A similar result is obtained for each State and Territory, except that in Louisiana upland and in Florida sea-island plantations, where the cost of cultivation was greater on plantations yielding a profit, the difference is added instead of subtracted. This shows that the principal cause of the losses is the small yield rather than any difference in the cost of cultivation.

Table 5 also gives the number of additional pounds of lint required to be produced on the loss plantations in order to equalize or offset all losses, and the total number of pounds of lint required to be produced in each State and Territory to prevent a loss. Of course, this applies only when the average cost of cultivation and price of lint are the same as in 1896.

TABLE 5.—*Excess in yield, value of same, and yield required to prevent loss.*

States and Territories.	Difference in yield (lint).			Excess in cost.		Value of excess in return.			Yield required to prevent loss.		
	Yield on profit plantations.	Yield on loss plantations.	Excess on profit plantations.	Excess on profit plantations.	Excess on loss plantations.	Average price of lint per pound.	Value of excess in yield.	Value less excess in cost.	Yield on loss plantations.	Additional yield required to prevent loss.	Total yield required to prevent loss.
Upland.	*Lbs.*	*Lbs.*	*Lbs.*			*Cents.*			*Lbs.*	*Lbs.*	*Lbs.*
Alabama	261.1	177.5	83.6	....	$1.18	6.60	$5.59	....	177.5	30.2	207.7
Arkansas	266.0	166.8	99.2	....	1.05	6.46	6.41	$5.36	166.8	38.9	205.7
Florida	252.7	163.1	89.6	....	.17	6.70	6.00	5.83	163.1	24.6	187.7
Georgia	262.1	186.0	76.1	....	1.09	6.73	5.12	4.03	186.0	19.6	205.6
Indian Territory	291.3	151.7	139.6	....	.50	6.45	9.00	8.50	151.7	32.5	184.2
Louisiana	358.6	179.6	179.0	$0.63	....	6.67	11.94	12.57	179.6	38.4	218.0
Mississippi	281.1	194.6	86.5	....	.77	6.74	5.83	5.06	194.6	30.1	224.7
Missouri	318.5	196.7	121.8	....	1.06	6.42	7.82	6.76	196.7	24.6	221.3
North Carolina	300.6	213.3	87.3	....	.83	6.96	6.08	5.25	213.3	28.8	242.1
Oklahoma	220.5	154.1	66.4	....	2.52	6.72	4.46	1.94	154.1	27.1	181.2
South Carolina	298.9	199.5	99.4	....	1.80	6.94	6.90	5.10	199.5	22.7	222.2
Tennessee	262.8	184.9	77.9	....	1.12	6.63	5.16	4.04	184.9	26.7	211.6
Texas	242.1	162.5	79.6	....	1.16	6.63	5.28	4.12	162.5	27.2	189.7
Virginia	281.4	181.8	99.6	....	2.83	6.90	6.87	4.04	181.8	42.9	224.7
Average	275.9	176.0	99.9	....	.44	6.70	6.69	6.25	176.0	30.4	206.4
Sea-island.											
Florida	168.9	98.6	70.3	.54	....	14.28	10.04	10.58	98.6	23.4	122.0
Georgia	210.3	158.6	51.7	....	.44	12.72	6.58	6.14	158.6	23.4	182.0
South Carolina	213.6	....	....	....	....	27.29	....	....	....	....	140.1
Average	186.0	110.1	75.9	1.03	....	15.57	11.82	....	110.1	23.4	133.5

RANGE IN COST OF CULTIVATION AND PRODUCTION.

As already stated, none of the estimates furnished to the Department in this investigation was rejected on account of the high or low cost of cultivation, or the high or low prices realized. The estimates were rejected when the errors could not be remedied, or where based upon experiments with only one or two acres, or, in a few instances, where the yield was so small as to amount to a failure of the crop.

Table 6 shows the lowest and highest charge for each item in the cost of cultivation, the lowest and highest yield, and price per pound, cost of picking per 100 pounds, and cost of production per pound in each State and Territory. It must be borne in mind, however, that the extremely low and high charges shown in this table are individual instances, and do not often occur. That they are frequently unreasonable must be admitted, but when all other charges seemed reasonable and the estimates otherwise intelligently made up, the fairest method of dealing with the investigation seemed to be to accept them all, no matter to what extremes the planter might seem to go in making up his estimate.

RENT.

The lowest charge for rent of land on upland plantations is 40 cents in Florida, while in Alabama, Arkansas, Georgia, and Texas it is as low as 50 cents per acre. The highest charge is $11.25 in Louisiana, while in North Carolina it is as high as $10.25; in South Carolina $9.30, and in Georgia $9.06. On sea-island plantations the lowest charge is $1 in Florida and Georgia, and the highest $20 per acre in Florida. No explanation can be made of the low charges, but the high charges are due to the rents being paid with a share of the crop where the yield is high. Notwithstanding these extreme charges, a reference to Table 1 shows an average charge on all upland plantations of $2.88, and of $2.36 on sea-island plantations, both of which appear to be reasonable.

PLOWING.

The lowest charge for plowing on upland plantations is 30 cents in Arkansas and 35 cents in Alabama, while in most of the other States it is as low as 40 and 50 cents per acre. On sea-island plantations it does not fall below 75 cents, except in Florida. On upland plantations the highest charge is $11.50 in Louisiana, $10 in Texas, and $9.50 in Arkansas and Mississippi. It may be urged that all charges above $5 appear too high, but on the other hand it may be said that some of the charges are too low. However, these extreme charges have not occurred often enough to affect a reasonable average, which is $2.81 for upland and $3.65 for sea-island plantations.

SEED AND PLANTING SEED.

The range of charges for these items, though low in some instances and high in others, appears to be reasonable, especially where high, because it sometimes happens that replanting must be resorted to in order to insure a good stand. The range is not included in Table 6, as the charges are comparatively small. The general average for all upland plantations is 21 cents for seed and 28 cents for planting seed, and on sea-island plantations 38 cents for seed and 46 cents for planting seed.

FERTILIZERS.

The lowest charge reported for fertilizers on upland plantations is 10 cents in Mississippi and Tennessee (in some instances no charges are made), and the highest $13 per acre in Georgia, while the lowest on sea-island plantations is 15 cents in South Carolina, and the highest $23 in Florida. But no significance need be attached to the range of charges for fertilizers, for the reason that their use and the amount used are purely a matter of judgment with the planter. Rent, plowing, chopping, hoeing, etc., are necessary expenses, and the prices paid are, to a large extent, governed by local custom. But in the use of fertilizers, and the amount used, the planter is governed to a greater or less extent by the character of his soil and his ability to purchase the amount he wants to use; and the price and amount paid depend upon whether the purchase is made on a cash or credit basis. The range of charges, however, while small in some cases, shows in most of the older States a liberal expenditure for this item; the general average for all States and Territories being $1.30 on upland and $3.35 on sea-island plantations.

DISTRIBUTING FERTILIZERS.

The cost of distributing fertilizers, like the planting of seed, is comparatively small, and is therefore omitted from Table 6. The average cost, as shown in Table 1, is 16 cents per acre, and ranges from 5 cents in Texas to 35 cents in Florida on upland plantations, and from 31 cents in Georgia to 44 cents in Florida on sea-island plantations.

CHOPPING AND HOEING.

Florida records the lowest charge, 10 cents per acre, for chopping and hoeing, and in three States—North Carolina, South Carolina, and Texas—it is as low as 20 cents on upland plantations. The lowest charge on sea-island plantations is 40 cents in Georgia. In Arkansas and Louisiana the charge runs as high as $6 on upland, and in South Carolina as high as $8 on sea-island plantations. No explanation can be made of the very low charges, but where they are unusually high it may often be attributed to grassy crops following excessive rains and necessitating repeated hoeings. The average on all upland plantations is $1.31, and on all sea-island plantations $1.73 per acre.

PICKING.

The cost per acre of picking on upland plantations ranges from 30 cents in Georgia and 50 cents in Alabama and Arkansas to $12 in Missouri and $11.25 in Arkansas. On sea-island plantations the range is from 50 cents in Florida to $15 in Georgia. No undue significance should be attached to such extreme figures, because cotton picking is not paid for by the acre, but per 100 pounds, and the range of average cost is shown in another column of the table. The average cost for picking, per acre, is $3.37 on upland, and $5.17 on sea-island plantations.

GINNING AND PRESSING.

The lowest charge on upland plantations is 10 cents for ginning and pressing 160 pounds in Georgia, and the highest $4.13 for 413 pounds in the same State. On sea-island plantations the lowest charge is 12 cents in Florida for ginning and pressing 100 pounds, and the highest $7.80 for 239 pounds in South Carolina. The general average for an acre on upland plantations is $1.08 and on sea-island plantations $1.99.

BAGGING AND TIES.

The cost of bagging and ties on upland plantations ranges from 10 cents for 130 pounds in Georgia to $2.50 for 250 pounds in the same State, and on sea-island plantations from 12 cents for 100 pounds in Georgia to $3 for 100 pounds in Florida. The average is 57 cents on upland and 62 cents on sea-island plantations for 1 acre.

MARKETING.

On upland plantations the cost of marketing ranges from 5 cents for 400 pounds in North Carolina to $5 for 500 pounds in Louisiana, and on sea-island plantations from 10 cents for 100 pounds in Florida to $4.50 for 376 pounds in South Carolina. But the ranges of cost for marketing may be readily accounted for, as the amount of the expense depends chiefly upon the distance to the market. Many planters sell their crops at the ginhouse and incur little or no expense, while many others ship to distant markets, and not only pay freight charges, but insurance, drayage, storage, weighing, and commissions for handling and selling. Such expenses are sometimes considerably increased by holding the crop from month to month for better prices. The average cost of marketing the product of an acre is 64 cents on upland and 91 cents on sea-island plantations.

REPAIRING IMPLEMENTS.

The lowest charge on any upland plantation for repairing implements is 1 cent in Louisiana (in some instances no charges are made), and the highest $3.20 in the same State, while 2 cents is the lowest in Georgia and $1.50 is the highest in each of the States of Florida, Georgia, and South Carolina on sea-island plantations. The average is 40 cents on upland and 42 cents on sea-island plantations.

OTHER EXPENSES.

If any other expense has been incurred in the cultivation of his crop, ample opportunity is afforded the planter to include it in "other expenses." That he has taken advantage of this is shown in the range of charges, which vary from 2 cents in Alabama (in some instances no charges are made) to $6 in Louisiana on upland plantations, and from 6 cents in South Carolina to $5 in the same State on sea-island plantations. The average on upland plantations is 41 cents, and on sea-island 51 cents, per acre.

TOTAL COST OF CULTIVATION.

The range in the total cost of cultivation is omitted from Table 6 because, with the exception of the cost of seeding and distributing fertilizers, the ranges in the cost of each item are already given. It may be of interest, however, to state that the lowest total cost on upland plantations is $4.32, reported from Cleburne County, Ark., and the highest $45.38, from Talladega County, Ala. Other States and Territories reporting a low total cost are: Florida, $5.10; Texas, $5.40; Indian Territory, $6.06; Louisiana, $6.55; North Carolina, $6.86, and Oklahoma, $6.30. Other States reporting a high total cost are: Arkansas, $31.40; Florida, $31.42; Georgia, $34.75; Louisiana, $34.05; Mississippi, $33.70; North Carolina, $35.90; South Carolina, $30.02, and

Texas, $30.90. The average total cost on all upland plantations is $15.42 per acre. On sea-island plantations the lowest cost is $7.42, in Levy County, Fla., and the highest $56.22, in Berkeley County, S. C. The average on all sea-island plantations is $21.95 per acre.

YIELD PER ACRE.

On upland plantations in every State except Florida, Missouri, and South Carolina a yield as low as 100 pounds of lint per acre is reported. Low yields are particularly noticeable in the reports from Arkansas, Indian and Oklahoma Territories, Louisiana, and Texas, where the crops were damaged by drought. The highest yield recorded is 750 pounds, in Arkansas and also in Georgia. In each of the States of Alabama, Arkansas, Florida, Louisiana, Mississippi, and South Carolina there are instances of yields ranging from 600 to 700 pounds, and in Missouri, North Carolina, Oklahoma, Tennessee, and Texas from 500 to 600 pounds. The average on all upland plantations is 255.6 pounds. The lowest yield on sea-island plantations is 67 pounds, in Florida, and the highest 500 pounds, in Florida and in Georgia. The average on all sea-island plantations is 168.2 pounds.

PRICE PER POUND.

Although from a business standpoint 1896 was an unfavorable year for the planter, owing to the general depression of the cotton industry, prices were fairly remunerative at the opening of the season. In September at the principal markets in the cotton States prices of middling upland ranged from $7\frac{3}{8}$ to $8\frac{1}{4}$ cents per pound. In October there was a decline, and the range was from 7 to $7\frac{7}{8}$ cents; a further decline in November, with the range from $6\frac{7}{8}$ to $7\frac{9}{16}$, and a still further decline in December, with the range from $6\frac{1}{2}$ to $7\frac{3}{8}$ cents per pound. There are several instances, as in Arkansas, Louisiana, Missouri, and Texas, where the price realized was as low as 5 cents per pound. The highest prices reported are 9 cents per pound in Alabama, Mississippi, and North Carolina, while all the other States except Tennessee report 8 cents or higher. The average on all upland plantations is 6.70 cents per pound. On sea-island plantations the range of prices is from 9 cents in Florida to 37 cents in South Carolina, the average on all being 15.57 cents per pound.

SEED AND ITS VALUE.

The ranges in the production of seed per acre and the price per bushel are not included in Table 6, but on upland plantations, where the yield is small, in every State except Missouri, as low as 5 and 6 bushels is reported, while Arkansas shows one instance of 50 bushels, Alabama 45, Florida and Georgia 44, and Mississippi 40, and the other States from 35 to 40 bushels per acre. The average on all upland plantations is 16 bushels to 255.6 pounds of lint, which is in conformity with the accepted rule to count 6 bushels of seed to every 100 pounds of lint, or 30 bushels to every 500-pound bale. On sea-island plantations the lowest yield is 4 bushels in Florida, and the highest 25 in Georgia, the average being 10.3 bushels to 168.2 pounds of lint per acre, a yet closer correspondence with the rule of counting. On upland plantations the price per bushel ranges from 5 and 6 cents to 40 and 50 cents, and on sea-island plantations from 7 to 50 cents. The high prices for upland seed are exceptional, and are no doubt for the "fancy" varieties. The average for upland is 11.9 cents, and for sea island 23.9 cents per bushel, twice as high.

PICKING, PER 100 POUNDS.

The range in the cost of picking upland cotton, the custom being to pay so much per hundred pounds for gathering the seed cotton, is from 22 cents in Arkansas, Georgia, and North Carolina to $1.28 in Arkansas. Except in Indian and Oklahoma Territories, instances of low cost are reported everywhere, while in Arkansas, Louisiana, Mississippi, and Texas there are figures as high as $1 and over, but these are exceptional cases. The average of 44 cents per hundred on all plantations seems reasonable, and closely conforms to the customary prices in most regions of the cotton belt. The cost for picking sea-island cotton ranges from 57 cents in Florida to $1.16 in South Carolina, the average in the three States being $1.03 per hundred. Owing to the character of the plant and its larger growth, it is much more troublesome and tedious to pick the cotton grown on the sea islands of South Carolina, hence its higher cost. It is an interesting fact, as shown in Table 10, that the average cost of picking is lowest in Virginia, the oldest cotton-growing State in the Union, and increases as we go south and westward to the newer plantations of Texas and the Territories.

COST OF PRODUCTION PER POUND.

The range in the cost of producing a pound of lint cotton on upland plantations, in the estimation of which the value of the seed is eliminated, is from 2.58 cents in Texas and 2.66 cents in Louisiana, the two lowest, to 12.35 cents in Arkansas and 11.39 cents in North Carolina, the two highest. The other States show a cost as low as from 3.10 to 4.38 cents and as high as from 7.62 to 11.30 cents per pound. The average on all upland plantations is 5.27 cents per pound. The cost of production on sea-island plantations ranges from 4.93 cents in Florida to 24.65 cents in the same State, the average for the three States being 11.59 cents per pound. While the cost in some instances appears extraordinarily low, in others it is remarkably high, but they occur so rarely as not to affect what seems to be a fair average. As in other cases of remarkably low or high items of cost, yield, and price, the figures in the table are confessedly extreme.

TABLE 6.—*Lowest and highest average cost, yield, and price, cost of picking and production per 100 pounds.*

States and Territories.	Rent.		Plowing.		Fertilizers.		Chopping and hoeing.		Picking.		Ginning and pressing.		Bagging and ties.	
	L.	H.	L.	H.	L.	H.	L.	H.	L.	H.	L.	H.	L.	H.
Upland.														
Alabama ...	$0.50	$6.72	$0.35	$7.00	$0.50	$9.73	$0.30	$5.00	$0.50	$9.89	$0.30	$3.00	$0.12	$1.60
Arkansas...	.50	6.50	.30	9.50	.25	4.50	.25	6.00	.50	11.25	.19	3.00	.13	1.60
Florida	.40	5.00	.50	5.00	.85	10.00	.10	3.00	1.00	7.52	.20	3.00	.10	1.80
Georgia.....	.50	9.06	.50	9.00	.50	13.00	.25	4.50	.30	8.00	.10	4.13	.10	2.50
Indian Ter..	.75	5.00	.50	5.00	.30	.30	.50	3.25	1.35	9.00	.35	3.50	.17	2.00
Louisiana...	1.00	11.25	.40	11.50	.15	6.00	.35	6.00	.80	11.20	.20	4.00	.14	1.00
Mississippi.	1.00	7.18	.50	9.50	.10	10.50	.35	4.00	1.20	8.50	.30	2.50	.15	1.50
Missouri....	2.00	4.50	1.00	6.25	.50	4.75	.50	2.50	2.00	12.00	.85	2.25	.35	1.50
N. Carolina .	1.00	10.25	.50	7.50	1.00	10.00	.20	4.00	1.20	6.80	.25	3.50	.15	2.00
Oklahoma ..	.75	3.00	.50	5.75	1.00	1.00	.30	4.00	.75	7.50	.25	2.50	.10	1.50
S. Carolina..	1.00	9.30	.50	7.50	.75	11.87	.20	2.25	.90	8.00	.15	3.40	.15	1.75
Tennessee..	1.50	5.00	.50	6.75	.10	3.00	.50	2.75	1.50	9.00	.40	2.50	.20	1.50
Texas	.50	6.45	.50	10.00	.25	5.00	.20	4.00	.40	10.00	.20	3.60	.11	1.40
Virginia	1.00	5.00	.75	5.00	1.00	6.00	.30	3.00	.90	4.00	.40	2.25	.25	1.75
Lowest ...	.40	......	.30	......	.10	......	.10	......	.30	......	.10	......	.10	......
Highest ..	......	11.25	......	11.50	......	13.00	......	6.00	......	12.00	......	4.13	......	2.50
Sea-island.														
Florida	1.00	20.00	.70	10.50	.75	23.00	.50	4.00	.50	13.00	.12	6.45	.16	3.00
Georgia.....	2.00	5.00	.75	10.00	.90	10.00	.40	3.25	.75	15.00	.75	5.00	.12	1.55
S. Carolina..	1.00	5.00	.90	5.25	.15	12.20	1.30	8.00	3.50	14.00	1.92	7.80	.25	1.00
Lowest ...	1.00	......	.70	......	.15	......	.40	......	.50	......	.12	......	.12	......
Highest ..	......	20.00	......	10.50	......	23.00	......	8.00	......	15.00	......	7.80	......	3.00

States and Territories.	Marketing.		Repairing implements.		Other expenses.		Yield.		Price.		Cost per 100 pounds.			
											Picking.		Production.	
	L.	H.	L.	H.	L.	H.	L.	H.	L.	H.	L.	H.	L.	H.
Upland.							*Lbs.*	*Lbs.*	*Cents.*	*Cents.*				
Alabama ...	$0.05	$3.25	$0.05	$2.00	$0.02	$3.00	100	642	6.00	9.00	$0.27	$0.72	$3.51	$10.25
Arkansas...	.05	4.25	.05	1.00	.05	1.00	100	750	5.00	8.75	.22	1.28	3.11	12.35
Florida	.10	2.85	.03	1.50	.10	2.00	120	627	6.00	8.00	.25	.54	3.23	7.62
Georgia.....	.05	4.00	.05	2.50	.02	4.21	100	750	6.00	8.00	.22	.54	3.40	9.60
Indian Ter..	.10	4.00	.10	2.30	.10	2.50	100	417	5.50	8.00	.51	.62	3.38	8.01
Louisiana ..	1.30	5.00	.01	3.20	.05	6.00	100	600	5.00	8.50	.30	1.00	2.66	10.62
Mississippi.	.05	4.50	.05	2.00	.05	3.25	100	667	5.50	9.00	.26	1.07	3.64	9.60
Missouri ...	.45	1.50	.10	1.00	.40	.80	130	550	5.00	8.00	.25	.75	3.96	8.77
N. Carolina .	.05	2.98	.05	1.50	.10	3.00	100	560	6.00	9.00	.22	.80	4.38	11.39
Oklahoma ..	.25	2.00	.05	2.00	.05	1.50	100	500	6.00	8.40	.50	.74	3.33	8.89
S. Carolina..	.10	2.80	.08	2.50	.07	3.00	138	600	5.50	8.00	.30	.50	3.28	7.99
Tennessee ..	.10	2.50	.10	1.50	.10	2.50	100	566	5.50	7.75	.31	.76	3.41	11.35
Texas	.05	4.00	.05	2.50	.05	4.75	100	560	5.00	8.00	.29	1.07	2.58	11.30
Virginia	.25	2.50	.10	1.00	.10	1.20	100	500	6.00	8.00	.27	.38	3.10	10.80
Lowest ...	.05	......	.01	......	.02	......	100	......	5.00	......	.22	......	2.58	......
Highest ..	......	5.00	......	3.20	......	6.00	......	750	......	9.00	......	1.28	......	12.35
Sea island.														
Florida	.10	2.00	.05	1.50	.10	2.00	67	500	9.00	22.00	.57	1.67	4.93	24.65
Georgia.....	.20	3.50	.02	1.50	.10	.80	80	500	10.00	15.00	.60	1.29	5.70	14.71
S. Carolina..	.40	4.50	.25	1.50	.06	5.00	96	376	10.00	37.00	1.16	1.39	13.18	17.75
Lowest ...	.10	......	.02	......	.06	......	67	......	9.00	......	.57	......	4.93	......
Highest ..	......	4.50	......	1.50	......	5.00	......	500	......	37.00	......	1.67	......	24.65

COST OF ITEMS TO PRODUCE 100 POUNDS OF LINT.

Table 7, showing the cost of each item in the production of 100 pounds of lint cotton, is based on the average cost on all upland and sea-island plantations in each State and Territory, as shown in Table 1.

The lowest cost per 100 pounds on upland plantations is $5.51 in Oklahoma, and the highest $6.29 in Arkansas. The lowest cost on sea-island plantations is $11.07 in Georgia, and the highest $17.89 in South Carolina. The average cost on all upland plantations is $6.03, and on all sea-island plantations $13.05 per 100 pounds.

TABLE 7.—*Cost of each item in the production of 100 pounds of lint cotton.*

States and Territories.	Rent.	Plowing.	Seed.	Planting seed.	Fertilizers.	Distributing fertilizers.	Chopping and hoeing.	Picking.	Ginning and pressing.	Bagging and ties.	Marketing.	Repairing implements.	Other expenses.	Total cost.
Upland.														
Alabama	$0.95	$1.25	$0.09	$0.10	$0.77	$0.10	$0.53	$1.20	$0.41	$0.22	$0.23	$0.16	$0.16	$6.17
Arkansas	1.30	1.23	.09	.12	.13	.04	.66	1.40	.49	.24	.29	.17	.13	6.29
Florida	.67	1.19	.12	.17	.86	.15	.48	1.33	.42	.24	.25	.14	.17	6.19
Georgia	.97	1.12	.09	.10	.91	.09	.48	1.16	.33	.21	.19	.16	.21	6.02
Indian Territory	1.03	.93	.06	.10	(*a*)	(*a*)	.62	1.61	.58	.25	.27	.16	.11	5.72
Louisiana	1.00	.95	.07	.09	.27	.04	.54	1.38	.44	.22	.39	.16	.15	5.70
Mississippi	1.10	1.11	.08	.10	.42	.07	.53	1.33	.44	.22	.28	.17	.17	6.02
Missouri	1.05	.78	.07	.16	.23	.03	.58	1.66	.46	.29	.30	.12	.09	5.82
North Carolina	1.30	1.03	.09	.11	.96	.09	.45	1.11	.38	.22	.20	.13	.12	6.10
Oklahoma	.88	.66	.06	.13	.01	(*a*)	.69	1.60	.57	.29	.35	.12	.15	5.51
South Carolina	.98	.93	.08	.08	1.04	.08	.36	1.18	.34	.21	.18	.14	.16	5.76
Tennessee	1.23	1.13	.10	.12	.13	.04	.56	1.40	.45	.24	.21	.16	.18	5.95
Texas	1.36	1.15	.07	.14	.07	.02	.50	1.52	.50	.22	.23	.16	.18	6.12
Virginia	.99	1.23	.10	.16	.89	.08	.34	1.08	.42	.27	.39	.11	.13	6.19
Average	1.13	1.10	.08	.11	.51	.06	.51	1.32	.42	.22	.25	.16	.16	6.03
Sea-island.														
Florida	1.42	2.40	.24	.32	1.77	.30	.88	2.02	.92	.42	.48	.28	.21	12.65
Georgia	1.34	2.08	.18	.18	1.57	.16	.64	2.93	.98	.30	.42	.18	.11	11.07
South Carolina	1.45	1.21	.26	.24	3.50	.15	2.20	3.91	2.48	.29	.98	.25	.97	17.89
Average	1.40	2.17	.23	.27	1.99	.24	1.03	3.08	1.18	.37	.54	.25	.30	13.05

a Expense trifling.

COST OF ITEMS TO PRODUCE A BALE OF COTTON.

The cost of each item in the production of a bale of cotton, as shown in the table below, is based on the cost per 100 pounds, as given in Table 7. The lowest cost of producing a 500-pound bale, the customary weight of a bale of upland, is $27.55 in Oklahoma, and the highest $31.45 in Arkansas. The lowest cost of producing a 350-pound bale, the customary weight of a bale of sea island, is $38.75 in Georgia and the highest $62.61 in South Carolina. The average cost of a bale of upland is $30.15 and of a bale of sea island $45.67. The cost of any fractional part of a bale of either may be easily arrived at by the use of the figures in Table 7.

TABLE 8.—*Cost of each item in the production of a 500-pound bale of cotton.*

States and Territories.	Rent.	Plowing.	Seed.	Planting seed.	Fertilizers.	Distributing fertilizers.	Chopping and hoeing.	Picking.	Ginning and pressing.	Bagging and ties.	Marketing.	Repairing implements.	Other expenses.	Total cost.
Upland (weight, 500 pounds).														
Alabama	$4.75	$6.25	$0.45	$0.50	$3.85	$0.50	$2.65	$6.00	$2.05	$1.10	$1.15	$0.80	$0.80	$30.85
Arkansas	6.50	6.15	.45	.60	.65	.20	3.30	7.00	2.45	1.20	1.45	.85	.65	31.45
Florida	3.35	5.95	.60	.85	4.30	.75	2.40	6.65	2.10	1.20	1.25	.70	.85	30.95
Georgia	4.85	5.60	.45	.50	4.55	.45	2.40	5.80	1.65	1.05	.95	.80	1.05	30.10
Indian Territory	5.15	4.65	.30	.50	.00	.00	3.10	8.05	2.90	1.25	1.35	.80	.55	28.60
Louisiana	5.00	4.75	.35	.45	1.35	.20	2.70	6.90	2.20	1.10	1.95	.80	.75	28.50
Mississippi	5.50	5.55	.40	.50	2.10	.35	2.65	6.65	2.20	1.10	1.40	.85	.85	30.10
Missouri	5.25	3.90	.35	.80	1.15	.15	2.90	8.30	2.30	1.45	1.50	.60	.45	29.10
North Carolina	6.50	5.15	.45	.55	4.80	.45	2.25	5.55	1.90	1.10	1.00	.65	.60	30.95
Oklahoma	4.40	3.30	.30	.65	.05	.00	3.45	8.00	2.85	1.45	1.75	.60	.75	27.55
South Carolina	4.90	4.65	.40	.40	5.20	.40	1.80	5.90	1.70	1.05	.90	.70	.80	28.80
Tennessee	6.15	5.65	.50	.60	.65	.20	2.80	7.00	2.25	1.20	1.05	.80	.90	29.75
Texas	6.80	5.75	.35	.70	.35	.10	2.50	7.60	2.50	1.10	1.15	.80	.90	30.60
Virginia	4.95	6.15	.50	.80	4.45	.40	1.70	5.40	2.10	1.35	1.95	.55	.65	30.95
Average	5.65	5.50	.40	.55	2.55	.30	2.55	6.60	2.10	1.10	1.25	.80	.80	30.15
Sea-island (weight, 350 pounds).														
Florida	4.97	8.71	.84	1.12	6.19	1.05	3.08	10.22	3.22	1.47	1.68	.98	.73	44.27
Georgia	4.69	7.28	.63	.63	5.49	.56	2.24	10.25	3.43	1.05	1.47	.63	.39	38.75
South Carolina	5.07	4.23	.91	.84	12.25	.53	7.70	13.69	8.68	1.01	3.43	.87	3.39	62.61
Average	4.90	7.59	.81	.95	6.97	.84	3.61	10.78	4.13	1.29	1.89	.87	1.05	45.67

PROPORTION OF EACH ITEM OF COST.

The proportion which each item of cost bears to the total cost of cultivating an acre and marketing its product is given in Table 9, and is based upon the average on all upland and sea-island plantations in each State and Territory. The smallest ratio on upland plantations is the cost of distributing fertilizers, and the highest the cost of picking. From lowest to highest the order of the items in the average cost on all upland plantations is as follows: First, distributing fertilizers; second, seed; third, planting seed; fourth, repairing implements; fifth, incidental expenses; sixth, bagging and ties; seventh, marketing; eighth, ginning and pressing; ninth, chopping and hoeing; tenth, fertilizers; eleventh, plowing; twelfth, rent, and thirteenth, picking. On sea-island plantations the lowest ratio is in the cost of seed, and the highest, as on upland plantations, in the cost of picking. The rank of each item from lowest to highest is in the following order: First, seed; second, distributing fertilizers; third, repairing implements; fourth, other expenses; fifth, planting seed; sixth, bagging and ties; seventh, marketing; eighth, chopping and hoeing; ninth, ginning and pressing; tenth, rent; eleventh, fertilizers; twelfth, plowing, and thirteenth, picking.

On upland plantations the same average percentage is given to distributing fertilizers as to seed, and the same to repairing implements as to other expenses. But, descending to fractions, the cost of distributing fertilizers is less by 0.37 of 1 per cent than that of seed, and other expenses 0.08 of 1 per cent less than that of repairing implements. Also on sea-island plantations the averages are the same for seed, planting seed, and distributing fertilizers, and for repairing implements and other expenses. There is a slight difference in each, when account is taken of fractions, and the proper order is here assigned to each.

TABLE 9.—*Percentage of each item to the total average cost of cultivation.*

States and Territories.	Rent.	Plowing.	Seed.	Planting seed.	Fertilizers.	Distributing fertilizers.	Chopping and hoeing.	Picking.	Ginning and pressing.	Bagging and ties.	Marketing.	Repairing implements.	Other expenses.	Total.
Alabama	15	20	1	2	12	2	8	19	7	4	4	3	3	100
Arkansas	21	20	1	2	2	1	10	22	8	4	4	3	2	100
Florida	11	19	2	3	14	2	8	21	7	4	4	2	3	100
Georgia	16	19	2	2	15	1	8	19	5	4	3	3	3	100
Indian Territory	18	16	1	2	....	....	11	28	10	4	5	3	2	100
Louisiana	17	17	1	1	5	1	9	24	8	4	7	3	3	100
Mississippi	18	18	1	2	7	1	9	22	7	4	5	3	3	100
Missouri	18	13	1	3	4	1	10	28	8	5	5	2	2	100
North Carolina	21	17	2	2	15	2	7	18	6	3	3	2	2	100
Oklahoma	16	12	1	2	....	....	13	29	11	5	6	2	3	100
South Carolina	17	16	1	1	18	1	6	21	6	4	3	3	3	100
Tennessee	21	19	2	2	2	1	9	23	7	4	4	3	3	100
Texas	22	19	1	2	1	.....	8	25	8	4	4	3	3	100
Virginia	16	20	2	3	14	1	6	17	7	4	6	2	2	100
Average	19	18	1	2	8	1	8	22	7	4	4	3	3	100
Order of the items	12	11	2	3	10	1	9	13	8	6	7	4	5	......
Sea-island.														
Florida	11	20	2	3	14	2	7	23	7	3	4	2	2	100
Georgia	12	19	2	2	14	1	6	26	9	3	4	1	1	100
South Carolina	8	7	1	1	20	1	12	22	14	2	6	1	5	100
Average	11	17	2	2	15	2	8	23	9	3	4	2	2	100
Order of the items	10	12	1	5	11	2	8	13	9	6	7	3	4	......

ORDER OF STATES AND TERRITORIES AS TO ITEMS OF COST AND PRODUCTION.

Table 10 shows the order of States and Territories for upland plantations as to each item of average cost of cultivation, total cost, pounds of lint produced, the price per pound realized, the total yield, profit realized, loss sustained, the cost of picking per 100 pounds, the cost of production per pound, and the number of plantations reporting profit and loss. The lowest total cost of cultivation is $11.50 in Oklahoma and the highest $18.05 in Louisiana. The lowest total return is $15.67 in Oklahoma and the highest $23.32 in Louisiana. The profit ranges from $4.28 in Texas to $7.83 in Louisiana, while the smallest loss is $1.33 in Georgia and the largest $3 in Virginia. The lowest cost of picking cotton per hundred pounds is 36 cents in Virginia and the highest 55 cents in Missouri. The lowest cost of production per pound is 4.72 cents in Oklahoma and the highest 5.61 cents in Arkansas. The smallest number of plantations reporting is 11 in Missouri and the greatest 683 in Texas.

TABLE 10.—*Order of States and Territories in the several items relating to average cost and production per acre.*

States and Territories.	Rent.	States and Territories.	Plowing.	States and Territories.	Fertilizers.
Florida	$1.55	Oklahoma	$1.38	Indian Territory	$0.01
Oklahoma	1.84	Missouri	2.28	Oklahoma	.03
Alabama	2.30	Indian Territory	2.36	Texas	.16
Georgia	2.44	Texas	2.56	Arkansas	.30
Virginia	2.56	Florida	2.73	Tennessee	.33
Indian Territory	2.64	South Carolina	2.74	Missouri	.66
South Carolina	2.88	Georgia	2.83	Louisiana	.85
Mississippi	2.93	Tennessee	2.83	Mississippi	1.12
Arkansas	3.00	Arkansas	2.88	Alabama	1.87
Missouri	3.00	Mississippi	2.94	Florida	1.99
Texas	3.03	Alabama	2.99	Georgia	2.30
Tennessee	3.09	North Carolina	3.00	Virginia	2.31
Louisiana	3.17	Louisiana	3.01	North Carolina	2.77
North Carolina	3.76	Virginia	3.16	South Carolina	3.05

States and Territories.	Chopping and hoeing.	States and Territories.	Picking.	States and Territories.	Ginning and pressing.
Virginia	$0.89	Virginia	$2.80	Georgia	$0.82
South Carolina	1.05	Alabama	2.90	Florida	.98
Texas	1.10	Georgia	2.91	South Carolina	.99
Florida	1.10	Florida	3.05	Alabama	1.00
Georgia	1.21	North Carolina	3.24	North Carolina	1.09
Alabama	1.28	Arkansas	3.24	Virginia	1.10
North Carolina	1.29	Oklahoma	3.31	Texas	1.11
Tennessee	1.42	Texas	3.37	Tennessee	1.13
Mississippi	1.42	South Carolina	3.51	Arkansas	1.13
Oklahoma	1.45	Tennessee	3.53	Mississippi	1.16
Arkansas	1.51	Mississippi	3.57	Oklahoma	1.20
Indian Territory	1.58	Indian Territory	4.08	Missouri	1.30
Missouri	1.66	Louisiana	4.36	Louisiana	1.38
Louisiana	1.72	Missouri	4.70	Indian Territory	1.40

States and Territories.	Bagging and ties.	States and Territories.	Marketing.	States and Territories.	Total cost.
Texas	$0.49	Georgia	$0.48	Oklahoma	$11.50
Alabama	.54	Texas	.52	Texas	13.60
Georgia	.54	Tennessee	.53	Florida	14.27
Arkansas	.55	South Carolina	.53	Arkansas	14.56
Florida	.56	Alabama	.56	Indian Territory	14.59
Mississippi	.59	Florida	.57	Alabama	14.93
Oklahoma	.60	North Carolina	.57	Tennessee	14.98
South Carolina	.61	Arkansas	.67	Georgia	15.17
Tennessee	.61	Indian Territory	.68	Mississippi	16.02
North Carolina	.63	Mississippi	.74	Virginia	16.05
Indian Territory	.65	Oklahoma	.74	Missouri	16.60
Virginia	.69	Missouri	.87	South Carolina	16.96
Louisiana	.71	Virginia	1.01	North Carolina	17.91
Missouri	.84	Louisiana	1.22	Louisiana	18.05

States and Territories.	Pounds of lint.	States and Territories.	Price per pound.	States and Territories.	Total return.
			Cents.		
Oklahoma	208	Missouri	6.42	Oklahoma	$15.67
Texas	222	Indian Territory	6.45	Texas	16.38
Florida	230	Arkansas	6.46	Arkansas	16.54
Arkansas	231	Tennessee	6.63	Florida	17.38
Alabama	242	Texas	6.63	Alabama	18.08
Tennessee	251	Louisiana	6.67	Indian Territory	18.17
Georgia	252	Alabama	6.69	Tennessee	18.44
Indian Territory	255	Florida	6.70	Georgia	19.42
Virginia	259	Oklahoma	6.72	Mississippi	19.65
Mississippi	266	Georgia	6.73	Virginia	19.95
Missouri	285	Mississippi	6.74	Missouri	20.49
North Carolina	289	Virginia	6.90	North Carolina	22.46
South Carolina	294	South Carolina	6.94	South Carolina	23.06
Louisiana	316	North Carolina	6.96	Louisiana	23.32

TABLE 10.—*Order of States and Territories in the several items relating to average cost and production per acre*—Continued.

States and Territories.	Profit.	States and Territories.	Loss.	States and Territories.	Cost of picking. *a*
Texas	$4.28	Georgia	$1.33	Virginia	$0.36
Tennessee	4.37	South Carolina	1.52	North Carolina	.37
Arkansas	4.43	Florida	1.58	Georgia	.39
Alabama	4.75	Missouri	1.68	Alabama	.40
Florida	4.80	Tennessee	1.77	South Carolina	.40
Mississippi	4.89	Texas	1.77	Florida	.44
Georgia	5.09	Oklahoma	1.78	Mississippi	.45
Oklahoma	5.44	Mississippi	1.95	Louisiana	.46
North Carolina	5.52	North Carolina	1.96	Tennessee	.47
Indian Territory	5.56	Alabama	2.00	Arkansas	.47
Missouri	5.74	Indian Territory	2.04	Texas	.51
Virginia	5.83	Louisiana	2.45	Oklahoma	.53
South Carolina	6.43	Arkansas	2.47	Indian Territory	.53
Louisiana	7.83	Virginia	3.00	Missouri	.55

States and Territories.	Cost of production. *b*	Number and per cent of farms reporting.			
		States and Territories.	Total.	States and Territories.	Profit.
	Cents.				*Pr. ct.*
Oklahoma	4.72	Missouri	11	Arkansas	65
South Carolina	4.87	Virginia	18	Missouri	73
Louisiana	5.01	Oklahoma	34	Indian Territory	74
Indian Territory	5.05	Florida	53	Texas	75
Missouri	5.06	Indian Territory	58	Florida	75
Georgia	5.23	Tennessee	111	Louisiana	77
Tennessee	5.26	South Carolina	181	Alabama	77
Florida	5.35	North Carolina	304	Virginia	78
Mississippi	5.36	Mississippi	322	Oklahoma	82
Texas	5.38	Louisiana	328	Mississippi	83
Alabama	5.38	Arkansas	337	Tennessee	86
North Carolina	5.39	Alabama	350	Georgia	87
Virginia	5.40	Georgia	545	North Carolina	87
Arkansas	5.61	Texas	683	South Carolina	96

a Per 100 pounds. *b* Per pound.

THE USE OF FERTILIZERS IN COTTON PRODUCTION.

One of the most interesting and instructive features of this investigation relates to the use of fertilizers. The States (see Table 1) expending the greatest average amount per acre for fertilizers, excepting Virginia, which produces a comparatively small crop, are Alabama, Florida, Georgia, North and South Carolina. Table 11 shows the relation between the average cost of the fertilizers used and the profit realized from an acre of cotton on upland and sea-island plantations in each of these States.

It will be observed that the average amounts expended for fertilizers are divided into six classes, ranging from "under $1" to "$6 and over," and that both profit and loss are given under each classification.

In South Carolina the total number of plantations reporting is 195, all of which used fertilizers. Of this number 186 show an average profit ranging from $4.78 on plantations where the average cost is $1.51 per acre, to $18.68 where the cost is $8.79 per acre, the average profit on all upland and sea island plantations being $7.83, while the average cost of fertilizers is $3.37 per acre. (The figures "under $1" are omitted because they are exceptional, only one plantation having reported.) In Georgia the total number of plantations reporting is

570, all but one of which used fertilizers, and 494 show an average profit ranging from $4.42 where the average cost is 73 cents per acre to $8.61 where the cost is $7.67 per acre, the average profit on all upland and sea-island plantations being $5.18, while the average cost of fertilizers is $2.34 per acre. In Florida the total number of plantations reporting is 125, and all but 14 used fertilizers. On 81 plantations the average profit ranges from $2.22 where the average cost is 81 cents per acre, to $19.82 where the cost is $12.50 per acre, the average profit on all upland and sea-island plantations being $7.17, while the average cost of fertilizers is $2.64 per acre.

In North Carolina the total number of plantations reporting is 304, and all but 4 used fertilizers. On 263 plantations the average profit ranges from $5.66 where the average cost is $1.38, to $7.80 where the cost is $7.23 per acre, the average profit on all plantations being $5.52 while the average cost of fertilizers is $2.80 per acre. In Alabama the total number of plantations reporting is 350, and all but 30 used fertilizers. On 243 plantations the average profit ranges from $3.28 where the average cost is 68 cents per acre, to $7.66 where the cost is $9.36 per acre, the average profit on all plantations being $4.88 while the average cost of fertilizers is $2.05 per acre.

In the five States the total number of plantations reporting is 1,544, on 1,495 of which fertilizers are used. Of this number 1,268 show an average profit ranging from $4.62 where the cost is 74 cents per acre, to $12.51 where the cost is $9.11 per acre, the average profit on all upland and sea-island plantations being $5.71 while the average cost of fertilizers is $2.52 per acre.

It is true, on the other hand, that in each State losses are reported, even where fertilizers are used, and that in some instances the losses are great in proportion to the cost of fertilizers. But some losses are to be expected, for the planter using fertilizers is subject to the same adverse conditions as the one who does not use them. The character of the soil, the seasons, and the cultivation, affect the results as much in one case as the other, and it sometimes happens that an injudicious application of fertilizers reduces the yield, and even where judiciously applied a drought may "burn" the plants and cut off the yield. But the number of losses reported in the five States are, after all, comparatively small, the percentage in each being as follows: Alabama, 24: Florida, 27; Georgia, 13; North Carolina, 12, and South Carolina 4 per cent; the total for all being only 15 per cent. In Alabama and Florida, where the percentage of losses is highest, the crops suffered from drought.

While it does not follow that the use of fertilizers necessarily insures an increased yield, certainly the results of this investigation imply that on the whole the use of fertilizers in Alabama, Florida, Georgia, North and South Carolina, in 1896, was a paying investment.

In connection with this it is a fact worthy of notice that the development of the phosphate industries of South Carolina began in 1867 and in Florida in 1888, and that a large number of cotton-seed oil mills were built in the cotton States between 1870 and 1880; that the value of the acid phosphates and of cotton-seed meal as fertilizers became a recognized fact among planters; that the development of these industries cheapened the cost of commercial fertilizers to such an extent that their use on the exhausted lands of some of the older cotton States became general, and that, in consequence, since 1870 all of the staple crops in those States, especially cotton, have greatly increased. This increased production in Georgia, North and South Carolina, is undoubtedly due to a great extent to the generous use of fertilizers and the development of a more intensive method of culture. The year 1859–60 perhaps witnessed the highest stage of agricultural development under the slave system. The census reports of that year show unprecedented crops. And yet, in 1896, according to the estimates of this Department, as shown in Table 12, in North Carolina the crops of cotton, oats, and tobacco are more than twice as great as in 1860, while there is only a slight difference in the yield of corn and wheat. In South Carolina the cotton crop is much more than two and a half times greater than in 1860, while, with the exception of wheat, all the other crops, especially oats and tobacco, are much greater. In Georgia the cotton crop is almost double that of 1860, while all other crops, except wheat and tobacco (the latter is an insignificant crop there), are much greater. Unfortunately, there are no data as to cotton acreage in any census before 1880.

TABLE 11.—*Relationship between the average cost of fertilizers and profit or loss in raising cotton in 1896.*

Classification of cost of fertilizers.	South Carolina.								
	Upland.			Sea-Island.			Total.		
	Number of farms reporting.	Average cost of fertilizers.	Average profit or loss.	Number of farms reporting.	Average cost of fertilizers.	Average profit or loss.	Number of farms reporting.	Average cost of fertilizers. (*a*)	Average profit or loss.
PROFIT.									
Under $1	1	$0.75	$8.54	......	......	......	1	$0.75	$8.54
$1 and under $2	28	1.50	4.64	1	$1.80	$8.71	29	1.51	4.78
$2 and under $3	76	2.17	5.43	......	......	......	76	2.17	5.43
$3 and under $4	21	3.21	6.36	2	3.00	20.26	23	3.19	7.56
$4 and under $5	22	4.18	8.64	......	......	......	22	4.18	8.64
$5 and under $6	13	5.12	8.06	3	5.50	20.54	16	5.19	10.40
$6 and over	12	7.95	11.09	8	10.06	30.06	20	8.79	18.68
Total	173	3.05	6.43	14	7.48	25.10	187	3.37	7.83
LOSS.									
Under $1	......	......	......	......	......	......	......	......	......
$1 and under $2	1	1.50	.90	......	......	......	1	1.51	.90
$2 and under $3	3	2.17	1.75	......	......	......	3	2.17	1.75
$3 and under $4	2	3.21	2.00	......	......	......	2	3.19	2.00
$4 and under $5	1	4.18	.42	......	......	......	1	4.18	.42
$5 and under $6	1	5.12	1.58	......	......	......	1	5.19	1.58
$6 and over	......	......	......	......	......	......	......	......	......
Total	8	3.05	1.52	......	......	......	8	3.37	1.52

a In computing the average cost of fertilizers per acre, the farms suffering a loss have been combined with those that made a profit, hence some disagreements, which are not errors, between this column and the similar column under "sea island" and "upland," in this table.

TABLE 11.—*Relationship between the average cost of fertilizers and profit or loss in raising cotton in 1896*—Continued.

Classification of cost of fertilizers.	Georgia.								
	Upland.			Sea-island.			Total.		
	Number of farms reporting.	Average cost of fertilizers.	Average profit or loss.	Number of farms reporting.	Average cost of fertilizers.	Average profit or loss.	Number of farms reporting.	Average cost of fertilizers.	Average profit or loss.
PROFIT.									
Under $1	6	$0.70	$4.42	......	......	......	6	$0.73	$4.42
$1 and under $2	116	1.42	4.05	......	......	......	116	1.42	4.05
$2 and under $3	277	2.18	4.87	12	$2.22	$9.86	289	2.18	5.07
$3 and under $4	34	3.16	5.63	1	3.50	10.10	35	3.17	5.76
$4 and under $5	19	4.11	8.35	3	4.19	1.91	22	4.12	7.47
$5 and under $6	11	5.16	10.32	2	5.00	3.50	13	5.13	9.27
$6 and over	12	7.47	8.62	1	10.00	8.49	13	7.67	8.61
Total	475	2.30	5.08	19	3.27	7.88	494	2.34	5.18
LOSS.									
Under $1	......	......	......	1	.90	1.91	1	.73	1.91
$1 and under $2	17	1.42	1.28	......	......	......	17	1.42	1.28
$2 and under $3	47	2.18	1.36	1	2.22	4.04	48	2.18	1.42
$3 and under $4	4	3.16	1.07	1	3.50	.79	5	3.17	1.01
$4 and under $5	1	4.11	2.10	1	4.19	1.70	2	4.12	1.90
$5 and under $6	1	5.16	2.64	1	5.00	4.90	2	5.13	3.77
$6 and over	......	......	......	......	......	......	......	......	......
Total	70	2.30	1.35	5	3.27	2.67	75	2.34	1.44

Classification of cost of fertilizers.	Florida.								
	Upland.			Sea-island.			Total.		
	Number of farms reporting.	Average cost of fertilizers.	Average profit or loss.	Number of farms reporting.	Average cost of fertilizers.	Average profit or loss.	Number of farms reporting.	Average cost of fertilizers.	Average profit or loss.
PROFIT.									
Under $1	......	......	......	5	$0.80	$2.22	5	$0.81	$2.22
$1 and under $2	12	$1.33	$4.25	12	1.40	9.10	24	1.37	6.67
$2 and under $3	16	2.28	4.66	12	2.21	7.71	28	2.25	5.97
$3 and under $4	2	3.00	1.30	9	3.00	5.86	11	3.00	5.03
$4 and under $5	1	4.00	7.35	1	4.10	4.30	2	4.07	5.82
$5 and under $6	......	......	......	7	5.00	13.71	7	5.00	13.71
$6 and over	2	9.50	16.90	2	15.50	22.75	4	12.50	19.82
Total	33	2.34	5.13	48	2.86	8.57	81	2.64	7.17
LOSS.									
Under $1	1	.85	1.72	......	......	......	1	.81	1.72
$1 and under $2	2	1.33	.85	5	1.40	1.52	7	1.37	1.33
$2 and under $3	9	2.28	1.77	9	2.21	2.65	18	2.25	2.21
$3 and under $4	......	......	......	1	3.00	7.47	1	3.00	7.47
$4 and under $5	......	......	......	1	4.10	11.65	1	4.07	11.65
$5 and under $6	......	......	......	2	5.00	5.08	2	5.00	5.08
$6 and over	......	......	......	......	......	......	......	......	......
Total	12	2.34	1.61	18	2.86	3.37	30	2.64	2.67

TABLE 11.—*Relationship between the average cost of fertilizers and profit or loss in raising cotton in 1896*—Continued.

Classification of cost of fertilizers.	North Carolina.			Alabama.			Average for the five States.			
	Number of farms reporting.	Average cost of fertilizers.	Average profit or loss.	Number of farms reporting.	Average cost of fertilizers.	Average profit or loss.	Number of farms reporting.	Average cost of fertilizers.	Average profit or loss.	Per-centage of increase of profit or loss.
PROFIT.										
Under $1	......	......	......	9	$0.68	$3.28	21	$0.74	$4.62	......
$1 and under $2	32	$1.38	$5.66	90	1.34	4.27	291	1.40	5.09	10.2
$2 and under $3	153	2.21	5.27	110	2.18	4.97	656	2.20	5.34	4.9
$3 and under $4	24	3.14	5.18	25	3.15	6.02	118	3.13	5.91	10.7
$4 and under $5	32	4.16	5.93	4	4.01	11.92	82	4.11	7.96	34.7
$5 and under $6	9	5.14	5.43	4	5.22	4.98	49	5.14	8.76	10.1
$6 and over	13	7.23	7.80	1	9.36	7.66	51	9.11	12.51	42.8
Total	263	2.80	5.52	243	2.05	4.88	1,268	2.52	5.71	......
LOSS.										
Under $1	......	......	......	1	.68	.81	3	.74	1.48	......
$1 and under $2	10	1.38	1.64	25	1.34	2.37	60	1.40	1.50	1.4
$2 and under $3	15	2.21	2.33	42	2.18	1.72	126	2.20	1.89	26.0
$3 and under $4	4	3.14	1.82	4	3.15	1.47	16	3.13	2.75	45.5
$4 and under $5	2	4.16	1.62	3	4.01	2.86	9	4.11	3.69	34.2
$5 and under $6	1	5.14	3.00	1	5.22	6.02	7	5.14	3.89	5.4
$6 and over	5	7.23	1.98	1	9.36	5.92	6	9.11	3.95	1.5
Total	37	2.80	2.02	77	2.05	2.06	227	2.52	1.91	......

TABLE 12.—*Staple crops of certain States, 1860–1896.*

NORTH CAROLINA.

Crops.	1860.	1870.	1880.	1890.	1896.
Cotton ....bales	145,514	144,935	389,598	336,261	521,795
Corn ....bushels	30,078,564	18,454,215	28,019,839	25,783,623	29,504,148
Oats ....do	2,781,860	3,220,105	3,838,068	4,512,762	5,777,256
Wheat ....do	4,743,706	2,859,879	3,397,393	4,292,035	4,621,922
Tobacco ....pounds	32,853,250	11,150,087	26,986,213	36,375,258	68,629,170

SOUTH CAROLINA.

Crops.	1860.	1870.	1880.	1890.	1896.
Cotton ....bales	353,412	224,500	522,548	747,190	936,463
Corn ....bushels	15,065,606	7,614,207	11,767,099	13,770,417	15,781,374
Oats ....do	936,974	613,593	2,715,505	3,019,119	2,954,798
Wheat ....do	1,285,631	783,610	962,358	658,351	957,902
Tobacco ....pounds	104,412	34,805	45,678	222,898	(*a*)

a No separate estimate for this State.

GEORGIA.

Crops.	1860.	1870.	1880.	1890.	1896.
Cotton ....bales	701,840	743,934	814,441	1,191,846	1,299,340
Corn ....bushels	30,776,293	17,646,459	23,202,018	29,261,422	32,829,654
Oats ....do	1,231,817	1,904,601	5,548,743	4,707,821	5,085,288
Wheat ....do	2,544,913	2,127,017	3,159,771	1,096,312	1,609,872
Tobacco ....pounds	919,318	288,596	228,590	263,752	(*a*)

a No separate estimate for this State.

PROPORTION OF VALUE OF LINT COTTON AND SEED.

Table 13 shows in each State and Territory what proportion the values of lint and seed, respectively, bear to the total value of the yield per acre. The lowest value of lint on upland plantations is $14.03 in Oklahoma, and the highest $21.12 per acre in Louisiana. The lowest value of seed is $1.58 in Arkansas, and the highest $2.62 in South Carolina, the average on all plantations being for lint $16.93 and for seed $1.90 per acre. The lowest value of lint on sea-island plantations is $21.13 in Florida, and the highest $58.29 per acre in South Carolina. The lowest value of seed is $2.15 in Georgia, and the highest $4.52 in South Carolina, the average on all plantations being for lint $26.19 and for seed $2.46 per acre. The percentage of value of lint ranges from 89 to 91, and of seed from 9 to 11 on upland plantations, the average being for lint 90 and for seed 10 per cent. The percentage of value of lint on sea-island plantations ranges from 91 to 93, and for seed from 7 to 9, the average being for lint 92 and for seed 8 per cent.

TABLE 13.—*Average value and percentage of lint cotton and seed in each State and Territory.*

UPLAND COTTON.

State.	Lint, value per acre.	Seed, value per acre.	Lint.	Seed.
			Per cent.	*Per cent.*
Alabama	$16.19	$1.89	90	10
Arkansas	14.90	1.58	90	10
Florida	15.46	1.92	89	11
Georgia	16.96	2.01	89	11
Indian Territory	16.46	1.71	91	9
Louisiana	21.12	2.20	91	9
Mississippi	17.93	1.72	91	9
Missouri	18.32	2.18	89	11
North Carolina	20.14	2.32	90	10
Oklahoma	14.03	1.64	90	10
South Carolina	20.44	2.62	89	11
Tennessee	16.68	1.75	91	9
Texas	14.73	1.65	90	10
Virginia	17.89	2.06	90	10
Average	16.93	1.90	90	10

SEA-ISLAND COTTON.

State.	Lint, value per acre.	Seed, value per acre.	Lint.	Seed.
Florida	21.13	2.21	91	9
Georgia	25.43	2.15	92	8
South Carolina	58.29	4.52	93	7
Average	26.19	2.46	92	8

COST OF COTTON PRODUCTION BY IRRIGATION.

It has been disclosed by this investigation that cotton is produced to a limited extent, though at a high rate of profit, in the counties of Menard, Pecos, and Ward, on the western plains of Texas, and in Washington County, in the extreme southwestern corner of Utah. The commissioner of agriculture of Texas, in his report for 1895, states that there were in Menard 20, Pecos 50, and Ward County 18 miles of irrigation canals, but only a small portion of the area under irrigation is reported as devoted to cotton culture. The canals in Menard County are watered from the San Saba River, and in Pecos and Ward counties from the Pecos River.

There were three estimates of the cost of production returned from Menard, 2 from Pecos, and 7 from Ward County (Table 14). The lowest cost of cultivation is $12.08 in Pecos, and the highest, $33.15, in Menard County, the average for the 12 plantations being $19.92, which is $6.32 higher than the average cost ($13.60) per acre on all other plantations in Texas, and $4.50 per acre higher than the average ($15.42) in all States and Territories.

The yield per acre, in pounds of lint, ranges from 166 pounds in Pecos to 750 pounds in Menard County, the average on all 12 plantations being 512.4 pounds, which is 290.3 pounds greater than the average (222.1 pounds) in Texas, and 256.8 pounds greater than the average (255.6 pounds) in all States and Territories. The lowest price realized for lint cotton is 6½ and the highest 7 cents per pound, the average on all plantations being 6.82 cents per pound, which is only slightly higher than the Texas average and the average for all States and Territories. The difference is not great enough to indicate any superiority in the staple produced by irrigation, though it is possible that the comparatively low prices in the irrigated district may be due to inaccessibility to the market and not to the quality of the fiber. The average price of seed is a fraction of a cent higher than the average in Texas and all States and Territories.

The value of lint and seed per acre ranges from $13.14 in Pecos to $57.50 in Menard, the average being $38.86 for the twelve plantations. This is $22.48 higher than the Texas average ($16.38) and $19.83 higher than the average ($19.03) in all States and Territories. The average profit ranges from $1.06 in Pecos to $32.33 in Menard County, the average on the twelve plantations being $18.94 per acre, which is $14.66 higher than the average ($4.28) of Texas plantations reporting a profit, and $13.74 higher than the average ($5.20) in all States and Territories reporting a profit. None of the twelve plantations reports a loss.

With the exception of the two plantations in Pecos County, where the yield per acre on one is 166 and on the other 400 pounds, the county average ranges from 500 to 750 pounds of lint cotton per acre. Indeed, with the two exceptions noted, the yield was so high as to lead to the conclusion that the planters estimated the yield in seed, instead of lint cotton. Correspondence developed the fact, however, that the estimates in all instances were correctly reported. As indicating the high yield on irrigated lands, Mr. G. Noyes, of Menard County, writes the Department that as much as 1,000 pounds of lint cotton per acre had been produced on his plantation. In 1896, on 67 acres, he produced 52,320 pounds, and in 1897, on 63 acres, 45,240 pounds of lint. In 1896 Mr. J. T. Westbrook, on 17 acres, produced 16,706 pounds; Mr. A. Pentecost, on 15½ acres, 15,265 pounds; Mr. G. R. Coleman, on 25 acres,

22,018 pounds, and Mr. M. Cantwell, on 40 acres, 21,299 pounds of lint. Mr. Noyes adds that it is a fact not generally known that more cotton to the acre can be produced on irrigated than on "dry" lands in Texas.

It will be noticed that the cost of production on these irrigated plantations is remarkably low, the average in Menard being 3.58 cents, in Pecos 5.86 cents, and in Ward County 2.41 cents per pound, the average for the twelve plantations being 3.09 cents per pound, which is 2.29 cents less than the average in Texas, and 2.18 cents per pound less than the cost on plantations in all States and Territories.

One estimate is reported from Washington County, Utah, which places the cost at 8.89 cents per pound. Although a profit of $4.45 per acre is reported on this farm, the high cost is apparently due to the exceptional charges for plowing, planting seed, picking, and marketing.

TABLE 14.—*Average cost of producing an acre of cotton in 1896, by irrigation, in Texas and Utah.*

State and county.	Rent.	Plowing.	Seed.	Planting seed.	Irrigation.	Chopping and hoeing.	Picking.	Ginning and pressing.	Bagging and ties.	Marketing.	Repairing implements.	Other expenses.	TOTAL COST.
TEXAS.													
Menard	$4.33	$2.58	$0.15	$0.13	$2.02	$1.38	$9.93	$2.89	$1.65	$1.56	$0.22	$0.83	$28.57
Pecos	1.95	2.28	.38	.62	1.00	1.62	3.75	2.88	.71	2.70	.50	.50	18.89
Ward	2.90	.99	.15	.15	1.24	.76	7.07	2.31	.69	.18	.07	(*a*)	16.51
Average	3.10	1.60	.19	.22	1.62	1.06	7.23	2.55	.94	.94	.18	.29	19.92
UTAH.													
Washington	3.00	7.50	.30	2.00	1.50	1.25	15.00	2.50	1.50	4.00	1.50	(*a*)	40.05

State and county.	Pounds of lint.	Price per pound.	Bushels of seed.	Price per bushel.	TOTAL RETURN.	PROFIT.	Number of farms reporting.	Cost of picking per 100 pounds.	Cost of production per pound.
TEXAS.		*Cents.*		*Cents.*					*Cents.*
Menard	677	6.75	43.4	10.0	$50.17	$21.60	3	$0.49	3.58
Pecos	283	7.00	17.0	13.5	22.01	3.12	2	.44	5.86
Ward	507	6.81	32.4	13.3	38.83	22.32	7	.46	2.41
Average	512.4	6.82	32.6	12.5	38.86	18.94	12	.47	3.09
UTAH.									
Washington	400	10.00	30.0	15.0	44.50	4.45	1	1.25	8.89

a Nothing reported.

THE COST OF COTTON PRODUCTION AT EXPERIMENT STATIONS.

An effort was made to ascertain the cost of cotton production by the intensive methods practiced at the various Government experiment stations, but reports were received from only three stations. The estimates made by the directors of the stations are given in Table 15.

It will be noticed that the average cost of cultivation at the three stations is $5.25 greater than the general average cost on all upland plantations (Table 1), the former being $20.67 and the latter $15.42 per acre. But the average value of lint and seed is $13.90 greater than the average on all upland plantations, the former being $32.93 and the latter $19.03. This is not due to any excess in the value of lint and seed, for the difference in the prices of each is slight, but to the excess in yield, the average on the experiment farms being 420 pounds as against an average of 255.6 pounds on all upland plantations, or 164.4 pounds greater on the experiment farms. The average profit per acre is $12.26, or $8.65 greater than the average net profit on all upland plantations, while the average cost of production of lint cotton is 4.09 cents per pound, or 1.18 cents less than the average cost on all upland plantations, the latter being 5.27 cents per pound.

TABLE 15.—*Average cost of producing an acre of cotton in 1896 at several experiment stations.*

	Rent.	Plowing.	Seed.	Planting seed.	Fertilizers.	Distributing fertilizers.	Chopping and hoeing.	Picking.	Ginning and pressing.	Bagging and ties.	Marketing.	Repairing implements.	Other expenses.	Total cost.
Auburn, Ala	$1.00	$3.92	$0.15	$0.40	$3.50	$0.50	$1.50	$2.70	$1.50	$0.75	$0.25	$0.50	$1.00	$17.67
Fayetteville, Ark	4.00	3.40	.20	.20	.00	.00	2.00	5.80	1.00	.87	.40	.25	.25	18.37
Experiment, Ga	5.00	1.87	.25	.25	8.00	.15	2.35	7.00	1.50	.80	.30	.50	1.00	28.97
Average	2.75	3.28	.19	.31	3.75	.29	1.84	4.55	1.38	.79	.30	.44	.81	20.67

	Pounds of lint.	Price per pound.	Bushels of seed.	Price per bushel.	Total yield.	Profit.	Number of experiments.	Cost of picking per 100 pounds.	Cost of production per pound.
		Cents.		*Cents.*				*Cents.*	*Cents.*
Auburn, Ala	300	7	18.0	14	$23.52	$5.85	2	.30	5.05
Fayetteville, Ark	410	7	27.5	9	31.17	12.80	1	.47	3.88
Experiment, Ga	670	7	44.0	15	53.50	24.53	1	.35	3.34
Average	420	7	26.9	13	32.93	12.26	4	.36	4.09

COST OF COTTON PRODUCTION PRIOR TO AND SINCE 1860.

It is a curious fact that from the beginning of the present century, when cotton first assumed importance as a staple crop, down to 1861, when under the slave system it attained supreme importance, no data in all that period of sixty years can be found giving any definite information as to the cost of cotton production in any State, or the smallest community of any State. During the slave period political economists wrote labored essays supporting the domestic economy and exploiting the agricultural resources of the cotton States, and during a long period of unexampled agricultural prosperity succeeded in convincing the planter that "cotton is king." This was a period (1800-1840) when cotton was in great demand, and prices were most of the time high.

Perhaps it is not surprising that in those days most planters did not care to trouble themselves with keeping accounts of the business affairs of the plantation. What did it matter so long as there was an active demand for every pound of cotton grown? The commission merchant was ever ready to advance half the value of the crop long before its maturity, and take it all at remunerative prices as soon as ready for the market. After a while prosperity led to overproduction and the inevitable result—low prices. But even when business depression and low prices followed, and the planter began concerning himself with his imperiled situation, the records do not show that he had any definite information as to what it was costing him to make his cotton. He only knew that he was losing money and getting into debt.

About 1840 began a series of annual conventions. held by the planters to "combine in their own defense" and find a remedy for "low and irregular prices." While they were "resolving" and searching for the remedies a short crop almost doubled the price (1849-50) and solved the problem—solved for the time being the problem of prices, but not of the cost of production.

During all that period of depression neither the proceedings of those conventions nor the periodical writers of the times throw any light on the question of the cost of raising cotton. However, the planter was not so much to blame, for none of the States encouraged the collection of agricultural statistics, and the Federal Government only to a limited extent. Moreover, under his system of domestic economy, it would have been a very difficult matter for the planter to arrive at any definite conclusion as to the cost of production, for the prime object was to make the plantation as nearly self-sustaining as possible, to produce —as was frequently the boast—everything required for man and beast, except "trace chains and wool hats." Hence, he not only "raised" negroes, but mules, horses, sheep, cattle, hogs, corn, oats, cane for his molasses, "tanbark for his tanyard," and spun his wool and cotton into yarns and wove them into cloth. His plantation was a veritable hive of industry, too complex in its economic arrangement to admit of precise calculations of cost. The interest on the amount of capital invested was the chief consideration.

Estimates of the cost of production were made, but they were based upon individual experience, and even then often included the growing of other things besides cotton. How. for instance, shall we arrive at any satisfactory conclusion as to the cost of production on the South Carolina plantation where $200 is credited to "increase in negroes," and $100 debited to "loss by death of old negro:" or where, on another plantation, "60 mules and mares, and one jack and one stud, average $60," are charged against "capital invested," and "80 cords of tan bark for his tanyard, $480," credited as part of the income? De Bow (Industrial Resources of the South and West, Vol. I, 1852) cites two estimates of the cost of cotton production, in which these items enter into the account of expenses and income.

There are to be found a few estimates that place the cost at a definite figure, as by the Southern Planter who (in "Notes on Political Economy as Applicable to the United States") fixes the cost in 1844 at 3 cents per pound; and by others, fixing it at 5 and 6 cents in 1849, 3 and 6 cents in 1850, 7⅝ cents in 1852, 4½ and 7½ cents in 1854, and 8 cents in 1855. But all of these are valueless, because they are only individual estimates. There is no means of ascertaining either the cost of rent and labor, which represent at least 65 to 70 per cent of the cost of cultivation, or the yield per acre, which is also of primary importance in determining the cost of production.

In 1845 farm labor was worth in North Carolina 50 to 75 cents per day, and from $7 to $8 per month; in South Carolina farm negroes hired for $5 per month, or 28 cents per day for men and less for women. In some parts of the State white laborers hired for $15 per month or $160 per annum, and negro laborers from $8 to $10 per month or $100 per annum; in Georgia farm labor was worth 75 cents per day or $15 per month, and in Alabama 30 cents per day or $6 per month; in Louisiana 50 cents per day or $12 to $15 per month, and in Mississippi 50 cents per day or $12 to $15 per month, including board and clothing. In Tennessee farm labor was worth 50 cents per day or $10 to $12 per month.—(Patent Office Report, 1845.)

In 1847 the wages of a man slave in Louisiana were $100 and of a woman $80 per annum, food and clothing furnished by the person hiring, and in Virginia $120 to $150 per annum and board.—(Patent Office Report, 1847.)

In 1849 white farm labor in Virginia hired at $1 to $2 per day with board, and slave farm labor at $60 to $80 per year with board and clothing, while in Georgia the average for farm hands was $5 to $8 per month, and slave hire by the year $40 to $60 for females and $50 to $90 for males. The same year, in Mississippi, slave labor was worth $15 per month "for common outdoor labor, the owner clothing them, paying physician's bills, taxes, the employer boarding them. When hired by the year on plantations, $70 to $75 for a full hand, the employer paying doctor's bills, taxes, etc."—(Patent Office Report, 1849.)

Olmsted, in his "Journeys and Explorations in the Cotton Kingdom" (1861), throws some light on the subject of wages paid to free labor in Virginia just prior to the civil war. He tells of a planter living in the neighborhood of Richmond who freed his slaves and employed Irish laborers on his farm. To some of them he paid $100 a year, but the average wages were $120 a year, including board. This planter told him that the wages paid for slaves when hired for agricultural labor were about the same as for free labor. But in case slaves were hired, in addition to money and board, the slave employer had to furnish clothing and lose the time in case of sickness. In North Carolina he found the rate of wages from 50 cents to $1 per day, or $8 per month. In Virginia the allowance of food to slaves was 1½ pecks of meal and 3 pounds of bacon a week, and on a large plantation on the Mississippi

River 1 peck of meal, 4 pints of salt, and 4 or sometimes as much as 5 pounds of bacon a week. But in addition to this, as a rule, every slave family was allowed a garden patch large enough to grow all the vegetables necessary for its consumption. The cost of clothing, per annum, for a hired hand was estimated at $30. In 1849 (Patent Office Report) the cost of boarding slave hands in Virginia, per annum, was estimated "for each grown person" as follows:

150 pounds bacon, at 7 cents	$10.50
12 bushels corn, at 40 cents	4.80
2 bushels wheat, at 85 cents	1.70
Sugar, molasses, vegetables, milk, fresh meat	5.00
Total cost of food	22.00

"Each hand," says Edward Ingle, speaking of the plantation system prior to 1860, "was given 4 pounds of clear meat and a peck of meal, with seasonable vegetables, each week."—(Southern Side Lights.)

The commissioner of labor of North Carolina, in his report for 1896, states that the average wages of farm labor in the State was $8.50 for men, $5 for women, and $3 for children. In addition to wages, rations to the average value of $3.90, and house, pasture, garden, fuel, fruit, etc., to the average value of $2.80 were furnished. It appears, therefore, that the rate of farm wages in North Carolina was 50 cents per month higher in 1896 than in 1845 and 1860, while the cost of rations was much higher in that State in 1896 than in Virginia in 1849; the former, according to the commissioner of labor, being $3.90, and the latter, as shown above, $1.83⅓ per month for each farm laborer. The Virginia estimate, however, was for slave labor, and the North Carolina estimate for free labor.

On the other hand, according to the results of some dietary investigations undertaken in 1895 and 1896 by Professors Atwater and Woods, of this Department, among the plantation negroes of the "Black Belt" in Alabama, the average cost of the animal and vegetable food consumed by each man seems to have been less than the cost of boarding slave hands in Virginia in 1849.

As a matter of comparison, the prices of some articles of food and clothing, and other items bearing upon the cost of cultivation and production of cotton in 1843 and 1896 are given below, in Table 16 (the prices being the highest and lowest on the 1st of September, October, November, and December of each year). The year 1843 is selected because the price of cotton was very nearly the same as in 1896. The prices of the commodities for 1843 are wholesale prices at Charleston, and those for 1896 at New Orleans, except for articles of clothing, which are Boston wholesale prices.

The price of mules in 1843 is that for which they sold that year in Mississippi, and for 1896 the average price in all the cotton States as reported to this Department.

TABLE 16.—*Comparative cost of items relating to cotton production.*

Items.	1843. Charleston.	1896. New Orleans.
Food:		
Bacon .... per pound..	\$0.03½ to \$0.05¾	\$0.04½ to \$0.05½
Mess pork .... per barrel..	7.00 to 11.00	7.25 to 9.00
Flour .... do....	6.00 to 6.50	3.50 to 5.00
Corn .... per bushel..	.37½ to .40	.27 to .36
Oats .... do....	.25 to .28	.25 to .27
Salt .... per sack..	1.75 to 2.00	.65 to .72½
Sugar, brown .... per pound..	.06 to .08	.02⅝ to .03⅜
Coffee, Rio .... do....	.06 to .08½	.10⅞ to .12½
Molasses, plantation .... per gallon..	.19 to .20	.04 to .11
Clothing:		
Shoes, brogans .... per pair..	1.25	.80 to 1.00
Shirtings, brown .... per yard..	.04½ to .08	.03¼ to .03¾
Prints .... do....	.07 to .20	.03½ to .05½
Plaids, cotton .... do....	.07 to .11	.03¾
Other items:		
Bagging, 2-pound Kentucky .... do....	.15 to .16	.06¼
Rope .... per pound..	.07 to .10	.05¼ to .05½
Iron ties .... do....	.07	.05¾
Pig iron .... per ton..	30.00	9.50 to 10.50
Mules .... each..	70.00 to 125.00	64.00
Freights:		
Columbia to Charleston .... per 100 pounds..	*a*.25 to .30	.20
Goldsboro to Wilmington .... do....	*b*.65 to .70	.23
New Orleans to New York .... do....	.30 to .37½	.32
New Orleans to Liverpool *c* .... per pound..	½ penny.	¼ to 17/64 penny.

a In 1855. *b* Prior to 1860. *c* In pence.

Whatever be the difference in the cost of maintaining farm labor under the slave and free labor systems—and it would be a distressing commentary upon free institutions if under the latter there had not been some increase, not in the relative cost of the articles consumed, but in the laborer's demand for more of the creature comforts—it is undoubtedly true that in recent years there has been a considerable reduction in the cost of some of the items entering into the cultivation and production of cotton. As compared with 1843, and the period prior to the civil war, this is particularly true with reference to bagging and ties and the cost of marketing.

In 1840, according to the Natchez Free Trader, Kentucky bagging was worth 25 cents per yard, and rope for binding bales 12½ cents per pound. Allowing 6 yards of bagging and 8 pounds of rope to the bale, the cost of wrapping a bale of 400 pounds, the average weight at that time, was \$2.50, as against \$1.10 for a 500-pound bale in 1896 (Table 8). Hazard's Commercial and Statistical Register says that "In January, 1840, the American Chamber of Commerce passed a resolution, 'That on and after the 1st of January, 1840, a bank commission of one-fourth per cent be generally charged in addition to the commission of 3 per cent on the sale of cotton.' This custom of charging a bank commission was in vogue before this date both in this country and in Liverpool."

With the view of ascertaining the difference in the cost of marketing cotton at Mobile in 1840 and 1897, the Department's special agent at Mobile was requested to duplicate for 1897 the itemized statement of cost, as published in Hunt's Merchants' Magazine (vol. 11) for 1840. The statement given below shows that in 1840 it cost \$18.15 to market a bale of middling cotton weighing 420 pounds, or 4.32 cents per pound, while in 1897, on account of the elimination of some of the charges, the cost was only $7.89 for a 500-pound bale, or 1.58 cents per pound, a saving of 2.74 cents since 1840.

Charges for marketing a bale of cotton, 1840 and 1897.

[The charges exhibited in this table were incurred at Mobile, Ala., exclusive of insurance, calculated on a bale of 420 pounds of middling upland cotton at 10 cents in 1840, with ocean freight at ⅜d.; and on a bale of 500 pounds of middling upland cotton at 5½ cents in 1897, ocean freight at $\frac{11}{32}$d.]

Charge.	In 1840.	In 1897.
Wharfage (if by river)	$0.10	a $0.08
Weighing	.12½	.10
Draying to press	.12½	.10
Storage	.20	.25
Factor's commissions	.80	.05
Add for freight to city (by river)	1.50	.75
Chargeable to planter	2.85	1.93
Brokerage	.25	.50
Storage until compressed	.12½	b .06
Drayage to vessel or lighter	.08	.00
Wharfage	.10	.04
Compressing	.00	.75
Commission on purchase	.80	c $0.00
Freight and primage	6.64½	2.46½
Chargeable to purchaser	8.00	3.75½

Charge.	In 1840.	In 1897.
Compressing	$0.80	d $0.00
Lighterage to lower bay	.25	.00
Stowing	.25	.35
Chargeable to vessel	1.30	.35
Total charges on a bale	12.15	6.03
Add port charges at Liverpool	6.00	1.86
Total, on both sides, per bale	18.15	7.89

a If by railroad, no wharfage charge.
b No charge if shipped in ten days.
c Included in charges for brokerage.
d Purchaser pays charge for compressing.

There was very little change from these charges down to 1850, according to the statement of a committee to a convention of cotton planters, held at Tallahassee, Fla., in 1851. The committee in their report say:

Taking the period of ten years, from 1840 to 1850, it is found that the average price in Liverpool was 2.95 cents per pound higher than the average during the same time in the seaports of the United States. * * * Thus it is shown that, exclusive of charges in interior towns, the expense paid by the planter would be nearly $17 per bale, and this, too, on a range of prices of only 7 cents and 7 mills in the American ports.

A cotton planter of Columbia, S. C., "of high respectability," in a letter to the "Plow, Loom and Anvil" (1848), says:

I find that planting cotton is no longer profitable; for after paying for bagging, rope, twine, freights, drayage, storage, insurance, and commissions, the cotton selling for 7 cents per pound, the bale amounts to $24.50; deducting the expense ($4) from the amount leaves $20.50, or nearly one dollar in every six.

The Department's special agent at Charleston furnishes the following information in regard to freight rates and charges for selling cotton in Charleston in 1898, and prior to 1860:

In 1855 the freight rate on cotton from Hamburg, S. C., to Charleston, for a 400-pound bale was $1.12½, and on less than 400 pounds 30 cents per 100 pounds, and from Columbia, S. C., the same rates. From points on the Greenville and Columbia Railroad it was $1.25 for a 400-pound bale, and 30 cents per 100 pounds for less than 400 pounds. From points on the Columbia and Charlotte Railroad the rates were the same as on the Greenville and Columbia Railroad. At the present time the rate from Columbia to Charleston is 20 cents per 100 pounds, and from Hamburg or Augusta 18 cents per 100 pounds. About the year 1860 the rate on the South Carolina Railroad (Augusta to Charleston) was uniformly $1.25 from all points to Charleston.

The storage on cotton (prior to 1860) was charged by the week, and not by the month as now, and was 8 cents for the first week and 4 cents for the intermediate weeks, and 8 cents for the last week, the rate being raised the last week to cover the extra labor incident to turning it over to the buyer. If the cotton was shipped by water, there was a charge of 4 cents for landing, and when the bale was delivered to the buyer there was a charge of 4 cents for shipping and 6 cents for weighing. Buyers did not then, as now, reweigh the cotton. Insurance was taken out in yearly and floating policies at a cost of 2½ per cent per annum, about the same as now, but the factor charged one-half per cent per month. Drayage was uniformly 12½ cents per bale: mending, if the bale was damaged, the same as now, 25 cents per bale. Commission for selling was the same as now, 2½ per cent on the gross proceeds. The following will indicate the comparative charges at present and prior to 1860:

Cotton charges at Charleston, S. C., prior to 1860, compared with 1898.

Charges.	Prior to 1860.		1898.	
1 bale, 400 pounds, at 12½ cents per pound		$50.00		
1 bale, 400 pounds, at 5¾ cents per pound				$23.00
Freight from Columbia	$1.25		$0.80	
Insurance, one month	.25		.40	
Storage, 1 month	.24		.50	
Drayage from railroad to warehouse	.13		.10	
Weighing	.06		......	
Shipping	.04		......	
Commissions, 2½ per cent	1.25	—3.22	.58	—2.38
Net proceeds		46.78		20.62

It should be noted that if the bale was sold within a week the charge for storage (prior to 1860) would be changed from 24 to 8 cents, and in some cases the insurance would be but 12½ cents for less than a week; and, also, that the above account of sale represents the charges against cotton upon which advances were made by the factor for plantation supplies and money to make the crop. On free cotton, i. e., cotton not shipped against advances, a charge of $1 per bale is made to cover all other charges, except freight on cotton sold within a month from the date of its receipt. If the cotton was on hand but one day the charges would be the same as for twenty-nine days. The rates last named are lower than they were five or six years ago, as warehouse charges have been reduced one-half, and insurance rates have fallen because the warehouses are better and safer.

One of the advantages enjoyed by the planter of to-day over his antebellum prototype, is found in the large number of banks in the interior towns. These banks advance means to the planter to make his crops, thus enabling him to sell his cotton in the local markets to mill buyers, speculators, and agents of exporters. The competition in the local interior markets between these buyers has frequently resulted in a higher range of prices than could be obtained in Charleston, and hence the cotton factorage business has declined to insignificant proportions, and the through and ship-side business has proportionately increased. Any shipper, whether a planter or merchant, who has on hand a lot of cotton, may ship it direct to exporters here at a cost of only 54 cents per bale, the charges being, drayage 10, wharfage 4, and compressing 40 cents per bale. Or, he may ship to a factor at a cost of 63 cents for drayage and compressing, commission charges added. The compress companies charge no storage in consideration of getting the compressing of the cotton. Landing cotton in Liverpool would cost, plus above charges, freight 37 to 40 cents per 100 pounds, insurance 1 per cent, free of commissions to shipper.

An unsuccessful effort was made to ascertain what changes, if any, have taken place in the past ten or twenty years in the freight rates on cotton from some of the principal inland points to the seaboard markets, and also to foreign ports on through bills of lading from inland points. Only one satisfactory reply could be given to the Department's request for this information. Mr. E. H. Hinton, traffic manager of the Central of Georgia Railway, has furnished the following comparative rates:

From Macon to Savannah proper, season 1876-77, 40 cents per 100 pounds. Shipside to Savannah, 43 cents per 100 pounds.

From Macon to Savannah proper, season 1886-87, 40 cents per 100 pounds. Shipside to Savannah. 43 cents per 100 pounds.

From Macon to Savannah, season 1896-97, including shipside delivery, September 1 to November 9, 1896, 34 cents: November 9. 1896. to January 20. 1897. 28 cents, and from January 20 to and including balance of season. 34 cents per 100 pounds. The prevailing ocean rate to Liverpool during the season 1896-97 was 50 cents per 100 pounds, which, added to the Macon to Savannah rate, would make the cost of freight from 78 to 84 cents per 100 pounds from Macon to Liverpool. Mr. George Pollock, general auditor of the Missouri, Kansas and Texas Railway, gives the rate from Waco to Galveston, as follows: 1886-87, 70 cents; 1896-97, 65 cents, and 1897-98, 60 cents per 100 pounds.

Mr. H. T. Newcomb, Bulletin No. 15, Division of Statistics, United States Department of Agriculture, gives the following rates, in cents, per 100 pounds, from New Orleans and Memphis:

Year.	From New Orleans to—			From Memphis to—	
	Boston.	New York.	Philadelphia.	New York.	Boston.
1880	60	55	55	74	79
1897	55	50	50	50	55

While these data show that there has been some reduction in inland freight rates on cotton, the most notable reduction has taken place in ocean rates to Liverpool, where the price of cotton is practically regulated for all other markets. The rate from New Orleans to Liverpool, according to the New Orleans Price Current, was as high as one-half of a penny in 1851, 1856, and 1857; three fourths of a penny in 1852, seven-eighths of a penny in 1853, and 1 penny per pound in 1861.

The above statistical and other data, as already intimated, are not given with the view of arriving at any definite conclusion as to the comparative cost of cotton production with slave and free labor, but rather that some side light might be thrown upon an economic system under which a large portion of the population of the country flourished for more than a half century.

We may at least conclude, however, that since the slave labor period there has been a considerable reduction in the cost of bagging and ties, and in the cost of marketing cotton—not in the home markets only, but what is of most importance, in the markets that consume the great bulk of the crop. As the foreign spinners consume the surplus, and as they practically regulate prices, any reduction in the cost of delivery to them must result in a corresponding increase in price to the planter.

THE COST OF COTTON PRODUCTION AT DIFFERENT PERIODS.

Having ascertained that the average cost of cotton production in 1896 is 5.27 cents per pound, the questions naturally arise: How does this compare with the cost in former periods? Has it increased or decreased, and does it appear that the minimum of cost has been reached? Unfortunately the data on the subject are too limited and incomplete to warrant a conclusion, or even to make a satisfactory comparison, but such as are available are given below, more as a matter of interest than of practical value.

UNDER THE SLAVE LABOR SYSTEM.

1822. Among the first estimates relating to the cost of production are two itemized statements that appeared, September 27, 1822, in a circular issued by Messrs. Benson, Cropper & Co., a well-known cotton commission house of one of the Southern ports. They are really not estimates of the cost of producing cotton, but rather statements showing the expenses connected with the conduct of two plantations, the amount of capital invested, and the interest realized upon the investment. The copy from the circular printed in the American Farmer, Volume IV, pages 308-9, is as follows, and is literal:

First estimate of cost on cotton plantations.

Food, 13 bushels of corn, or 1 peck per week, at 70 cents per bushel	$9.10
1 hat, $1.50; 2 pair shoes, $2.50; 1 blanket, $3	7.00
6 yards plains, at 75 cents, $4.50; doctor and physic, $1	5.50
One suit of osnaburgs	1.50
Tools, vehicles, and horses	1.00
Tax	1.50
	25.60

One hundred negroes are equal to 60 good working hands.

100 average negroes worth now perhaps $350 each		$35,000
100 average negroes or 60 working hands will cultivate each 3½ acres, or 210 acres, worth per acre $50		10,500
Planter's capital		45,500
If 1 working hand cultivates 3½ acres, which give 900 pounds of clean cotton, 60 working hands, or 100 average hands, will cultivate 210 acres, which yield 54,000 pounds clean cotton, which at 11 cents per pound is gross		5,940
Deduct the expense of keeping 100 hands, at $24, in lieu of $25.60, the estimate	$2.400	
Factorage, 2½ per cent on $5,940	148	
Carriage, rent, drayage, and labor on 185 bags or 54,000 pound weight, at $2.50	[sic] 712	
Bagging, at 90 cents per bale	[sic] 256	
		[sic] 5,316
Leaves net profit of 100 negroes, or 60 working hands, at 11 cents	[sic] 2,342	

Then it appears that a capital of $45,500 in land and negroes yields, if the cotton sell at 11 cents per pound, $2,324, or $5\frac{1}{10}$ per cent.

Second estimate of cost on cotton plantations.

Cost of keeping one negro a year on a cotton plantation:

Food, 13 bushels of corn, or 1 peck per week, at 70 cents per bushel........	$9.10
[Touching this item, this planter says that he appoints a certain portion of his negroes to cultivate breadstuff for those employed in his plantations, and that whether he cultivate it or buy it, it will cost as above.]	
1 pair of shoes, $1.25; 1 blanket in 3 years, at $3, is $1....................	2.25
6 yards of plaids, at 75 cents, $4.50; doctor and physic, $1	5.50
1 suit osnaburgs for summer..	1.50
Tools, vehicles, and horses	1.50
Tax	1.00
	20.85

This planter says that on an average, $20 will defray the expense per head, and these items come near it. The negro, out of his own earnings, buys a hat and any more shoes he may require.

But out of 100 average hands, 50 only are workers, the other 50 being rendered noneffective by infancy, infirmity, or from being used for domestic purposes.

100 average negroes, worth $400 each	$40,000
100 average negroes, or 50 working hands, will cultivate each 3½ acres, or 175 acres, worth per acre $80..	14,000
Amount of capital in negroes and land	54,000

The land is only worth $20 an acre, but a plantation must have at least four times the quantity that is actually employed for cotton, seeing that it soon gets exhausted. It is too expensive to restore it by manure, and it lies in fallow until the remainder of the estate has undergone exhaustion, so that $80 is really the cost of an acre of the land actually in use.

The average gangs of negroes would, not long ago, have commanded $425 each, so that the above is a low estimate.

If 1 working hand cultivates 3½ acres, which will yield 900 pounds of clean cotton, 50 hands will cultivate 175 acres, which will yield 45,000 pounds of clean cotton, and which, at 10 cents per pound, is...........		$4,500.00
Deduct expense of keeping 100 hands, at $20....................	$2,000.00	
Factorage on $4,500, at 2½ per cent	112.50	
Carriage, rent, drayage, and labor on 150 bags, or 45,000-pound weight, $2.50 each	375.00	
Bagging, at 90 cents per bale	135.00	
		2,622.50
Net profit of 100 average or 50 working hands, at 10 cents..........		1,877.50

So that on a capital of negroes and land, amounting to $54,000, there is a profit of 3 per cent and twenty-five fifty-fourths of 1 per cent, at 10 cents per pound.

[Patent Office Report, 1844.]

1843. As to the cost of production in 1843, the editor of the Southern Quarterly Review (1845, Vol. III), commenting on an address by General Hamilton, of South Carolina, says that cotton could not be grown in South Carolina at a profit for less than 8 cents per pound. At that time it was selling at only 6 cents. Dr. McCloud, of Alabama, writing to the Commissioner of Patents in 1844, says: "My experiments in improving the culture of the cotton plant are rapidly gaining ground among planters, and I think I have reduced it to a positive demonstration that cotton may be grown on the improved plan of manure and checks and sold in the market by the planter at 3 cents per pound, at least more profitably than it can be grown and sold on the ordinary plan of the country at 6 cents to 8 cents per pound." A Mississippi correspondent, writing to the Commissioner on the subject of the overproduction of cotton (1844), says: "The consequence is prices are below the cost of production; we can not grow it for 4 cents net, at the present high price of negroes, etc."

[Extracts from "Notes on Political Economy as Applicable to the United States, by a Southern Planter."]

1844. Let us now calculate what cotton can be grown for when prices get down to a mere support for master and slave. With the proper economy, by the owner living on his place, deriving his household and table expenses from it, and clothing and feeding his own slaves, his annual expenses, consisting of salt, iron, medicine, taxes, wrapping for his cotton, and overseer's wages, do not exceed 2 cents per pound on the product of the crop. All over that is a profit in their sense—that is, over and above annual expenses. I will give the details to make this clear. A plantation of 50 hands makes the average of 7 bales to the hand, weighing 450 pounds. This is 350 bales. Suppose 2 cents for expenses. This amounts to $3,150 on the crop. This crop, say, sells for 4 cents a pound, net, and, clear of charges for transportation, insurance, and commission for selling, leaves $3,150 profit for the luxuries of the owner, who gets his necessaries out of the plantation by living on it. This is a very pretty sum; and half of it would be ample for him, which would reduce cotton to 3 cents. As to insurance, unfortunately, the slaves not only insure themselves, but give a large increase, which grows up with the owner's children and furnishes them with outfits by the time they need them. Now, I will go into a calculation to show that 2 cents a pound cover the annual expenses. Here follow the items, taking a plantation of 50 hands as a basis:

For overseer	$500
For salt	20
Iron	30
Medicines	20
Doctor's bill *	100
Bagging and rope (12½ cents for the first and 5 cents for the second)	300
Taxes	100
Sundry small things	100
Total	1,170

The writer speaks from experience, for he is a planter of cotton and owns slaves. All this amounts to $1,170, much below the allowance of 2 cents a pound, amounting, as we have seen, to $3,150. I only wish to show that we can grow cotton for 3 cents a pound and have a living profit. The cotton culture, then, is sure to go on in this country at any price, from 3 cents up, that the market warrants, and with increased energies. These facts warrant us in asserting, which we do broadly and unqualifiedly, that we can grow cotton cheaper than any other people on earth, not even excepting the Hindoos. The consequence of this will be that we will take the market of the world and keep it supplied with cotton.

[S. B., in Skinner's Journal of Agriculture, Vol. II.]

1846. A very fair average crop of cotton from an acre is 150 pounds of ginned cotton. It is generally agreed, and I think fairly, that a hand, including his finding and lost time, costs about 50 cents per day, and a hand and a horse $1. These sums are about fair daily wages. The expenses of cultivating an acre of cotton may be estimated as follows:

To breaking up one acre	$1.00
Bedding and preparing for planting	1.00
Planting	.50
Replanting and thinning	.50
Plowing and scraping 4 times	2.00
Hoeing	2.00
Gathering	2.50
Ginning, packing, rope and bagging	1.50
Rent of land	1.50
Total	12.50

To pay the rate of wages stated, the price of 150 pounds of cotton grown on an acre at the estimated cost of $12.50 must be 8⅓ cents per pound net at the gin house. But for five years past the net price at the gin house has scarcely averaged 6 cents, and establishing an annual loss of 25 cents in its culture in South Carolina, and I believe in Georgia.

* For you can contract by the year, and it is often done, at $2 a head.

[Solon Robinson, in National Intelligencer, 1849.]

1849. The cost of making 331,136 pounds of cotton last year upon one of the best plantations of South Carolina was $17,894.48, or a fraction over 5 cents and 4 mills a pound, including freight and commission, as well as interest upon a fair valuation of property.

The cost, exclusive of freight and commission and including interest, of making 128,000 pounds upon the "canebrake lands of Alabama" last year was $6,676.80, a fraction over 5 cents and 2 mills a pound. This is considered the richest cotton land in the world, and although the crop was called a small one, it was probably about an average one. The field hands upon this place numbered 75, counting all over 12 years old, which gives a fraction less than four and one-third bales to each. Now this crop has to be hauled over about 25 miles of the worst roads in the world when wet, as they usually are at the time the crop is ready to go to market, and then down the difficult and dangerous navigation of the Tombigbee River.

I am satisfied that these two crops give a better showing than three-fourths of the cotton crops of the United States. My own opinion is that whenever cotton is below 6 cents it does not pay interest upon the capital invested, except perhaps in some few instances.

Below I give a table of items of expense upon the first plantation mentioned. This is owned by Col. J. M. Williams, of Society Hill, and lies upon what is called the swamp lands of the Pedee River. These items are necessary to show that I have not stated the expenses too high:

The capital consists of 4,200 acres of land (2,700 in cultivation), at $15 ..	$63,000.00
254 slaves, at $350 each, average old and young	89,900.00
60 mules and mares, and 1 jack and 1 stud, average $60	3,720.00
200 head of cattle, at $10	2,000.00
500 head of hogs, at $2	1,000.00
23 carts and 6 wagons	520.00
60 bull-tongue plows, 60 shaving plows, 25 turning plows, 15 drill plows, 15 harrows, at an average of $1.50 each	262.00
All other plantation tools, estimated worth	1,000.00
Total ....(sic)..	161,000.00

Cash expenses:

Interest is only counted on the first five items, $158,620, at 7 per cent.	11,103.00
3,980 yards Dundee bagging, at 16 cents (5 yards to a bale)	636.80
3,184 pounds of rope, at 6 cents	191.04
Taxes on 254 slaves, at 76 cents	193.04
Taxes on land	70.00
3 overseers' wages	900.00
Medical attendance, $1.25 per head	317.00
Bill of yearly supply of iron, average	100.00
Plows and other tools purchased, annual average	100.00
200 pairs of shoes, $175; annual supply of hats, $100	275.00
Bill of cotton and woolen cloth	810.00
100 cotton comforters, in lieu of bed blankets	125.00
100 oilcloth capotes (New York cost)	87.50
20 small woolen blankets for infants	25.00
Calico dress and handkerchief for each woman and girl (extra of other clothing)	82.00
Christmas presents given in lieu of "negro crop"	175.00
50 sacks of salt	80.00
Annual average outlay for iron and wood work for carts and wagons.	100.00
Lime and plaster bought last year	194.00
Annual average outlay for gin, bitts, etc	80.00
400 gallons molasses	100.00
3 kegs of tobacco, $60; 2 barrels of flour, $10	70.00
Five-sixths of a cent a pound on cotton for freight and commission..	2,069.60
Total	17,879.48

The crop of cotton at 6 cents will amount to	19,868.16

Colonel Williams has also credited this place with the additional items drawn from it:

13,500 pounds of bacon taken for home, place, and factory	$675.00
Beef and butter for home, place, and factory, and sales	500.00
1,100 bushels of corn and meal for home, place, and factory, and sales	550.00
80 cords of tan bark for his tanyard	480.00
Charges to others for blacksmith work	100.00
Mutton and wool for home use and sales	125.00
Total	22,298.16
Profits over and above interest and expenses upon this total	4,403.68

Counting cotton only at 6 cents, profits are $1,973.68; counting it at 7 cents ($23,179.52), and profits are $5,285.04. It is proper to state that part of the crop was sold at 7 cents, and it may average that.

Now, it must be borne in mind that this is one of the best plantations, as well in soil as management, and that this was an extraordinarily good crop. It must also be assumed that the land will continue to maintain its fertility and value and that the same hands will keep the buildings in repair, as no allowance is made in the expense account for such repairs, or there will be a loss under that head.

Most of the corn and meal credited comes from a toll mill on the place. All the cloth and shoes are manufactured by Colonel Williams, but upon a distinct place.

The place mentioned in Alabama belongs to Robert Montague, esq., of Marengo County.

The items of valuation are:

1,100 acres of land, at $25	$27,500.00
120 slaves, at $400	48,000.00
4 wagons	400.00
5 yoke of oxen, at $30	150.00
30 mules and horses, at $75	2,250.00
4,000 bushels of corn on hand for plantation use, at 35 cents	1,400.00
Fodder and oats on hand for plantation use	200.00
40 head of cattle, at $5, for plantation use	200.00
70 head of sheep, at $2, for plantation use	140.00
250 head of hogs for plantation use	600.00
20,000 pounds bacon and pork for plantation use	1,000.00
Plows and all other tools for plantation use	500.00
Total	82,210.00

Interest on capital, at 7 per cent	5,756.80
Cash expenses, taxes, average	100.00
Blankets, hats, and shoes (other clothing all homemade)	250.00
Medical bill, average not exceeding	40.00
500 pounds of iron, $30; hoes, spades, etc., $30	60.00
Average outlay for mules over what are raised	100.00
Average expense yearly for machinery repairs	20.00
Bagging and rope	350.00
Total	6,676.80

This crop (28,000 pounds), at 6 cents net, will leave a balance of $1,004.20, which is just about enough to pay the owner common wages of an overseer, which business he attends to himself.

[Report Commissioner of Patents, 1849.]

Mr. Simeon D. Oliver, of De Soto County, Miss., estimated the cost of production at about 6 cents; Mr. Pope, of Tennessee, at 6 cents; and Mr. Samuel D. Graham, of Coosa County, Ala., at 5 cents per pound. Mr. Thomas H. Head, of Clark County, Ark., estimated the cost of producing a bale (400 pounds) at $25, where the average yield was 1,200 pounds per acre.

Upon well-managed cotton plantations, making a support of corn, meat, etc., 4 bales of 500 pounds each per hand is a fair average. The average price of cotton for eight or ten years past may be set down at 6 cents per pound. Therefore 2,000 pounds, at 6 cents, will amount to $120.00

Expenses on 4 bales:			
Freight	$4.00		
Commissions, 2½ per cent	3.00		
Bagging and rope	7.00		
Storage, drayage, and weighage	75		
Insurance, fire, and river	1.50		
		$16.25	
Expenses per hand:			
Clothing and taxes	$14.50		
Ten per cent on mule and horse capital	10.00		
Wear and tear of farming ustensils	5.00		
		$29.50	
Expenses of making the 4 bales			$45.75
Clear profit per hand			$74.25

This calculation is a fair average gain per hand throughout this locality.

[Report Commissioner Patents, 1850.]

1850. Mr. John M. Swoope, of Lawrence County, Ala., estimated the cost at 6 cents, Mr. J. A. Brown, of Talladega County, Ala., at 3 cents. and Mr. John H. Davis, of Laurens County, S. C., at 6 to 8 cents, though the cost, he said, varied greatly.

[Report Commissioner Patents. 1852.]

1852. Mr. H. W. Huntington, of Catahoula Parish, La., estimated the cost at 7⅝ cents per pound.

[Report Commissioner Patents. 1854.]

1854. Mr. J. H. Forman, of Chambers County, Ala., estimated the cost at 7½ and Mr. John Finlayson, of central Florida, at 4½ cents per pound.

[Report Commissioner Patents, 1855.]

1855. Mr. J. J. Pratt, of Cherokee County, Ala., estimated the cost at 8 cents per pound.

The same year the Soil of the South estimated the cost of raising a pound of cotton at 8 cents and a fraction. "We make no charge," it says, "for corn or bacon, which is supposed to be raised at home. Thus it is seen that. taking the average production of the country to be 2,000 pounds of ginned cotton, or 4 bales [presumably 4 bales to the hand], and estimating that by economy the planter makes all his own supplies, it actually costs him 8 cents for every pound he makes."

[Plow, Loom, and Anvil, 1855.]

A Vicksburg, Miss., cotton planter, writing to the National Intelligencer in 1855 to correct the statement of the editor that cotton could be made on the Mississippi River at a cost of 4 cents per pound, after a carefully itemized statement of the cost of conducting a plantation of 1,600 acres, 1,000 of which was cleared land, and worked with 75 effective hands worth $600 each and 50 mules worth $130 each, the corn and meat being produced on the plantation, states that the total yield for an average of ten years would be about 600 bales of 400 pounds each, the yield per acre being a bale. At 8 cents per pound this would be equivalent to just about 8 per cent on the invested capital in the plantation, $150,000, or a profit of $12,000 net. This plantation was equipped with a steam gin and other up-to-date improvements.

UNDER THE FREE-LABOR SYSTEM.

[Southern Cultivator, 1870.]

1870. An estimate made by a Bibb County, Ga., planter, which included all the items of cost and marketing and the feed for one animal for seven months, but which did not include rent, makes the cost of production a little less than 9½ cents per pound, on land yielding 340 pounds of lint cotton per acre. An estimate made by E. M. Pendleton, of Hancock County, Ga., places the cost of production, cultivated on the tenant system, at 10.90 cents per pound, the yield per acre being 200 pounds of lint cotton. Another estimate on the tenant system, by T. M. Turner, of the same State, places the cost at 10.82 cents per pound, and on the wage system at 12.11 cents per pound. The yield was on the basis of 200 pounds produced upon an acre, with cotton worth at Augusta 13⅝ cents per pound.

[Rural Carolinian, May, 1871.]

Mr. William C. Coker, a member of the Pomological and Farmers' Club, of Society Hill, S. C., in an essay on the "Cost of producing cotton," says: "I have found that the hire of labor, cost of fertilizers, expense of maintaining plantation and implements in good working order, and a very moderate allowance for rent of land and use of capital, have amounted fully to 14 cents for each pound of cotton I have sold in the year 1870, and about 16 cents in 1869. In this estimate, the whole of the plantation expenses have been charged to the cotton, for, whatever else was produced, was consumed by men and animals engaged in making the cotton, and was, in part, produced for that purpose. The amount of corn, forage and grain, made in those years was about sufficient for the plantation animals; that consumed by the laborers was purchased, and the cost included in the above estimate." As a basis of calculation, he estimated it would require twenty-five days' work for each acre of cotton; "the cost of a full day's labor, with all incidental expenses, such as furnishing the labor with tools, etc., 66⅔ cents, or if one-third of the cost of mule feed was added, 80 cents. This gives $20 per acre as the bare cost of cultivation. Putting the production at 130 pounds per acre, we have about 15¼ cents as the cost of a pound in the one item of labor." The above calculation supposes the labor to be devoted exclusively to cotton culture.

[Resources of Tennessee, 1874, p. 103, Killebrew.]

1872. Mr. John L. Dickson, of Dickson, Ala., gives the Memphis Appeal of a recent date, says Killebrew, the following as the approximate cost of the production of cotton. If this calculation is correct, it will be seen that there is a dead loss of 3 cents per pound on all cotton grown, a conclusion which the pinched condition of the planters throughout the South would seem to justify. The general estimate of cost is, for new bottoms, 12½ cents per pound, and for uplands 15 cents, an average for both localities being 13¾ cents:

Wages of hand 12 months, at $12.50 per month	$150.00
Board of hand 12 months, at $5 per month	60.00
Half feed of mule	37.50
Interest on 36 acres of land at $5.61 per acre, at 10 per cent	20.19
Interest on half cost of mule $75, at 10 per cent	7.50
Half wear of same, 10 per cent	7.50
Expense of manager or overseer	20.00
Salt	1.00
Iron and blacksmith work	3.50
Annual expense of tools and gear	3.00
Ginning and baling, actual cost	12.00
Bagging and rope	6.00
Total (sic)	328.00

Product, 1,883⅓ pounds; cost, $17\frac{3}{10}$ cents per pound; average size of farms in the ten cotton States, $220\frac{7}{10}$ acres; proportion of improved to unimproved lands, 3 to 3.5 acres; average number of acres cultivated in cotton per hand, 10; per mule, 20; proportion of land on each farm per hand, 36 acres; average value of land in farms in 10 cotton States, $5.61; average yield per acre, from 1867 to 1872, in 10 cotton States, 188⅓ pounds; average per hand, from 1867 to 1872, in 10 cotton States, 1,883⅓ pounds.

[From Cotton Plant.]

1877. In December, 1877, the commissioner of agriculture of Georgia sent out a circular asking planters to make an estimate of the lowest price at which cotton could be produced on plantations making their supplies at home, and on plantations where bacon, flour, sirup, and more or less corn are purchased. He says the answers to his circular were "not the result of mere theoretical calculation, but of the practical experience of years."

The results were tabulated as follows:

Question addressed to planters.	North Georgia.	Middle Georgia.	Southwest Georgia.	East Georgia.	Southeast Georgia.	General average.*a*
	Cents.	*Cents.*	*Cents.*	*Cents.*	*Cents.*	*Cents.*
Average estimate of lowest price at which cotton can be produced, supplies all made at home	8.7	9.5	9	9.6	12	9.25
Average estimate where bacon, flour, sirup, and more or less corn are purchased	12.5	15	13.3	14.5	18	14

a Much cotton made in southeast Georgia is sea island and does not enter into this general average.

The low estimate for north Georgia, where supplies are purchased, is accounted for on the ground of the cheapness in that part of the State of the supplies used as compared with other sections of the State. The general average cost, 9.25 cents, where supplies were made at home, he says, "is, perhaps, not more than the average price received throughout the fall season of 1877 for all grades of cotton."

1880. ALABAMA: *Pine level region.*—About 1 per cent of the land produces, without fertilizers, a bale to the acre, at a cost of 3 cents a pound; 2 per cent three-fourths of a bale, costing 3.4 cents; 15 per cent half a bale, costing 4 cents; 30 per cent produces one-third of a bale, costing 5.8 cents. *Pine hills region.*—The estimates for this region 8 cents, which include charges for interest on plant, rent, and management.

1880. ARKANSAS: *Prairie region.*—Ten estimates, ranging from 3 to 8½ cents per pound; average, 6.2 cents. *Oak and hickory region.*—Nine estimates, 4 to 9 cents; average, 6.2 cents. *Alluvial region.*—Seven estimates, 4 to 10 cents, average; 7 cents. *Red loam lands.*—Ten estimates, 3.4 to 8.5 cents; average, 6.1 cents per pound.

1880. GEORGIA: *Pine level region.*—The cost of producing short staple was estimated at 8 to 10 cents per pound. *Pine hills region.*—Estimates place the cost in this region at 3 to 6 cents under good management, with all necessary supplies.

1880. LOUISIANA: *Oak and hickory region.*—Seven estimates, ranging from 4½ to 8 cents; average, 6.8 cents per pound. *Alluvial region.*—Nine estimates, 5½ to 9 cents; average, 7.4 cents per pound.

1880. MISSISSIPPI: *Pine level region.*—In this region cotton seems to have been produced cheaper than anywhere else in the State, the lowest estimate for the whole State as to cost of production, 4 cents, being given. *Prairie region.*—One estimate, 11 cents per pound of lint. *Oak and hickory region.*—One estimate, 4½ cents per pound. *Bluff and brown loam table-lands.*—Four estimates vary from 5½ to 10 cents; average, 7.2 cents per pound. *Alluvial region.*—Twenty-eight estimates, 5 to 9 cents; average, 7.4 cents.

1880. NORTH CAROLINA: *Pine level region.*—Five estimates of the cost of production ranged from 5½ cents per pound of lint to 10 cents, the average being 7.3 cents. *Pine hills region.*—Three estimates, 5½ to 10 cents: average, 7 cents. *Piedmont region.*—Four estimates, 4.6 to 10 cents; average, 6.2 cents per pound.

1880. SOUTH CAROLINA.—The cost of producing short staples in the interior of the State was placed at 6½ cents and of growing sea-island cotton at from 15 to 21 cents per pound of lint, with a net profit per acre of $38 to $78. *Pine hills region.*—Eleven estimates, 6 to 10¾ cents; average, 8 cents per pound. *Piedmont region.*—Eight estimates, 5.71 to 8.25 cents; average, 6.91 cents per pound.

1880. TENNESSEE.—The estimates varied from 3½ to 10 cents and averaged 8½ cents per pound.

1880. TEXAS: *Black prairie region.*—Fourteen estimates, ranging from 3½ to 9½ cents, average 5.3 cents. *Coast prairies.*—Seven estimates, 1½ to 9½ cents, average 6½ cents. *Red loam prairie.*—Two estimates, each 1½ cents. *Oak and hickory region.*—Twelve estimates, 3½ to 9½ cents, average 6.1 cents. *Alluvial region.*—Five estimates, 3½ to 7 cents, average 5.2 cents per pound.

[L. S. Lake in Report of Senate Committee on Agriculture, 53d Congress, 3d session.]

1892. *In the Memphis, Tenn., cotton region.*—I am confident the cost of production of lint cotton is considerably greater to the large farmer or planter than to the small farmers or renters. Farm labor has never been thoroughly systematized since the civil war or since the negroes were freed. As a rule it is very imperfectly disciplined indeed, and the undiscipline of the few who strive for the better things. Waste, carelessness, stubbornness, apathy, insubordination, destructiveness, and theft cause the large farmer's cotton to cost him quite high. I think it costs such farmers now, delivered as specified, fully 7 cents per pound; with the seed deducted, 6 cents per pound. The small white farmer, with his family, makes cotton the cheapest, though somewhat at the expense of the comfort and instruction of his family. I allude to the small farmer who owns his own land. He makes cotton at a cost of about 6 cents per pound of lint. Deducting the value of the seed he can make it at 5 cents. As to the renter, he does not make cotton as cheaply as the small landowning farmer. on account of his slipshod, unambitious methods; but by reason of the economy of his stomach, habilaments, and house or cabin, by pinching he outclasses the big farmer, and probably makes cotton at a cost of 6½ cents per pound, 5½ with the seed credited.

[R. H. Speight, in same report.]

1892. NORTH CAROLINA, *Edgecombe County.*—The average cost of cultivating a 1-horse crop of 25 acres of cotton for the last three years has been about $250; picking, packing, and baling ready for market, about $8 per bale of 500 pounds, making the total cost, if a bale of 500 pounds is produced per acre, of $450, or $18 per bale of 500 pounds, at 3⅗ cents per pound. On land producing three fourths, one-half, and one-third of a bale the cost will be the same, less the difference in picking, ginning, and baling. At what point of reduced production it ceases to be profitable depends upon the price. If 200 pounds are produced it would cost $13.20 per acre to produce and put upon the market. At 8 cents per pound there would be a net profit of $2.80 per acre.

[W. E. Ardrey, in same report.]

1892. NORTH CAROLINA, *Mecklenburg County.*—One bale of cotton, 500 pounds per acre, without commercial fertilizers, I think can be produced for $25, or at the cost of 5 cents per pound (fertilizers will pay 10 per cent); 375 pounds lint, per acre, at a cost of $30, or 6 per cent (fertilizers 8 per cent); 250 pounds per acre, at a cost of $35, or 7 per cent (fertilizers will pay 7 per cent); 166 pounds of lint, per acre, at a cost of $40, or 8 per cent (fertilizers will pay 5 per cent); below this, cotton does not pay for production (fertilizers will not pay).

[J. W. Watts, in same report.]

1892. SOUTH CAROLINA, *Laurens County.*—It is considered good farming to raise, gather, and prepare for market a bale of cotton weighing 500 pounds, at a cost of from $20 to $25. The cost increases as the yield per acre decreases. It is of very doubtful propriety to grow cotton on land that will not produce more than 200 pounds of lint per acre with fertilizers.

[W. E. Dargan, in same report.]

1892. SOUTH CAROLINA, *Darlington County.*—The cost of raising and marketing 500 pounds of lint cotton per acre would be about 5 cents per pound, but as we have no lands to yield that, we use fertilizers, which makes it cost us about 7 cents per pound, and those who make less of course do it at a greater expense.

[H. Hayne Crum, in same report.]

1892. SOUTH CAROLINA, *Barnwell County.*—The cost of raising, gathering, and preparing for market one bale of cotton weighing 500 pounds of lint on 1 acre of land without manure is $24.42, or 4¾ cents per pound; three-fourths of a bale per acre without manure $20.40, or 5¼ cents per pound; half a bale per acre without manure, $14.50, or 5¾ cents per pound; one-third of a bale per acre without manure, $12.23, or 7¼ cents per pound.

[J. H. Harrison, in same report.]

1892. SOUTH CAROLINA, *Greenville County.*—The actual cost of producing 500 pounds of lint cotton with fertilizers is about 7 cents per pound.

[S. Y. Stribling, in same report.]

1892. SOUTH CAROLINA, *Oconee County.*—Cotton could be raised for 5 cents per pound on land that will yield 500 pounds of lint per acre without fertilizers; on land that would make three-fourths of a bale it would cost 5¾ cents; on land producing one-half bale to the acre it would cost 6¾ cents; on land producing one-third of a bale per acre it would cost 8 cents per pound. Cotton raising ceases to be profitable when we make less than one-half bale per acre. The use of fertilizers will add 33 per cent to 12½ per cent, respectively, on the above qualities of land.

[Col. Hiram Hawkins, in same report.]

1892. ALABAMA, *Barbour County.*—The cost of cotton raising in the past ten years has diminished. In other words, the cost of production is less now than ten years ago, or five years ago. The cotton planter is learning to use more economy on the farm, buys less of what he can raise at home, and by organized cooperation he has learned to buy fertilizers, goods, and implements cheaper than as an individual. Rent of land is also cheaper. Labor, considering its productive capacity, about the same cost. Farm animals are some cheaper, and more of them are raised on the farm. The cost of raising 1 bale of lint cotton (500 pounds) on land producing 1 bale to the acre without fertilizers, or rents, $15; on land producing three-fourths bale to the acre, $17.35; on land producing one half bale to the acre, $22; on land producing one-third bale to the acre, $29. Cotton raising will cease to be profitable when production is 150 pounds or less per acre, as only 150 pounds per acre will leave little on the margin for rents or profit. One-fourth of the lint cotton would be considered fair rent.

[S. C. M. Amason, in same report.]

1892. ALABAMA, *Sumter County.*—There has been a decrease in the cost of raising a given quantity of lint cotton. This decrease of cotton culture is owing to the decline of the prices of staple goods, rent of land, cost of labor and farm animals, and a little to the use of improved implements. I do not think that cotton can be profitably raised for less than 8 cents per pound on any kind of land.

[J. R. McLendon, in same report.]

1892. ALABAMA, *Montgomery County.*—The average production of lint to the acre, 150 pounds. The average production is increasing, owing to better cultivation and more fertilizers. The cost of cultivation has decreased, owing to better cultivation, better tools, more cotton made on less land. It will cost $15 to produce a bale of cotton on land yielding 500 pounds of lint to the acre. On less than a bale to the acre the cost of cultivation will increase rather than decrease, because the poorer the land the slower the growth of the plant, and consequently the grass and weeds will come up later, causing not unfrequently an extra plowing and hoeing on poor grades of land. Where the yield falls below half a bale to the acre profits are absorbed.

[J. R. Cowan, in same report.]

1892. ALABAMA, *Clarke County*.—The average production of lint cotton per acre for the last three years, I should say, is not over 200 to 250 pounds. The average yield has been on the increase, from the use of fertilizers, for several years, until 1892–93. Commercial fertilizers were largely abandoned in 1892, but the use of home made manures is steadily increasing. The cost of raising a given quantity of cotton is somewhat reduced. Implements are certainly improved, but it is found very difficult to introduce or secure their general use. As an illustration, I might say that perhaps not over 75 per cent of the cotton raisers use as simple and profitable an implement as the planter, but still sow the seed with their hands. The tendency is to cheapen rents, and farm animals cost less money, but were as easily bought when they cost more. I put the cost of raising a 500-pound bale of cotton on 1 acre at about $23, including transportation to market. On 1 acre producing three-fourths of a bale, $18.50; one-half bale, $14.95, and one-third bale, $10.50.

[Gen. S. D. Lee, in same report.]

1892. MISSISSIPPI, *Lowndes County*.—About one bale to every 4 or 5 acres is the average production on the very best lands. The average production per acre is diminishing, due in a large measure to the gradual decrease in the fertility of the soil and the lack of an effort to build up the soil by the use of fertilizers, restorative crops, or any similar means. The cultivation of the crop is about the same, if anything worse, where negro labor is employed, the teams not being as good as they were or as well taken care of. The cost of raising a given quantity of cotton in the last ten years has been increased, as it takes more land to make that given quantity and consequently more labor to cultivate the increased land required to raise it. The rent of land is becoming less and less because of the increased care and cultivation, and less yield owing to its loss of fertility. I do not believe it pays to cultivate land in cotton which produces less than one-third of a bale to the acre, and the planter will have to get 8 cents a pound for his cotton to meet his expenses with the production. If he gets less, he raises cotton at a loss. The use of green fertilizers, such as red clover, cowpeas, and melilotus, pay handsomely on these prairie lands, and in two years will cause them to produce three-quarters of a bale to the acre. No commercial fertilizers have been found which will give anything like as favorable results on prairie lands.

[L. B. Brown, in same report.]

1892. MISSISSIPPI, *Clarke County*.—The average production is about one-third of a bale of lint cotton per acre for the last three years. The average production per acre is diminishing, chiefly from long and continued cultivation without help (manures). The average cost of raising a given quantity of cotton, say 500 pounds of lint, has been very uniform for the last two years. It will cost 5 cents per pound to make cotton on land that will produce 1 bale of cotton per acre, without fertilizers; 6 cents per pound on land that produces three-fourths of a bale to the acre; 7 cents per pound on land that will produce one-half bale, and 8½ cents on land that will produce one-third of a bale per acre.

[Hon. William H. Stovall, in same report.]

1892. MISSISSIPPI, *Coahoma County*.—I should say that the average yield of lint per acre is about 250 pounds. There is no special change in the average production per acre in recent years. No fertilizers used in this country except stock peas, and the methods of cultivation remain about the same. I think the present cost of raising cotton is less than it was ten years ago. Wages are lower; supplies (except meat) are lower, and implements are perhaps a shade cheaper; rents are not so high; farm animals are some cheaper. Improved implements contribute some to the reduction of cost, but not largely. Very little cotton is raised as a wage crop. The universal custom, with rare exception, is to let the laborer work for a share in the crop or as a renter. As to the cost of producing cotton we will take the case of a small farmer, who rents the land and hires the labor done, and assume that he makes 500 pounds of lint per acre. Land that will produce that much lint is very rare and valuable, and should easily rent for $8 per acre:

Say 18 acres, at $8 per acre	$144.00
Rent of one mule, usual price	30.00
Feed of mule for 12 months (hay, at $16 per ton; corn, 50 cents per bushel)	60.00
Use of implements, $1 per acre	18.00
Blacksmith bill	1.50
Seed, 2 bushels to acre, at 30 to 60 cents per acre	10.80
Planting and cultivation, at $6.50 per acre	117.00
Gathering 1,670 pounds seed cotton (lint is about 30 per cent average of seed cotton) per acre on 18 acres is 30,060 pounds of seed cotton, at 50 cents per hundred	150.30
(It may be assumed that the seed will pay for the ginning and wrapping.)	
To this add cost of hauling in seed cotton to ginhouse and hauling off the bales, say $1 per bale	18.00
Total cost of 18 bales is	$549.60

Or cost of 1 bale, 500 pounds, is $31.59, or $6\frac{3}{10}$ cents per pound.

The above is a very conservative estimate; 18 acres are used because that is the usual crop for one mule. Now, if this same land only made three-fourths of a bale, or 375 pounds of lint, it would stand thus:

All items as before, except gathering and hauling	$381.30
Gathering 22,500 pounds seed cotton, at 50 cents	112.00
Hauling to and from gin	13.50
Total	507.30

One-eighteenth is $28.29, or $7\frac{54}{100}$ cents per pound.

If the production be one-third of a bale, or 166 pounds of lint, it would cost as follows:

Items as before	$381.30
Gathering 9,954 pounds seed cotton, at 50 cents	49.77
Hauling to and from gin	6.00
Total	437.07

One-eighteenth of this is $18.83. 166 pounds lint, costing $18.83, is $11\frac{34}{100}$ cents per pound.

[D. Street, in same report.]

1892. MISSISSIPPI, *Alcorn County.*—The average production of lint per acre is 150 pounds. The production per acre is decreasing, owing to the soil becoming impoverished. There has been within the past ten years a decrease in the cost of producing cotton. Farm animals and all farm implements are lower in price and labor some lower, while some articles of provisions are lower. The cost of raising and marketing 1 bale of 500 pounds of lint cotton on land that will produce this amount per acre without fertilizer is $22.88; the same on land producing three-fourths of a bale per acre, $23.64; the same, one-half bale per acre, $26.50; the same, one-third bale per acre, $31.75. It will be seen that with cotton at the present price, about $6\frac{1}{2}$ cents per pound on the farm, it can not be profitably produced on land yielding less than one-third bale per acre without fertilizers.

[T. B. Ford, in same report.]

1892. MISSISSIPPI, *Marion County.*—The average yield per acre is 200 to 250 pounds. The cost of raising a given amount of cotton, for the past ten years, remains about the same. The cost of raising cotton, 500 pounds to the bale, and where one acre makes a bale without fertilizing, is, under the most favorable circumstances, 4 cents a pound; three-fourths of a bale, $4\frac{1}{2}$ cents; one-half bale, 5 cents; one-third of a bale, $6\frac{1}{2}$ cents per pound.

[G. J. Finley, in same report.]

1892. MISSISSIPPI, *Marshall County.*—The average yield per acre is not over one-third bale per acre. The yield is diminishing, caused chiefly by the wearing out of the land and washing of the soil. In the matter of cultivation perhaps we are improving. There has been a slight decrease in the cost of raising cotton. Land is cheaper; therefore rents are cheaper. Implements have been improved, and are cheaper; more land per mule and hand can be cultivated; labor is cheaper necessarily, because we could not pay as much as three, ten, or twenty years ago on account of depressed prices. Farm animals are a little cheaper, and the feeding can be done cheaper, more mowers being used and more hay saved. Under rather favorable conditions I produced cotton in 1891 at about 7 cents. Last year, under unfavorable climatic conditions, the crop in my district cost at least 10 cents to produce, and was made at a money loss to all who hired labor, and at a labor loss to all who grew it with their own labor. The making of less than one-third bale per acre in upland is attended by loss, with no profit at one-third bale.

[T. R. Henderson, in same report.]

1892. MISSISSIPPI, *Leflore County.*—The cost of production is about the same as ten years ago. The cost of raising, gathering, and preparing for market a given quantity of cotton (as one 500-pound bale) on land producing without fertilizers one bale of cotton (say 500 pounds lint) per acre would be $28; cost of same on land producing three-fourths bale per acre would be $30; cost of same on land producing one-half bale to the acre would be $32.50, and cost of same on land producing one-third of a bale to the acre would be $35. It ceases to be profitable to raise cotton on land producing less than one-half bale to the acre.

[A. J. Phelps, in same report.]

1892. MISSISSIPPI, *Sharkey County.*—For large bodies of land the average production for the last three years has been 300 pounds of lint per acre. The average production is diminishing from the nonattention to some system of fertilization and drainage. The cultivation has been about the same. There has been no appreciable increase or decrease in the cost of raising a given quantity of cotton during the past ten years. If any, it has been in the rent of land 20 per cent. Cash land rent formerly rated at $8 per acre. It now rates more nearly $6. The cost of production where the yield is 500 pounds of lint per acre is 3.90 cents; where it is three-fourths of a bale, or 375 pounds of lint, it is 4.63 cents per pound; where it is one-half a bale, or 250 pounds of lint, the cost is 6.20 cents per pound; where the yield is one-third of a bale, or 166⅔ pounds of lint, the cost is 8½ cents per pound.

[A. V. Roberts, in same report.]

1892. LOUISIANA, *De Soto Parish.*—The average yield of lint cotton per acre is not more than 175 pounds. There has been a decrease in the cost of raising cotton, for while the more intelligent have decreased the cost by better cultivation with improved implements and fertilization the less progressive have been compelled to do so, for they had to live on less; they could not get advances. The cost of production on land making a 500-pound bale is less than 3 cents per pound; on land making three-fourths of a bale, about 3½ cents per pound; on land making a half bale, 4½ cents per pound, and on land making one third of a bale, 5 cents per pound.

[J. B. McGehee, in same report.]

1892. LOUISIANA, *West Feliciana Parish.*—The average yield of lint per acre is 200 pounds. There is a decrease in the cost of production, caused chiefly by the inability to get credit, forcing the production of the maximum crop at a minimum of expense. The cost is $17.50 for 1 acre producing a 500-pound bale of lint cotton; three-fourths of a bale, $16 per acre; one-half bale, $14.25; one-third of a bale, $12.50.

[W. R. Ross, in same report.]

1892. TEXAS, *Dallas County.*—The average production of lint cotton per acre during the last three years in this district has been about 160 pounds per acre. The average production is slightly increasing, but not because of fertilizers, as we use none at all. It is the result of improved cultivation. There is a decrease in the cost of production by reason of the use of agricultural machinery of an improved kind. On land producing from one-half to 1 bale of cotton per acre it is raised and prepared for market at a cost of 5 cents per pound. The cost is a little more on land not producing so heavily. It is not profitable to raise cotton on land producing less than 100 pounds of lint cotton to the acre.

The following extracts are from the same report, same year:

NORTH CAROLINA, *Cleveland County.*—The cost of production on 32 acres, yielding 23 bales, weighing 11,500 pounds (gross), 6 cents per pound. Value of seed deducted.—[Burwell Blanton.]

NORTH CAROLINA, *Vance County.*—The cost of production on 40 acres, yielding 20 bales, weighing 9,000 pounds (gross), 9½ cents per pound. Value of seed included.—[W. S. Parker.]

NORTH CAROLINA, *Edgecombe County.*—The cost of production on 40 acres, yielding 32 bales, weighing 15,980 pounds (gross), 7 cents per pound. Value of seed deducted. The cost of production on 25 acres, yielding 30 bales, weighing 13,400 pounds (gross), 5½ cents per pound. Value of seed deducted.—[A. B. Noble.]

The cost of production on 1 acre, 350 pounds (gross), 6¼ cents per pound. Value of seed deducted.—[R. F. Lenhardt.]

The cost of production on 36 acres, yielding 22 bales, weighing 9,526 pounds (gross), 6¾ cents per pound. Value of seed deducted.—[J. W. Rosamond.]

SOUTH CAROLINA, *Richland County.*—The cost of production on 50 acres, yielding 40 bales, weighing 20,000 pounds (gross), 7 cents per pound. Value of seed deducted.—[Thomas Taylor.]

GEORGIA, *Harris County.*—The cost of production on 500 acres, yielding 200 bales, weighing 100,000 pounds (gross), 7 cents per pound. Value of seed deducted.—[L. D. Hutchinson.]

GEORGIA, *Lincoln County.*—The cost of production on 20 acres, yielding 20 bales, weighing 10,000 pounds (gross), 4⅙ cents per pound. Value of seed deducted.—[T. B. Hollenshead.]

GEORGIA, *Baker County.*—It cost 7½ cents per pound to produce 22 bales, weighing 11,000 pounds (gross), on 65 acres, with the value of the seed deducted.—[J. O. Perry.]

GEORGIA, *Lee County.*—It cost 6.92 cents per pound to produce 21,500 pounds (gross), 43 bales, on 180 acres, with the value of the seed deducted.—[E. B. Martin.]

It cost 6⅓ cents per pound to make on 35 acres, 12 bales, weighing 6,000 pounds (gross), value of the seed deducted.—[W. H. Mattox.]

GEORGIA, *Dekalb County.*—It cost 8½ cents per pound to make on 1 acre 266 pounds (gross), the value of the seed being deducted.—[T. J. Flake.]

GEORGIA, *Jones County.*—It cost 6¼ cents per pound to make on 150 acres, 62 bales, weighing 28,520 pounds (gross), the value of the seed deducted.—[W. H. Barron.]

ALABAMA, *Dale County.*—It cost 7¾ cents per pound to make on 75 acres, 25 bales, weighing 12,500 pounds (gross), the value of the seed deducted.—[J. W. Dowling.]

ALABAMA, *Chambers County.*—It cost 8 cents to make on 25 acres, 8 bales, weighing 4,000 pounds (gross), the value of the seed being deducted.—[J. M. Vernon.]

ALABAMA, *Pike County.*—It cost 4⅞ cents to make on 30 acres, 15 bales, weighing 7,500 pounds (gross), the value of the seed being deducted.—[C. J. Knox.]

ALABAMA, *Autauga County.*—Yield on 50 acres, 50 bales, weighing 25,000 pounds (gross), value of seed deducted, 5 cents per pound.—[C. S. G. Doster.]

ALABAMA, *Hale County.*—Yield on 150 acres, 64 bales, weighing 32,000 pounds (gross), value of seed deducted, 8 cents per pound.—[Garrier Bros.]

ALABAMA, *Montgomery County.*—Yield on 360 acres, 236 bales, weighing 118,000 pounds (gross), value of seed deducted, 7¼ cents per pound.—[W. M. Browder.]

MISSISSIPPI, *Copiah County.*—Yield on 45 acres, 23 bales, weighing 11,500 pounds (gross), value of seed deducted, 6½ cents per pound.—[W. M. Kethley.]

MISSISSIPPI, *Yalobusha County.*—Yield on 10 acres, 7 bales, weighing 3,500 pounds (gross), value of seed deducted, 6¼ cents per pound.—[D. R. Pittman.]

MISSISSIPPI, *Wilkinson County.*—Yield on 75 acres, 40 bales, weighing 18,000 pounds (gross), value of seed deducted, 9½ cents per pound.—[E. J. McGehee.]

MISSISSIPPI, *Marshall County.*—Yield on 12 acres, 6 bales, weighing 2,700 pounds (gross), 6½ cents per pound, value of seed deducted.—[G. J. Finley.]

LOUISIANA, *East Feliciana Parish.*—Yield on 1 acre, 300 pounds (gross), value of seed deducted, 7 cents per pound.—[E. A. Scott.]

ARKANSAS, *Mississippi County.*—Yield on 1 acre, 187 pounds (gross), 8½ cents per pound, value of seed deducted.—[W. H. Grider.]

LOUISIANA, *Concordia Parish.*—Yield on 500 acres, 400 bales, weighing 200,000 pounds (gross), 4$\frac{17}{20}$ cents per pound, value of seed deducted.—[B. Z. Wade.]

The rent of land was put at only $1 in this estimate.

LOUISIANA, *Point Coupee Parish.*—Yield on 1 acre, 1 bale, weighing 400 pounds (gross), 5¾ cents per pound, value of seed deducted.—[James Vignes.]

LOUISIANA, *Bienville Parish.*—Yield on 15 acres, 5 bales, weighing 2,500 pounds (gross), 10½ cents per pound, value of seed deducted.—[James Brice.]

LOUISIANA, *Red River Parish.*—Yield on 2,000 acres, 2,000 bales, weighing 1,000,000 pounds (gross), 5½ cents per pound, value of seed deducted.—[B. W. Marston.]

ARKANSAS, *Jefferson County.*—Yield on 33 acres, 22 bales, weighing 8,743 pounds (gross), 8¾ cents per pound, value of seed deducted.—[R. B. Donelson.]

ARKANSAS, *Cleveland County.*—Yield on 100 acres, 33 bales, weighing 16,500 pounds (gross), 5½ cents per pound, value of seed deducted.—[G. C. Atwood.]

ARKANSAS, *Lonoke County.*—Yield on 25 acres, 12 bales, weighing 6,000 pounds (gross), 7$\frac{1}{12}$ cents per pound, value of seed deducted.—[J. M. Neely.]

ARKANSAS, *Johnson County.*—Yield on 121 acres, 99 bales, weighing 45,500 pounds (gross), 4 cents per pound, value of seed deducted.—[W. R. Rogers.]

[North Carolina Commissioner of Labor, Ninth Annual Report.]

1894. NORTH CAROLINA.—We find that the average cost to produce a bale of cotton (400 pounds), that is, from the time the ground is broken until it is bagged, will run to $22.50 throughout the State.

[J. R. Connell, in Report of Commissioner of Labor, North Carolina, 1895.]

1894. NORTH CAROLINA, *Gaston County.*—Cost of cotton crop for the year 1894, as follows:

To 28 days' plowing (1 horse), $1.00	$28.00
To 28 days' hoeing, at 60 cents	6.60
To picking 4,400 pounds seed cotton, 40 cents	17.60
To hauling to gin	2.00
To hauling to market	2.00
To 1 sack of acid	1.70
	57.90
By 88 bushels seed, at 12½ cents	11.00
Made 3 bales, weighing 1,490 pounds, at a cost of	46.90

which is 3.15 cents per pound, after deducting one-fourth for land rent. Cotton has cost me from 3.15 cents in 1894, to 7½ cents in 1893, which was one-half cent more than I got for it. The next highest cost was 6 cents, in 1889, but I sold that year for 9¾ and 10 cents.

[A. J. Denning, in Report of Commissioner of Labor of North Carolina, 1895.]

1894. NORTH CAROLINA, *Bertie County*.—Actual cost to raise a bale of cotton on 1 acre of land:

To knocking down old stalks	$0.20	
To siding off old rows	.37	
To 75 loads good compost	7.50	
To hauling and drilling same	3.50	
To 200 pounds guano	2.50	
To bedding up land	1.75	
To 1½ bushels seed	.20	
Planting	.75	
To scraping and chopping out	2.25	
To grassing	1.25	
To 3 days other plowing, at $1.50	4.50	
To picking 1,500 pounds cotton, at 30 cents	4.50	
To hauling to gin	1.50	
To ginning	1.50	
To bagging and ties	1.25	
		$33.27
Credit—		
By 1 bale cotton, 500 pounds, at 7 cents	35.00	
By 33 bushels seed, at 12½ cents	4.12	
		39.12
Profit		5.85

THE COST OF COTTON PRODUCTION IN 1876 AND 1897.

In 1877 Mr. J. R. Dodge, statistician of this Department, undertook an investigation into the cost of cotton production per pound, and the price per pound realized in the home markets in 1876. The investigation was carried on through the Department's county correspondents in the ten principal cotton States. The following is the statistician's report giving the results of the investigation:

COST AND PRICE.

It is not practicable to obtain the exact cost of production, for the reason that few cultivators keep systematic accounts. It is perhaps easier to approximate the real cost of cotton than of other products of agriculture. Being a prominent specialty, sometimes monopolizing the resources of cultivation, it is less complicated than mixed farming. The price obtained is that at home markets, making the aggregate value less than the commercial value of cotton at shipping ports. Our correspondents have promptly responded to this part of the circular, and their returns (in districts with similar conditions) have been remarkably uniform, but of course less so as to cost than as to price. The State averages are as follows, in cents and fractions per pound, of upland cotton:

States.	Cost.	Price.
	Cents.	*Cents.*
North Carolina	9.3	9.8
South Carolina	9.4	9.7
Georgia	9.3	9.8
Florida	8.7	9.2
Alabama	9.9	10.1
Mississippi	9.8	10.2
Louisiana	9.7	10.2
Texas	8.0	9.1
Arkansas	9.0	9.9
Tennessee	9.0	9.8

This gives to Texas the largest proportion of profit, or 11 mills per pound; Arkansas, 9; Tennessee, 8; the others, 2 to 5, the average slightly exceeding half a cent; being $2.60 per average bale, making the net profit to the cultivators $11,500,000, in round numbers, in an aggregate of about 205,000,000. This is within a fraction of 6 per cent of the gross receipts, and, if assumed to be substantially correct, is too small a margin for a good season. It illustrates the necessity of increased returns. How shall they be obtained? By increasing the yield and diminishing the cost of supplies. Both ends are reached by a single operation—the adoption of a restorative rotation, which involves animal production and green manuring, a cheapening of fertilizers and supplies for man and beast, a partial protection of the soil from washing and waste, a large yield at a small cost, and increase of fertility instead of exhaustion.

Alabama reported during the past season the lowest averages of condition, resulting in the lowest yield per acre. It now returns the smallest margin of profit, only 2 mills per pound. In South Carolina, where low condition also prevailed, the net profit made is but 3 mills.

Some correspondents make the cost per pound to those who pay high rates of interest upon indebtedness for high-priced supplies twice as much as to those who produce their own supplies. In every State the cultivator who buys least saves most, according to universal testimony. Those who make cotton a surplus product are getting rich; in a sense, the crop becomes all profit.

So great is the waste attendant upon large operations on a credit basis, and involved in the prevalent irresponsible management under the share system, that the counties with large plantations and heavy aggregate production generally give the smallest net profit. In Mississippi the cost per pound in several such counties averages more than the price received. A few large counties in Arkansas make the cost 2 cents greater than the price. The principal districts in North Carolina average 10 cents for cost and the same for price. The districts of heaviest production in Texas only make an average of 2 to 3 mills net profit, while the average of the State exceeds 1 cent. In Louisiana, the districts of heavy production make a better showing, yet here there are some of the largest that return cost higher than price.

Here is convincing proof of two things: The superior economy of small holdings, and the wastefulness of the share system, especially with large gangs of hands.

In order to make a fairer comparison of the cost of production and price per pound in 1876 with that in 1896, the figures reported by the Statistician, being in currency are reduced to the gold basis, and, as presented below in Table 17, show the cost of production per pound and the price per pound in 1876 in the ten principal cotton States, as compared with the cost and price in the same States in 1896. The per cent of decrease in cost and price and the profit for each year are also shown in the table.

TABLE 17.—*Showing comparative cost of production and price per pound of cotton (in gold), 1876–1896.*

States.	Cost per pound.			Price per pound.			Profit.	
	1876.	1896.	Per cent of decrease.	1876.	1896.	Per cent of decrease.	1876.	1896.
	Cents.	*Cents.*		*Cents.*	*Cents.*		*Cents.*	*Cents.*
Alabama	8.88	5.38	39.4	9.06	6.69	26.1	0.18	1.31
Arkansas	8.07	5.61	30.5	8.88	6.46	27.3	.81	.85
Florida	7.80	5.35	31.4	8.25	6.75	18.2	.45	1.40
Georgia	8.34	5.23	37.3	8.79	6.73	23.4	.45	1.50
Louisiana	8.70	5.01	42.4	9.15	6.67	27.1	.45	1.66
Mississippi	8.79	5.36	39.0	9.15	6.74	26.3	.36	1.38
North Carolina	8.34	5.39	35.4	8.79	6.96	20.8	.45	1.57
South Carolina	8.43	4.87	42.2	8.70	6.94	20.2	.27	2.07
Tennessee	8.07	5.26	34.8	8.79	6.63	24.6	.72	1.37
Texas	7.17	5.38	25.0	8.16	6.63	18.7	.99	1.25
Average for 10 States	8.32	5.29	36.4	8.83	6.71	24.0	.51	1.42

The comparisons in the above table show that in every State there has been a considerable reduction since 1876 in the cost of making cotton, the decrease ranging from 1.79 cents in Texas to 3.69 cents per pound in Louisiana. The average cost of production per pound in the ten States is 8.32 cents in 1876 and 5.29 cents in 1896, which is 3.03 cents, or 36.4 per cent less than in 1876. On the other hand, there has been a considerable reduction in price since 1876, the decrease ranging from 1.50 cents in Florida to 2.42 cents in Arkansas. The average price per pound in the ten States is 8.83 cents in 1876 and 6.71 cents in 1896, which is 2.12 cents, or 24 per cent, less than in 1876. The difference in the profit ranges from .04 of 1 cent in Arkansas to 1.80 cents in South Carolina. The average profit in 1876 is .51 cent and 1.42 cents in 1896, or .91 cent greater in 1896.

But that there has been a reduction, and a great reduction, in the cost of making cotton since 1876 should not be a matter of surprise, because, as is well known, the price of almost every article that enters into the cost of making a cotton crop has greatly fallen in the twenty years. The question of greatest importance is, whether the reduction in the cost of making cotton has been greater or less than the reduction in the prices realized by the planter for his cotton. The figures above show that the decrease in the cost of production is 3.03 cents per pound, or 36.4 per cent, while the decrease in prices is 2.12 cents per pound, or 24 per cent. The decrease in the average cost of production, therefore, is .91 cent a pound greater than the decrease in the price per pound, and the planter is the gainer to that extent. In other words, since 1876, the planter by thrift and economy has forced down the cost of production 12.4 per cent more than the decline in the price of cotton, which has enabled him to make a profit of about 1 cent a pound according to the showing of these two investigations.

In order to compare the cost of production with the cost of plantation supplies, picking cotton, and freight rates, in 1876 and 1896, considerable pains have been taken to ascertain the cost of the items enumerated below in Table 18, most of which have a direct bearing upon the cost of making cotton. The prices of all articles of food, bagging and ties, freight rates from New Orleans to New York and Liverpool, are taken from the daily market quotations at New Orleans, and are the average prices the first of each month. The cost of clothing and implements are the manufacturers' wholesale prices, furnished by well-established and reliable firms. The cost of guano and crude phosphates is based upon the export value of these fertilizers at the custom-houses, and the cost of standard fertilizers is the price at Atlanta, obtained from a reliable dealer of that city. The price of mules is the average price in the ten principal cotton States, as reported to this Department, and the price of picking cotton is the average price in those States, as ascertained by a special investigation made by this Department. The freight rates from Atlanta to Charleston and Atlanta to New York are furnished by the Clyde Steamship Line, of New York; the rates from

Macon to Savannah by the Central of Georgia Railway, and from Memphis by the Department's special agent in that city. The price of cotton is the price realized by the planter, as reported to this Department, and the price of cotton-seed is taken from the daily quotations at Memphis, the largest cotton-seed market in the country, and is the average price the first of each month. All prices for 1876 are reduced to the gold basis and are thus made uniform, as to value, with those of 1896.

TABLE 18.—*Showing gold prices of plantation supplies and products, 1876–1896.*

Supplies and products.	1876.	1896.	Per cent of increase.	Per cent of decrease.
FOOD.				
Bacon (clear sides) .... per pound..	\$0.10$\frac{1}{2}$	\$0.05$\frac{1}{2}$	....	52
Mess pork (prime) .... per barrel..	17.92	8.73	....	51
Corn (mixed) .... per bushel..	.53$\frac{7}{10}$	.34$\frac{1}{2}$	....	36
Oats (mixed) .... do....	.39$\frac{1}{5}$	.26$\frac{1}{2}$	....	32
Flour (choice) .... per barrel..	3.28	3.73	14	....
Sugar (com. plant) .... per pound..	.06$\frac{1}{2}$	.03$\frac{1}{4}$	....	51
Molasses (com. plant) .... per gallon	.34$\frac{9}{10}$	.07$\frac{1}{4}$	....	79
Coffee (com. Rio) .... per pound..	.14$\frac{1}{2}$	.12$\frac{1}{10}$	....	17
Salt (coarse La.) .... per sack..	.79$\frac{7}{10}$	.65	....	19
CLOTHING.				
Shoes (brogans) .... per pair..	1.12$\frac{1}{2}$	.80	....	29
Shirtings (bleached 4-4) .... per yard..	.11$\frac{7}{10}$	.08	....	32
Plaids (standard 27-inch) .... do....	.09	.04$\frac{1}{5}$	....	53
Calico (prints) .... do....	.06$\frac{1}{2}$	.04$\frac{1}{5}$	....	35
IMPLEMENTS.				
Cotton gins (standard) .... per saw..	4.04	3.50	....	13
Cotton planters (Dow) .... each..	7.18	4.50	....	37
Plows (single horse) .... do...	4.40	3.35	....	24
Trace chains .... per pair..	.27	.15	....	44
Hoes (8-inch) .... per dozen..	4.20	1.85	....	56
Wagons (double horse) .... each..	67.35	50.00	....	26
OTHER SUPPLIES.				
Bagging (2-pound) .... per yard..	.12$\frac{1}{10}$	.05$\frac{3}{4}$	....	54
Ties (arrow) .... per bundle..	3.06	.93	....	70
Fertilizers (guano) .... per ton..	33.83	10.25	....	70
Fertilizers (crude phosphate) .... do....	18.11	7.46	....	59
Fertilizers (standard brand) .... do....	12.21	19.05	....	55
Mules (average plant) .... each..	72.33	64.00	....	12
LABOR.				
Picking cotton .... per 100 pounds..	.60	.45	....	25
TRANSPORTATION (*per 100 pounds*).				
New Orleans to Liverpool	1.17	.38	....	69
New Orleans to New York (water)	.48	.32	....	33
Atlanta to Charleston	.49$\frac{3}{5}$	.43	....	13
Atlanta to New York via Charleston	.89$\frac{1}{5}$	.57$\frac{1}{2}$	....	36
Macon to Savannah (ship side)	.38$\frac{3}{5}$	.28	....	27
Memphis to New York (all rail)	.85	.50$\frac{1}{2}$	....	41
Memphis to New York (river and rail)	.93	.47$\frac{1}{2}$	....	49
Memphis to Fall River (all rail)	.93	.55$\frac{1}{2}$	....	40
Memphis to Fall River (river and rail)	.88	.52$\frac{1}{2}$	....	40
PLANTATION PRODUCTS.				
Cotton (at plantation) .... per pound..	.08$\frac{1}{3}$	.06$\frac{7}{10}$	....	24
Cotton seed .... per ton..	6.74	7.95	18	....

It will be noticed that with one exception—that of flour—there has been a reduction in every article enumerated, and that, with the exception of coffee, salt, cotton gins, and mules, the percentage of reduction is greater than the percentage of reduction in the price of cotton. It should, however, be remembered that the prices quoted are wholesale and not retail prices to the planter. As there is no means of ascertaining the latter, there is likewise no way of ascertaining the true relation between the reduction in the price of supplies and the reduction in the price of cotton, or the cost of production. On the other hand, as has already been ascertained, there has been a reduction of 36.4 per cent in the cost of making cotton in 1896 as compared with 1876, and there has also been an increase of 18 per cent in the value of cotton seed since 1876.

The large percentage of reduction in the cost of transportation, particularly in ocean rates to Liverpool, is of especial significance in view of the fact that that market has so much to do with regulating the price of cotton. Of still more importance is the fall in the cost of picking, the most expensive item connected with cotton cultivation. The price of this labor is largely controlled by the price of cotton, but the percentage of reduction is shown to be somewhat in favor of the planter. But the chief value of these comparative prices consists in the fact established that there has been a great decrease in the price of almost every article entering into the cost of making cotton. Of course some of the articles—food articles especially—are subject to fluctuations, but there are others, such as implements and fertilizers, and also freight rates, the prices of which are comparatively steady, the tendency being downward rather than upward.

One of the most extensive Southern manufacturers of fertilizers, at Port Royal, S. C., furnishes the following data and prices, per ton of 2,000 pounds, in bags, of two grades of fertilizer:

	1886.	1896.	1898.
Complete fertilizer	$20.00	$16.00	$13.50
Acid phosphate	13.00	8.50	8.00

By complete fertilizer is meant one that contains the three elements of phosphoric acid in available form, ammonia, and potash; and by acid phosphate, acidulated phosphate rock that contains only one element of phosphoric acid in available form. To arrive at the prices paid by the planter at his depot, a fair average would be an addition of $8 per ton, for freight and profit, to the above prices for complete fertilizer, and $5 per ton to that of acid phosphate. The price of these fertilizers in 1876 was about 25 per cent higher than in 1886.

The Hon. Charles E. Pearce, of Missouri, who has made an exhaustive study of the subject, furnishes the Department with the following interesting and valuable data in regard to bagging:

Prior to 1866 bagging manufactured in the United States was chiefly made from flax fiber and flax and hemp fiber mixed, the percentage of the latter, however, being small. The supply of bagging which was imported from Dundee and East India was made from jute. Jute butts (i. e., fiber decorticated from the butt end of the jute stalks) came into use in the United States for bagging manufacture about 1866. The American manufacture about 1870, under the operations of the Morrill tariff law and subsequent acts, became sufficient to supply the home market. Prior to that time a large proportion of the supply was imported from Dundee and East India. The average price of standard-weight bagging for 30 years prior to 1870 was about 17 cents per linear yard. Owing to the exigencies of the times prices fluctuated very greatly during that period. Since 1870 the price has rapidly declined, owing to various causes, such as the great increase of the Indian jute crop, reductions in the cost of transportation, improvements in processes of manufacture, etc. Allowing for fluctuations in raw material consequent upon crop conditions and occasional speculative control at Calcutta and the operations of the East India Jute Association, the cost of bagging to consumers has been steadily downward to the present time.

Taking the 15th of September as the time when, by reason of accumulated warehouse, insurance, and interest charges, the cost generally reaches the maximum, the following table exhibits the prices of two-pound bagging per linear yard, on or about that date from 1860 to 1896:

	Cents.
In 1860 Indian bagging fetched per linear yard	16½
In 1861 Kentucky bagging fetched per linear yard	16½
In 1863 Indian bagging fetched per linear yard	20
In 1865 Indian bagging fetched per linear yard	27

The average market price for two-pound bagging September 15, in United States was—

In 1866	35
In 1867	23
In 1868	20¾
In 1869	22
In 1870	30
In 1871	19
In 1872	13½
In 1873	12¾
In 1874	13
In 1875	12¾
In 1876	11¼
In 1881	10¾
In 1886	9¼
In 1891, free on board, New York, average for year	6
In 1896, free on board, New York, average for year	5

So great has been the reduction in the wholesale cost of plantation supplies that the conclusion seems reasonable that if that reduction has not inured to the advantage of the planter the fault is chargeable to the conditions of the retail trade, for, while there has been a general fall of about 40 per cent in the wholesale prices of supplies, the decrease in the price of cotton is 24 per cent, while that in the cost of making cotton is 36.4 per cent a pound, with an increase of 18 per cent in the value of seed.

CAN THE COST OF RAISING COTTON BE REDUCED?

The average cost of cultivating an acre of cotton in 1896 was $15.42 and the average cost of making a pound of lint 5.27 cents. Is it possible, by thrift or economy, or by improved methods of cultivation, to reduce this cost? Some planters have, no doubt, reached the lowest cost under present conditions, but there is a large class, and particularly that class operating large plantations on the share system, and the share croppers as well, who may reduce the cost:

(1) By making the plantation more self-sustaining.

(2) By improving the labor system.

(3) By adopting the intensive method of cultivation.

(4) By reducing the acreage.

(1) *By making the plantation more self-sustaining.*—There is far more involved in this proposition than is at first apparent. In plain language it means "living at home;" it means the production on the plantation of everything possible that is consumed on the plantation by man and beast. It means more than this. It means fewer crop liens and mortgages, less cotton and better prices.

There has been a large and very encouraging increase in the production of food crops in the cotton States for several years, but even as late as 1890, the census shows that in those States, with the exception of Texas, the corn and wheat crops, and the number of hogs, were nothing like so large as in 1860, although in 1890 there were nearly 6,000,000 more people to be fed. It is estimated that from 1860 to 1890 the population of the cotton States increased 87 per cent while the grain crops increased only 37 per cent, and that in seven of the ten cotton States, on the basis of the increased population, the production of corn and oats was 150,000,000 bushels short of the requirements of the population. It is a mistake to assume that the enormous crops of recent years are altogether due to the increased acreage in Texas. In the season of 1897, the cotton States, not including Texas, produced over 2,750,000 more bales of cotton than they did in 1860. It is also a fact that the amount of live stock, except in Texas, was less in 1880 than in 1860, and that even now, in proportion to the population, it is less than in 1860.

The merchants are still advancing large quantities of food supplies to the planters, the greater portion of which could be made on the plantation. Much of the merchant's profit on these supplies would go to the planter, and every cent thus saved would be just that much reduction in the cost of making cotton. Moreover, whenever the plantations become as nearly as possible self-sustaining the cotton acreage will be decreased, and the amount of cotton produced will more nearly meet the demands of commerce. When this adjustment takes place remunerative prices are sure to follow. The planter and tenant and the live stock, must be fed from the products of the plantation; the merchant's profits on these advances must be saved before any reduction is made in the cost of making cotton. The planter who "lives at home" is the one who makes cotton at the least cost and gets some profit from raising it.

(2) *By improving the labor system.*—Labor is by far the most important and expensive item connected with cotton cultivation. In fact, from the first spring plowing to the last picking in the fall and the delivery of the cotton in the market, more than 50 per cent of its cost is expended in plowing, seeding, fertilizing, chopping to a stand, hoeing, picking, and other incidental labor. It would therefore appear that any material reduction in cost of making cotton must depend upon some reduction

in wages. But this does not necessarily follow. In cotton production, particularly, it is not so much the wages of the labor as its efficiency that counts in the end, because only a small part of the crop is made by hired laborers. More than one-fourth of the total crop is made by share croppers, who are mostly negroes. Competent authorities estimate that of the laborers engaged in cotton cultivation more than one-half, or from 50 to 60 per cent, are negroes, and that, generally speaking, there has been a great depreciation in the efficiency of this labor. "The concurrent testimony of farmers and others," says Otken,* "is that the value of the work of negroes on the farm, as compared with the same kind of work done in slave time under humane masters, and that work under no effective supervision to-day, may be thus expressed: The value of the work done by old slave negroes is 50 per cent of what it was in the olden times; that of the younger negro men, 30 per cent; and that of the colored females 20 per cent." Is it not the system of labor under which the negroes are employed that is largely responsible for this condition? There are only a small number of planters who discipline their labor as is done by the managers of other industries, while there are yet a large number of plantations wholly given over to negro tenants and share croppers, over whom little or no supervision is exercised, except in the matter of the collection of rents. What is needed to reduce the cost of cotton production on these plantations is intelligent direction and control of the labor, and such discipline as will exact o the laborer his undivided attention to the cultivation of the crops and the keeping up of all needed repairs.

(3) *By adopting the intensive method of cultivation.*—How to obtain the largest possible yield of cotton per acre is a proposition which should engage the earnest attention of every planter. Much depends upon the seasons, but not all. Mr. David Dickson (of Georgia), who was the first planter to introduce the use of commercial fertilizers in cotton cultivation, formulated a "compound" (in 1869) which he declared had never failed to grow good crops and bring satisfactory dividends, no matter what might be the season. But, first of all, the most careful attention should be paid to the selection of seed for planting, for no cultivated plant deteriorates so rapidly when this is neglected. It used to be the custom, still followed to some extent, for planters to change their seed by sending to a distant market for a fresh supply; but by a rigid selection from his own fields this expense might be avoided. The too common method of saving seed for planting† is to take a sufficient number of bushels just as they come from the gin, or, perhaps, to buy them from an oil mill. No attention has been given to the selection of the individual plants from which those seeds came, and those from the poorest, least prolific, and latest maturing are taken together with those from the best. The first pickings give the best

* Ills of the South (1894), page 110.

† Professor Tracy—The Cotton Plant, page 215.

seed, and if the seed be saved from the best stalks only, the practice will soon bring a marked improvement.

Such was the abundance and cheapness of new lands, not many years ago, that the cotton planter found it more profitable to clear up the "new ground" than to fertilize the old worn-out field. But the results of the war, the abolition of slavery, and the introduction of chemical manures, completely revolutionized the methods of cotton culture* in some of the Southern States. This is particularly true of Georgia and and North and South Carolina, where, in the past twenty years, notwithstanding the decline in the price of cotton, there has been a great increase in the use of fertilizers. There are, however, large cotton areas in Alabama, Mississippi, and Tennessee where little or no attention is paid to fertilizing the soil. The records show † that in 1897, Alabama used only 96,154 tons of commercial fertilizer (which was 19,631 tons less than was used in 1891), while Mississippi used only 42,550 and Tennessee 25,883 tons. The same year North Carolina used 203,097, South Carolina 240,000, and Georgia 401,979 tons. If it be assumed that all of the commercial fertilizers purchased by the following States was applied to cotton cultivation, the number of pounds used per acre and its value in 1896 would be as follows: North Carolina, 305 pounds, $2.29; Florida, 200 pounds, $2.20; South Carolina, 198 pounds, $1.39; Georgia, 194 pounds, $1.35; Alabama, 75 pounds, 53 cents; Tennessee, 43 pounds, 53 cents, and Mississippi, 23 pounds, 20 cents. The average yield per acre in Alabama for the period 1874 to 1894, inclusive (omitting four years of the period), was only 146 pounds of lint.

What may be accomplished by the intensive methods of culture is well illustrated by Mr. Harry Hammond in his admirable article on the culture of cotton in the Cotton Plant, p. 234. "The lands of Marlboro County, S. C.," he says, "were thought to be exhausted in the early part of this century, and numbers of the population emigrated to the fresh lands of Alabama. A great change has taken place in that county in recent years. Very little of the land now lies fallow. Cropping is continuous, and there is a systematic rotation of crops. Cotton is planted on the same land every fourth year. Green manuring with the cowpea sown broadcast has been extensively practiced, and, when cotton is laid by, peas are often drilled between the rows where the beds for the next year's cotton crop are to be thrown up. All of the cotton seed, or its equivalent in meal, is returned to the soil, either alone or composted with stable manure, woods mold, and superphosphate of lime. In 1880 an average of $4.77 per acre for each acre in cotton was expended in commercial fertilizers. In 1890, in this county, 32,306 bales were produced on 58,836 acres, or very nearly a bale to 1.8 acres, a yield not exceeded anywhere except in the alluvium of the Mississippi River."

Whatever will insure a greater yield than heretofore from a given acreage, whether it be a more careful selection of seed, a more generous

* Professor White—Cotton Plant, page 172.

† George K. Holmes, Bulletin 13. Division of Statistics, U. S. Dept. Agr.

and judicious use of fertilizers, a cleaner cultivation, a more careful picking of the seed cotton, and other improved methods, should be carefully studied and adopted.

(4) *By reducing the acreage.*—The principal cause of the decline in the price of cotton since 1890 is overproduction. This is a truth so well known and recognized, even by the planters themselves, that it is scarcely necessary to attempt to prove it by an array of figures. However, the following table (19), in periods of five years, showing the "visible supply," or surplus cotton on hand at the close of each year; the total world's consumption (in bales of 500 pounds), the crops of the United States (in commercial bales), the average price of middling upland (in New York), and the value of the crop, may present such a contrast as to be of some interest. For the sake of uniformity commercial figures only are used.*

TABLE 19.—*Showing visible supply, consumption, United States crops, and values.*

Year.	Visible supply.	Total consumption.	United States crops.	Price per pound.	Value of crops.
				Cents.	
1884-85	984,000	7,344,000	5,706,165	10.54	$289,245,503
1885-86	968,000	8,000,000	6,575,691	9.44	313,989,245
1886-87	999,000	8,375,000	6,505,087	10.25	296,957,221
1887-88	772,000	8,751,000	7,046,833	10.27	333,526,605
1888-89	682,000	9,117,000	6,938,290	10.71	337,825,340
Average	881,000	8,317,400	6,554,413	10.24	314,308,783
1893-94	1,800,000	10,283,000	7,549,817	7.67	292,932,899
1894-95	2,180,000	11,097,000	9,901,251	6.50	288,918,504
1895-96	1,231,000	11,113,000	7,157,346	8.16	292,234,437
1896-97	1,654,000	11,334,000	8,757,964	7.72	327,547,854
1897-98	1,641,000	11,968,000	11,199,994	6.22	338,432,458
Average	1,581,200	11,159,000	8,913,274	7.25	308,013,230

It will be seen from the above figures that during the first period the average "visible supply" for the five years was 881,000 bales as against a total average consumption of 8,317,000 bales, whereas the average "visible supply" for the five years of the second period was 1,581,200 as against a total average consumption of 11,159,000 bales. Therefore, from 1893-94 to 1897-98 the "visible supply" was 79 per cent greater than during the period 1884-85 to 1888-89, while the consumption during the latter was only 34 per cent greater than during the former period. In other words, the average surplus supply, by reason of the larger crops in this country, has outrun the average world's consumption, the increase in the former being 45 per cent more than that in the latter, as shown above.

The planter can not hope to realize a profit on his cotton so long as he makes more than the spinners can consume. The remarkable increase in the consumption of cotton since 1890 would seem to justify an increase in the crops, but this increased consumption is largely due to the unusually low prices of the raw material. The American planter

* "Cotton Movement and Fluctuations." (1898.) Latham, Alexander & Co.

has overdone the business of raising cotton, and unless the acreage now planted is reduced, must consent to adjust himself to 5-cent cotton, or even 3½ and 4 cent, as in 1842, when the supply overran the demand. The situation is just as bad now as it was in the spring of 1895, when the planters held a convention at Jackson, Miss., and resolved to reduce the acreage as the only sure remedy against low prices. For a while the remedy worked admirably, the next season's area in cotton being reduced more than 3,500,000 acres, so that prices advanced 1½ to 2 cents a pound. The efforts put forth by the planters in 1895 are well worth repeating. But if every planter would only grow his own food supplies, the change in the acreage from cotton to food crops would go a long way toward accomplishing the desired purpose.

COST OF COTTON PRODUCTION BY COUNTIES.

The following tables will show the average cost of cultivation and total yield, the average cost of picking per 100 pounds, and the average cost of production per pound of lint; also the number of plantations reporting in each county of every State and Territory. The plantations showing a profit are separated from those showing a loss for the purpose of disclosing as far as possible the causes of the profit or loss in each county.

According to the census of 1890, there were 725 counties in the cotton States producing 400 bales of cotton and over. The Department's circular was sent to all these counties, and all but 20 were heard from. The following are the counties in each State from which no reports were received: Baldwin County, Ala.; Wakulla County, Fla.; Bryan, Habersham, and Murray counties, Ga.; Jackson Parish, La.; Ripley and Stoddard counties, Mo.; Chowan and Granville counties, N. C.; Polk, Rutherford, and Williamson counties, Tenn.; and Bandera, Fisher, Frio, Haskell, Jackson, Mason, and Scurry counties, Tex. All counties in the States of Arkansas, Mississippi, South Carolina, and Virginia producing 400 bales of cotton and over are represented in this investigation.

TABLE 20.—*Average cost of producing an acre of cotton in 1896 on farms showing a* ***PROFIT****, by counties.*

[Wherever a blank occurs in these tables it means that no expense was incurred.]

ALABAMA.

County.	Rent.	Plowing.	Seeds.	Planting seed.	Fertilizers.	Distributing fertilizers.	Chopping and hoeing.	Picking.	Ginning and pressing.	Bagging and ties.	Marketing.	Repairing implements.	Other expenses.	TOTAL COST.	Pounds of lint.	Price per pound.	Bushels of seed.	Price per bushel.	TOTAL RETURN.	PROFIT.	Number of farms reporting.	Cost of picking per 100 pounds.	Cost of production per pound.
																Cents.		Cents.					Cents.
Autauga	$1.25	$1.63	$0.11	$0.14	$1.38	$0.10	$0.72	$2.05	$1.00	$0.49	$0.52	......	$0.13	$9.52	166	6.75	13.0	11.0	$12.64	$3.12	2	$0.41	4.87
Barbour	2.06	2.21	.21	.12	1.90	.16	1.30	1.84	.61	.48	.40	$0.26	.34	11.89	199	6.69	13.0	11.1	14.77	2.88	4	.31	5.25
Bibb	2.00	2.67	.33	.32	1.92	.33	1.08	3.60	1.25	.75	.75	.50	.42	15.92	247	7.00	15.7	15.8	19.94	4.02	3	.49	5.44
Blount	2.00	3.25	.18	.30	1.76	.21	.79	3.33	1.18	.49	.56	.43	.34	14.82	270	6.50	16.9	12.6	19.79	4.97	7	.41	4.70
Bullock	2.00	1.82	.28	.21	1.79	.16	1.21	3.15	.89	.48	.25	.40	.46	13.10	221	6.64	14.3	11.8	16.55	3.45	7	.48	5.16
Butler	1.75	2.00	.18	.18	1.62	.18	1.35	2.40	.78	.36	.30	.43	......	11.53	175	6.88	11.0	11.2	13.31	1.78	2	.46	5.89
Calhoun	2.58	3.14	.24	.30	1.52	.17	1.25	2.73	.87	.65	.39	.35	.43	14.62	244	6.76	14.8	12.6	18.19	3.57	6	.37	5.23
Chambers	2.33	2.38	.23	.20	2.06	.20	1.17	2.63	.92	.58	.36	.46	.64	14.16	260	6.90	16.0	12.2	20.00	5.84	6	.34	4.70
Cherokee	2.77	3.22	.21	.25	1.48	.18	1.50	2.59	1.24	.59	.38	.47	.31	15.19	232	6.91	15.3	14.4	18.23	3.04	6	.37	5.60
Chilton	2.13	3.16	.17	.25	1.79	.21	.94	3.09	1.08	.45	.65	.30	.20	14.42	264	6.98	16.6	13.4	20.67	6.25	8	.39	4.62
Choctaw	1.75	2.12	.19	.34	1.81	.24	.84	2.70	.86	.52	.35	.12	.23	12.07	239	6.44	14.8	10.6	16.87	4.80	4	.38	4.39
Clarke	2.32	3.07	.13	.30	2.55	.28	.98	3.48	1.45	.78	1.48	.54	.12	17.48	326	6.79	19.5	10.8	24.18	6.70	10	.36	4.71
Clay	2.00	3.67	.17	.23	1.83	.22	1.08	3.17	.86	.67	.75	.18	.08	14.91	250	6.67	15.0	11.7	18.36	3.45	3	.42	5.26
Cleburne	3.21	2.62	.25	.29	1.87	.29	.78	3.06	.92	.59	.69	.81	.10	15.48	292	6.88	17.0	12.5	22.10	6.62	4	.35	4.58
Coffee	2.00	2.25	.14	.22	2.00	.30	1.05	3.12	1.32	.68	.50	.25	.50	14.33	325	6.75	19.5	15.0	25.05	10.72	2	.32	3.51
Colbert	2.25	2.22	.31	.28	1.00	.16	.94	3.85	1.25	.74	1.09	.64	.55	15.28	285	7.06	18.8	21.8	27.21	11.93	4	.45	3.92
Conecuh	1.62	3.81	.17	.21	1.99	.19	1.41	2.88	1.19	.65	1.22	.48	.19	16.01	262	6.75	16.8	13.8	19.90	3.89	4	.37	5.23
Coosa	2.31	3.00	.53	.21	1.85	.20	1.45	3.21	.88	.55	.56	.38	.74	15.87	265	6.99	16.2	13.0	20.67	4.80	5	.40	5.19
Covington	2.00	2.83	.20	.30	2.75	.38	2.05	2.84	.68	.58	.67	.47	.24	15.99	300	6.75	16.7	15.0	22.88	6.89	3	.32	4.50
Crenshaw	1.59	3.00	.20	.20	2.03	.23	1.23	3.08	.59	.41	.77	.20	.42	13.95	267	6.33	16.0	11.0	18.59	4.64	3	.38	4.57
Cullman	2.75	2.75	.18	.21	1.41	.21	1.25	3.05	.92	.68	.49	.20	.06	14.16	233	6.44	14.5	14.4	17.00	2.84	4	.44	5.18
Dale	2.17	2.50	.16	.25	1.50	.21	1.13	2.25	.63	.31	.28	.19	.45	12.03	188	6.81	12.5	14.4	14.53	2.50	4	.40	5.44
Dallas	1.87	2.87	.24	.22	1.58	.19	1.30	2.85	1.00	.58	.74	.64	.20	14.28	231	6.88	14.8	12.0	17.64	3.36	4	.41	5.41
Dekalb	4.76	2.30	.22	.27	1.89	.25	1.85	3.86	1.09	.63	.57	.40	.66	18.75	313	6.80	19.2	14.0	23.97	5.22	5	.41	5.13
Elmore	2.00	2.85	.15	.25	2.34	.21	1.10	3.15	1.14	.50	.58	.44	.53	15.24	277	6.90	16.6	11.0	20.97	5.73	5	.38	4.84
Etowah	3.08	3.50	.23	.33	2.40	.27	1.50	3.20	1.38	.63	.58	.38	.68	18.16	264	6.53	16.0	15.0	19.44	1.28	3	.40	5.97
Fayette	1.84	2.80	.29	.24	1.79	.25	1.21	2.82	1.20	.48	.66	.24	.31	14.13	271	6.62	18.7	11.2	19.93	5.80	6	.35	4.44
Franklin	2.20	4.10	.24	.30	1.70	.40	1.90	3.04	1.43	.76	.37	.50	.10	17.04	256	6.95	15.6	10.5	19.36	2.32	5	.40	6.02
Geneva	1.75	2.05	.12	.16	1.42	.13	1.35	2.28	.56	.34	.39	.28	.18	11.01	188	6.39	11.8	12.6	13.53	2.52	5	.40	5.06
Greene	2.00	2.80	.24	.31	1.30	.14	.96	2.13	.85	.49	.53	.12	.68	12.55	217	6.85	13.4	11.9	16.49	3.94	5	.33	5.05
Hale	2.63	2.56	.21	.40	1.59	.30	1.32	2.78	.52	.41	.40	.40	.31	13.83	228	6.78	14.8	12.1	17.15	3.32	4	.41	5.28
Henry	1.70	2.95	.18	.33	2.18	.22	.89	3.41	.81	.37	.40	.20	.38	14.02	226	6.90	13.2	14.0	17.30	3.28	5	.50	5.38

TABLE 20.—*Average cost of producing an acre of cotton in 1896 on farms showing a **PROFIT**, by counties*—Continued.

[Wherever a blank occurs in these tables it means that no expense was incurred.]

ALABAMA—Continued.

County.	Rent.	Plowing.	Seeds.	Planting seed.	Fertilizers.	Distributing fertilizers.	Chopping and hoeing.	Picking.	Ginning and pressing.	Bagging and ties.	Marketing.	Repairing implements.	Other expenses.	TOTAL COST.	Pounds of lint.	Price per pound.	Bushels of seed.	Price per bushel.	TOTAL RETURN.	PROFIT.	Number of farms reporting.	Cost of picking per 100 pounds.	Cost of production per pound.
																Cents.		Cents.					Cents.
Jackson	$2.67	$2.33	$0.25	$0.23	$1.30	$0.15	$0.83	$2.75	$1.18	$0.72	$0.44	$0.22	$0.90	$13.97	217	6.58	12.3	10.0	$15.48	$1.51	3	$0.42	5.87
Jefferson	3.67	5.50	.26	.25	2.67	.67	1.75	5.76	2.17	.93	.75	.55	.30	25.23	411	6.50	21.7	16.7	30.64	5.41	3	.47	5.14
Lamar	2.00	2.69	.20	.17	2.21	.20	1.19	3.35	.88	.49	.75	.27	.72	15.12	260	6.50	17.2	10.8	18.83	3.71	4	.43	5.10
Lauderdale	2.17	2.20	.23	.28	.50	.05	1.30	3.04	1.01	.49	.21	.58	.35	12.41	228	6.50	13.8	12.1	16.42	4.01	5	.44	4.71
Lawrence	2.66	3.67	.28	.42	2.50	.50	1.25	3.80	1.17	.62	.50	.83	.05	18.25	300	6.54	18.7	11.0	21.78	3.53	3	.42	5.40
Lee	1.77	3.00	.21	.25	2.26	.23	1.28	2.47	.88	.46	.39	.44	.40	14.04	271	6.93	16.9	14.1	21.34	7.30	7	.30	4.30
Limestone	2.38	1.81	.24	.25	.62	.10	1.14	3.08	1.23	.74	.22	.30	.30	12.41	274	6.71	16.5	10.9	21.21	8.80	4	.37	3.87
Lowndes	2.20	2.71	.23	.26	2.16	.30	1.31	3.08	1.21	.56	.95	.26	.16	15.39	292	6.85	16.6	11.2	21.70	6.31	5	.35	4.63
Madison	2.12	1.59	.17	.20	.59	.11	.88	2.83	.81	.48	.24	.38	.30	10.70	192	6.62	12.3	12.6	14.28	3.58	6	.49	4.77
Marengo	2.25	2.75	.17	.38	1.25	.25	1.75	3.20	.81	.75	.50	.30	.60	14.96	325	6.50	20.5	13.5	23.82	8.86	2	.33	3.75
Marion	2.92	3.08	.22	.17	1.52	.22	1.38	3.20	1.27	.53	.69	.33	.38	15.91	258	6.50	16.0	10.0	18.35	2.44	6	.41	5.55
Marshall	1.73	3.00	.18	.25	1.07	.22	1.50	2.96	.81	.44	.30	.40	.50	13.36	225	6.50	13.7	10.0	15.99	2.63	3	.44	5.33
Monroe	2.00	4.25	.17	.24	2.35	.17	1.41	3.33	1.17	.57	1.48	.50	.93	18.57	308	6.83	17.3	10.0	22.73	4.16	3	.36	5.47
Montgomery	2.35	3.36	.27	.24	1.78	.17	1.04	3.10	.93	.48	.45	.43	.55	15.15	257	6.32	15.7	11.8	18.18	3.03	5	.40	5.18
Morgan	2.31	1.50	.20	.21	1.46	.20	1.11	2.52	.53	.37	.38	.32	.31	11.42	204	6.62	12.2	11.8	14.93	3.51	4	.41	4.89
Perry	2.25	2.34	.20	.28	.62	.12	.96	2.65	1.00	.75	.55	.43	.18	12.33	208	6.50	13.5	12.5	15.24	2.91	2	.42	5.12
Pickens	2.00	3.00	.16	.18	1.00	.20	1.25	1.92	.70	.60	.85	.38	.20	12.44	275	6.75	16.5	10.0	20.02	7.58	2	.23	3.92
Pike	2.25	1.99	.20	.28	2.28	.15	1.09	2.46	.79	.39	.53	.25	.47	13.13	201	6.50	12.4	12.9	14.57	1.44	6	.41	5.74
Randolph	3.33	3.00	.13	.20	1.96	.30	1.67	3.08	1.00	.47	.54	.43	.33	16.44	247	7.00	15.3	10.0	18.80	2.36	3	.42	6.04
Russell	1.72	2.13	.26	.16	2.25	.14	.94	1.56	.59	.44	.51	.36	.19	11.25	194	6.50	11.8	14.5	14.16	2.91	4	.27	4.92
St. Clair	2.85	4.44	.25	.30	1.89	.35	1.50	3.65	1.30	.52	.26	.29	.28	17.88	319	6.81	18.8	15.0	24.53	6.65	4	.38	4.72
Shelby	2.50	3.70	.21	.20	1.88	.18	1.59	3.00	.85	.51	.47	.17	.15	15.41	263	6.80	17.0	12.2	19.81	4.40	5	.38	5.07
Sumter	2.00	2.55	.25	.32	1.12	.12	.65	2.38	.92	.38	.38	.30	.35	11.72	234	6.50	10.5	10.5	16.26	4.54	2	.34	4.54
Talladega	4.04	3.29	.31	.28	2.72	.52	1.18	3.71	1.29	.58	.49	.31	.53	19.25	342	6.83	20.0	14.4	26.54	7.29	6	.36	4.79
Tallapoosa	2.77	3.20	.19	.28	2.80	.45	2.08	3.83	1.53	.71	.70	.55	.21	19.30	357	6.45	22.4	10.5	24.98	5.68	5	.36	4.75
Tuscaloosa	2.13	2.39	.23	.25	1.09	.18	.95	2.22	.92	.52	.30	.10	.31	11.59	204	6.79	14.0	13.3	15.59	4.00	4	.36	4.77
Walker	2.18	2.68	.24	.29	2.32	.24	1.28	4.07	1.28	.67	.39	.35	.08	16.07	290	6.52	20.3	13.6	21.74	5.67	7	.47	4.59
Washington	2.25	5.88	.20	.25	1.50	.25	2.37	5.60	1.75	1.00	1.50	.75	1.50	24.80	450	7.00	27.0	12.5	34.88	10.08	2	.41	4.76
Wilcox	1.88	2.25	.20	.17	2.50	.13	1.10	2.49	1.25	.56	.71	.24	.64	14.12	250	6.68	15.8	11.8	18.97	4.85	4	.33	4.90
Winston	2.43	3.67	.22	.32	1.57	.33	1.58	3.93	1.88	.98	.75	.19	.33	18.18	397	6.92	23.3	13.3	30.63	12.45	3	.33	3.80

ARKANSAS.

																Cents.		Cents.					Cents.
Arkansas	$3.00	$3.88	$0.22	$0.27	......	......	$2.20	$3.15	$1.25	$0.70	$1.25	$0.38	$0.75	$17.05	262	7.25	15.8	12.5	$20.65	$3.60	2	$.40	5.75
Ashley	3.12	2.75	.21	.21	$1.00	$0.19	1.56	2.44	1.21	.62	.55	.88	.19	14.93	228	6.50	13.5	9.5	15.89	.96	4	.36	5.99
Baxter	3.81	3.75	.21	.21	.50	.04	1.66	3.70	.99	.65	.68	.15	......	16.35	271	6.25	19.8	10.0	18.82	2.47	4	.46	5.30
Boone	2.00	1.50	.20	.25	......	......	1.00	4.00	2.25	.75	.75	.25	1.50	14.45	333	6.00	20.0	15.0	22.98	8.53	1	.40	3.44
Bradley	2.00	2.75	.20	.38	1.10	.38	1.75	3.75	1.51	.97	.50	.38	1.05	16.72	250	6.38	14.5	10.0	17.20	.48	2	.50	6.11
Calhoun	2.00	4.00	.25	.50	2.50	.50	2.00	2.50	1.00	.50	.50	.50	......	16.75	250	6.25	15.0	15.0	17.88	1.13	1	.33	5.80
Chicot	5.00	1.10	.20	1.00	......	......	2.85	4.80	2.00	.90	2.35	.10	1.10	21.40	400	7.00	26.0	7.0	29.82	8.42	1	.40	4.90
Clark	1.53	2.63	.15	.26	.50	.12	.75	1.79	.65	.66	.63	.61	.09	10.37	182	6.55	11.5	11.9	13.35	2.98	4	.33	4.95
Clay	3.50	2.15	.14	.47	......	......	1.28	4.82	2.27	.82	1.10	.10	.16	16.81	317	6.83	21.0	10.0	23.93	7.12	3	.51	4.64
Cleburne	1.50	1.50	.20	.22	1.50	.12	.75	1.50	1.08	.44	.15	.33	.05	9.34	175	6.88	10.0	12.2	13.42	4.08	2	.29	4.64
Cleveland	2.50	1.83	.15	.22	.50	.08	1.20	2.58	.67	.70	.68	.39	.19	11.69	232	6.17	13.3	10.0	15.53	3.84	3	.37	4.47
Columbia	1.83	2.83	.17	.23	1.05	.15	.50	2.22	.72	.37	.58	.20	.23	11.08	203	6.12	12.7	10.8	13.85	2.77	3	.36	4.78
Conway	3.31	2.08	.22	.22	.38	.03	1.65	3.30	1.01	.48	.42	.44	......	13.54	219	6.32	11.9	12.5	15.39	1.85	4	.50	5.50
Craighead	3.50	2.94	.17	.24	......	......	1.88	5.66	1.75	.58	.61	.56	......	17.89	358	6.76	22.1	9.6	26.26	8.37	4	.53	4.40
Crawford	3.00	3.12	.18	.19	......	......	1.84	3.18	1.07	.54	.59	.25	.22	14.18	222	6.49	13.4	11.3	15.94	1.76	5	.48	5.71
Crittenden	4.80	3.34	.37	.39	......	......	2.04	5.40	1.73	.71	1.81	.27	1.07	22.02	353	7.03	25.4	14.0	28.16	6.14	5	.52	5.23
Cross	3.12	3.04	.21	.30	......	......	1.50	2.60	.81	.36	.18	.44	......	12.56	202	6.10	13.0	9.1	13.53	.97	4	.43	5.63
Dallas	1.50	2.25	.12	1.00	......	......	1.30	2.00	.50	.30	.35	.50	......	9.82	170	7.00	10.0	12.5	13.15	3.33	1	.39	5.04
Desha	5.00	2.80	.25	.18	1.00	.05	1.75	7.12	2.00	.90	1.88	.12	.25	23.30	500	7.00	32.5	14.5	38.75	15.45	2	.47	3.72
Drew	2.00	3.25	.28	.55	1.75	.62	.75	2.48	.79	.80	.40	.38	.12	14.17	216	6.00	13.0	10.2	14.39	.22	2	.38	5.95
Faulkner	2.65	2.45	.15	.34	.10	.04	1.15	2.72	1.25	.44	.43	.37	.38	12.47	232	6.65	13.5	10.0	16.81	4.34	5	.39	4.79
Franklin	2.82	2.58	.13	.22	......	......	1.34	2.53	1.08	.49	.15	.12	.33	11.79	240	6.25	14.7	10.3	16.48	4.69	3	.35	4.28
Fulton	2.50	2.81	.20	.41	......	......	1.25	3.10	1.11	.42	.70	.41	.13	13.04	204	6.75	12.5	11.2	15.17	2.13	4	.51	5.71
Garland	1.75	4.75	.23	.28	......	......	2.00	2.50	1.62	.70	1.50	.10	......	15.43	250	6.25	11.5	10.0	16.78	1.35	2	.33	5.71
Grant	3.83	3.46	.17	.25	.33	.17	1.50	3.73	.87	.57	1.00	.30	.38	16.56	264	6.25	18.7	12.5	18.88	2.32	3	.47	5.39
Greene	4.50	5.00	.30	1.00	......	......	3.00	5.00	.75	.60	.60	.25	......	21.00	335	7.00	20.0	10.0	25.45	4.45	1	.50	5.67
Hempstead	2.50	2.50	.22	.45	......	......	2.38	3.18	1.42	.92	.98	.13	1.00	15.68	216	7.50	12.5	8.8	17.12	1.44	2	.49	6.75
Hot Spring	2.50	3.50	.12	.13	.75	.12	.50	2.08	1.10	.42	.75	.50	.25	12.72	320	6.25	20.0	13.8	22.60	9.88	2	.22	3.11
Independence	3.12	3.25	.21	.37	.30	.45	1.75	3.82	1.30	.54	.60	.34	.20	16.25	276	6.80	16.5	9.6	20.26	4.01	5	.46	5.31
Izard	2.25	2.12	.16	.34	......	......	.88	1.90	.72	.32	.29	.10	......	9.08	154	6.50	9.0	10.0	10.76	1.68	4	.41	5.31
Jackson	3.88	2.25	.15	.32	......	......	1.50	5.06	1.08	.44	.50	.60	.42	16.20	324	6.62	18.8	9.2	23.08	6.88	2	.52	4.47
Jefferson	4.36	2.21	.28	.14	......	......	1.58	3.96	1.29	.69	.88	.43	1.27	17.09	304	6.75	20.9	9.2	22.61	5.52	7	.43	4.99
Johnson	2.50	1.84	.18	.21	......	......	1.33	2.02	1.24	.41	.32	.36	......	10.41	194	6.46	11.7	10.0	13.60	3.19	7	.35	4.76
Lafayette	2.50	1.75	.17	.19	......	......	1.32	3.85	1.60	.52	1.84	.44	.62	14.80	319	6.66	18.6	10.0	23.36	8.56	4	.40	4.06
Lawrence	2.42	1.50	.27	.61	......	......	1.55	4.67	1.46	.61	1.26	.56	.41	15.32	272	6.33	18.7	10.0	19.12	3.80	3	.57	4.94
Lee	3.00	2.63	.12	.32	......	......	1.50	4.75	1.68	.60	.80	.25	.50	16.15	312	6.75	19.5	9.8	23.09	6.94	2	.51	4.56
Lincoln	3.56	1.96	.18	.26	.78	.11	1.38	3.25	1.06	.56	.58	.25	.21	14.14	271	6.69	16.2	11.3	20.40	6.26	4	.40	4.54
Little River	2.75	2.17	.15	.23	......	......	2.08	3.73	1.10	.42	.70	.20	.34	13.87	267	6.50	16.7	11.7	18.71	4.84	3	.47	4.46
Logan	1.50	2.98	.12	.30	.75	.25	1.25	3.28	1.54	.75	.37	.90	1.00	14.99	285	6.62	17.5	10.0	21.06	6.07	2	.38	4.65
Lonoke	4.00	2.25	.35	.62	......	......	3.50	5.60	1.42	.98	.62	.13	.50	19.97	325	6.50	21.0	12.2	24.08	4.11	2	.57	5.36
Marion	3.50	3.17	.15	.30	......	......	1.67	4.17	1.10	.58	1.41	.13	.18	16.36	257	7.04	16.0	11.7	20.01	3.65	3	.54	5.64
Miller	2.90	2.30	.18	.18	.20	.05	1.55	3.38	1.15	.68	.55	.08	......	13.20	245	6.10	16.0	10.8	16.66	3.46	5	.46	4.68
Mississippi	4.50	1.21	.28	.37	......	......	1.87	7.43	1.70	.82	1.47	.79	......	20.44	369	6.50	23.7	10.0	26.26	5.82	3	.67	4.90
Monroe	3.00	.75	.28	.35	......	......	1.12	2.35	.66	.38	.32	.20	.05	9.46	175	6.25	13.0	12.5	11.82	2.36	2	.45	4.48
Montgomery	2.50	1.87	.30	.23	......	......	1.75	3.34	.80	.48	.97	.40	.35	12.99	217	6.00	12.6	13.0	14.49	1.50	5	.51	5.23
Nevada	2.00	1.69	.12	.16	.81	.15	.78	2.01	1.06	.39	.41	.56	.32	10.46	179	6.42	10.5	11.9	12.74	2.28	4	.37	5.15
Newton	3.00	3.75	.25	.62	......	......	2.12	3.50	1.70	.68	1.92	.63	.75	18.92	252	7.75	15.0	11.2	21.21	2.29	2	.46	6.84
Ouachita	2.50	3.75	.10	.33	2.33	.42	.92	3.08	1.36	.63	.33	.20	.19	16.14	288	6.17	17.0	10.0	19.30	3.16	3	.36	5.01

TABLE 20.—*Average cost of producing an acre of cotton in 1896 on farms showing a* ***PROFIT****, by counties*—Continued.

[Wherever a blank occurs in these tables it means that no expense was incurred.]

ARKANSAS—Continued.

County.	Rent.	Plowing.	Seeds.	Planting seed.	Fertilizers.	Distributing fertilizers.	Chopping and hoeing.	Picking.	Ginning and pressing.	Bagging and ties.	Marketing.	Repairing implements.	Other expenses.	TOTAL COST.	Pounds of lint.	Price per pound.	Bushels of seed.	Price per bushel.	TOTAL RETURN.	PROFIT.	Number of farms reporting.	Cost of picking per 100 pounds.	Cost of production per pound.
																Cents.		*Cents.*					*Cents.*
Perry	$4.17	$3.00	$0.15	$0.23	......	......	$1.67	$5.00	$1.63	$0.55	$1.12	$0.75	......	$18.27	347	6.58	21.0	10.0	$24.96	$6.69	3	$0.48	4.66
Phillips	3.50	1.88	.18	.25	......	......	2.12	4.00	.75	1.48	.55	.25	$0.13	15.09	250	7.12	16.5	11.2	19.61	4.52	2	.53	5.30
Pike	3.97	3.75	.20	.20	......	......	2.25	2.40	.58	.58	.37	.52	......	14.82	231	7.00	14.0	11.2	17.69	2.87	2	.35	5.74
Poinsott	4.33	2.83	.32	.27	......	......	2.58	6.67	2.33	1.00	1.50	.30	.33	22.46	433	7.58	26.3	11.8	35.26	12.80	3	.51	4.47
Polk	3.00	3.00	.20	.20	$2.50	$0.20	1.00	5.00	1.75	.65	.50	.25	.30	18.55	331	6.00	20.0	12.5	22.54	3.99	1	.50	4.81
Pope	3.38	1.63	.21	.15	......	......	1.62	2.95	.82	.60	.56	.60	.38	12.90	239	6.38	15.2	12.4	17.18	4.28	4	.41	4.61
Prairie	4.50	2.50	.18	.22	......	......	1.12	3.10	1.00	.38	.62	.10	.38	14.10	266	6.50	16.5	8.2	18.50	4.40	2	.39	4.79
Pulaski	3.86	2.86	.25	.18	.86	.25	1.59	5.85	1.83	.79	.84	.76	.36	20.28	357	6.46	24.3	10.3	25.44	5.16	7	.55	4.98
Randolph	3.12	2.39	.14	.22	......	......	1.94	4.88	1.21	.71	.41	.18	.61	15.81	317	7.02	19.0	9.4	24.30	8.49	4	.51	4.42
St. Francis	3.00	2.08	.34	.26	.33	.08	1.00	3.92	1.08	.57	.92	.68	.68	14.94	293	6.17	15.7	11.0	20.06	5.12	3	.45	4.51
Saline	2.50	2.25	.21	.27	......	......	1.00	4.10	1.19	.78	.86	.25	.25	13.66	305	6.50	19.0	13.1	23.22	9.56	4	.45	3.66
Scott	2.83	2.00	.18	.28	......	......	1.28	3.91	1.12	.58	.67	.70	.50	14.08	272	5.67	16.0	10.0	16.90	2.82	3	.48	4.59
Searcy	3.50	2.00	.20	.25	......	......	2.75	3.50	1.50	.50	1.50	1.00	......	16.70	300	5.00	18.0	10.0	16.80	.10	1	.39	4.97
Sebastian	2.83	3.27	.18	.43	.08	.08	1.21	4.42	1.44	.74	.48	.33	.22	15.71	269	6.48	16.7	11.5	19.19	3.48	6	.55	5.13
Sevier	3.37	3.69	.17	.21	.88	.38	1.18	3.95	1.05	.48	.79	.50	......	16.65	308	6.56	20.2	11.2	22.46	5.81	4	.43	4.67
Sharp	2.50	2.17	.16	.22	......	......	1.08	2.50	.57	.30	.30	.25	.12	10.17	193	6.63	11.3	10.0	14.15	3.98	3	.43	4.68
Stone	5.00	1.00	.12	.12	......	......	1.00	2.25	.90	.30	.25	.10	......	11.04	200	6.00	12.0	8.0	12.96	1.92	1	.38	5.04
Union	2.00	1.63	.10	.22	1.00	.12	.75	2.60	1.00	.63	.63	.25	.12	11.05	250	6.25	14.0	10.0	17.15	6.10	2	.35	3.86
Van Buren	2.00	1.50	.20	.25	......	......	1.00	2.00	1.00	1.40	1.00	.50	......	10.85	250	6.00	15.0	10.0	16.50	5.65	1	.27	3.74
White	2.55	2.20	.18	.31	......	......	1.40	2.61	1.21	.50	.45	.34	.34	12.09	203	6.60	12.8	11.5	14.86	2.77	5	.43	5.23
Woodruff	3.34	2.88	.33	.30	......	......	1.17	3.45	1.05	.47	.23	.08	......	13.30	256	6.25	15.3	10.0	17.45	4.15	3	.45	4.60
Yell	3.20	1.50	.16	.20	......	......	1.08	4.17	1.03	.57	.48	.25	.05	12.69	270	6.25	16.6	11.4	18.97	6.28	5	.51	4.00

FLORIDA.

UPLAND.

																Cents.		*Cents.*					*Cent.*
Calhoun	$0.83	$2.67	$0.25	$0.27	$1.90	$0.40	$1.27	$3.00	$0.78	$0.76	$0.43	$0.07	$0.58	$13.23	222	6.92	12.9	13.7	17.16	$3.93	3	$0.45	5.16
Escambia	2.00	1.75	.20	.07	2.00	.07	.50	2.45	.95	.40	.72	.50	.16	11.77	233	6.50	15.0	20.0	18.14	6.37	1	.35	3.76
Gadsden	1.14	2.83	.34	.88	4.50	.75	1.28	5.23	1.75	.77	.42	.34	1.24	21.47	358	6.71	22.8	16.7	28.15	6.68	3	.49	4.93
Holmes	1.77	3.17	.20	.42	1.99	.33	.83	3.33	1.34	.84	.50	.25	.03	15.00	206	7.17	12.7	16.7	16.72	1.72	3	.54	6.25
Jackson	1.46	3.01	.34	.35	2.08	.34	1.60	3.23	.78	.52	.63	.47	.22	15.03	228	6.46	14.8	10.8	16.88	1.65	6	.45	5.64
Jefferson	1.75	1.75	.46	.32	2.67	.54	.62	3.41	.84	.54	.36	.18	.40	13.84	274	6.83	18.8	11.9	21.28	7.45	6	.41	4.23
Leon	1.22	2.11	.37	.24	.56	.13	.90	2.31	.65	.35	.29	.32	.26	9.71	180	6.49	12.2	11.6	13.03	3.32	8	.43	4.61
Liberty	2.00	5.00	.20	.50	2.00	.25	.50	7.50	2.00	1.25	......	......	.16	21.36	498	7.00	35.0	15.0	40.11	18.75	1	.50	3.23
Madison	1.50	3.00	.12	.75	1.00	.75	1.50	2.40	1.25	.50	.75	.50	.15	14.17	200	7.00	16.0	12.0	15.92	1.75	1	.40	6.12
Putnam	1.00	1.00	.20	1.00	1.00	.50	3.00	3.00	2.75	.50	1.00	.75	.25	15.95	400	7.50	24.0	10.0	32.40	16.45	1	.25	3.39
Walton	2.44	2.75	.18	.55	2.56	.35	1.12	3.98	1.50	.75	.97	.38	......	17.53	289	7.06	17.5	13.8	22.82	5.29	4	.46	5.23
Washington	1.83	3.33	.18	.58	2.25	.42	1.25	3.25	1.03	.66	.75	1.08	.18	16.79	250	6.92	15.7	14.2	19.52	2.73	3	.43	5.82

SEA ISLAND.

																Cents.		*Cents*					*Cents.*
Alachua	$1.78	$3.28	$0.29	$0.35	$2.45	$0.27	$1.17	$4.97	$1.51	$0.52	$0.46	$0.38	$0.20	$17.63	154	12.68	9.6	20.5	$21.07	$3.44	8	$1.08	10.17
Baker	2.00	2.00	.50	.45	1.50	.25	2.25	5.00	1.25	.50	1.00	......	......	16.70	125	15.00	8.0	25.0	20.75	4.05	1	1.33	11.76
Bradford	11.00	3.75	.50	.25	2.25	.18	.50	7.50	1.80	.40	.25	.75	1.12	30.25	300	16.50	20.0	35.0	56.50	26.25	2	.83	7.75
Clay	4.10	4.90	.42	1.20	8.10	1.00	2.50	5.90	2.15	1.12	.80	.10	.06	32.35	240	16.00	14.8	22.4	40.51	8.16	5	.82	12.10
Columbia	1.40	3.35	.22	.25	1.90	.15	1.10	3.90	1.11	.48	.46	.31	.19	14.82	129	14.20	7.1	21.0	19.76	4.94	5	1.01	10.33
Gadsden	1.50	4.50	.25	.75	2.25	.50	1.25	3.00	2.00	.75	.75	1.00	1.20	19.70	175	14.00	10.0	20.0	26.50	6.80	1	.57	10.11
Hamilton	1.75	3.50	.50	.50	1.18	.10	.62	3.12	1.00	.23	.23	.15	.12	13.00	113	14.25	9.0	20.0	18.10	5.10	2	.92	9.91
Lafayette	1.50	6.34	.33	.25	3.83	1.08	.92	5.67	1.70	.78	.67	.58	.27	23.92	233	14.25	13.0	20.8	35.48	11.56	3	.81	9.11
Levy	1.58	5.12	.40	.49	3.17	.71	.92	4.06	1.48	.66	.42	.58	.31	19.90	168	14.17	11.3	24.2	27.30	7.40	6	.81	10.22
Madison	1.25	2.34	.23	.20	1.08	.23	1.13	2.50	.84	1.15	.32	.23	.30	12.15	108	13.67	6.0	30.0	16.48	4.33	3	.77	9.58
Marion	1.64	2.70	.41	.53	2.11	.36	1.23	3.79	1.32	.62	.75	.36	.32	16.14	121	16.86	7.9	32.1	22.22	6.08	7	1.04	11.24
Nassau	1.25	6.00	.25	1.50	2.90	.25	.50	3.00	.70	.30	1.25	......	......	17.90	107	15.75	7.0	25.0	18.60	.70	1	.93	15.09
Putnam	1.75	2.00	.62	.55	1.88	.55	1.50	7.55	3.60	.80	1.20	.05	.15	22.20	251	15.50	15.0	25.0	50.43	28.23	2	1.00	7.35
St. Johns	3.00	4.00	.40	.50	5.00	.50	.50	10.00	2.50	2.00	1.50	.50	.25	30.65	500	15.00	30.0	20.0	81.00	50.35	1	.67	4.93
Suwanee	1.50	3.00	.25	.25	.80	.40	1.70	2.25	.30	.45	.25	.10	......	11.25	100	12.00	4.5	25.0	13.12	1.87	1	.75	10.12
Taylor	1.42	2.17	.25	.20	.84	.25	1.33	3.33	1.00	.30	......	.33	.08	11.50	108	15.50	6.3	33.3	19.29	7.79	3	1.03	8.71

TABLE 20.—*Average cost of producing an acre of cotton in 1896 on farms showing a* ***PROFIT***, *by counties*—Continued.

[Wherever a blank occurs in these tables it means that no expense was incurred.]

GEORGIA.

UPLAND.

County.	Rent.	Plowing.	Seeds.	Planting seed.	Fertilizers.	Distributing fertilizers.	Chopping and hoeing.	Picking.	Ginning and pressing.	Bagging and ties.	Marketing.	Repairing implements.	Other expenses.	TOTAL COST.	Pounds of lint.	Price per pound.	Bushels of seed.	Price per bushel.	TOTAL RETURN.	PROFIT.	Number of farms reporting.	Cost of picking per 100 pounds.	Cost of production per pound.
																Cents.		*Cents.*					*Cents.*
Baker	$2.05	$2.74	$0.18	$0.14	$1.82	$0.13	$1.04	$2.68	$0.71	$0.37	$0.29	$0.10	$0.08	$12.33	214	6.75	14.3	11.2	$16.33	$4.00	5	$0.42	5.01
Baldwin	2.03	4.33	.60	.45	2.95	.31	.72	3.94	1.12	.50	.63	.30	.80	18.68	350	7.17	21.3	11.7	27.69	9.01	3	.37	4.51
Banks	3.41	2.81	.22	.32	2.19	.25	1.00	3.33	.91	.65	.28	.35	.90	16.62	250	7.12	15.5	13.8	19.94	3.32	4	.44	5.79
Bartow	3.10	3.12	.39	.21	2.23	.28	1.25	3.29	.95	.48	.29	.34	.52	16.45	267	7.00	16.2	13.1	21.10	4.65	7	.41	5.37
Berrien	2.17	3.67	.18	.30	1.93	.15	.67	2.67	.72	.52	.43	.20	.76	14.37	222	6.67	13.3	12.7	16.37	2.00	3	.40	5.71
Bibb	2.20	1.85	.28	.21	2.49	.19	1.03	2.52	.92	.96	.55	.38	.57	14.15	253	7.12	16.3	10.5	20.07	5.92	5	.33	4.92
Brooks	1.50	2.64	.25	.21	2.69	.18	1.20	3.99	1.12	.72	.75	.30	.06	15.61	304	6.62	19.8	13.0	22.38	6.77	4	.44	4.29
Bullock	2.00	1.75	.12	.18	2.25	.18	1.00	2.90	1.50	.70	2.05	.28	.77	15.68	250	7.12	18.0	12.5	20.07	4.39	2	.39	5.37
Burke	2.00	3.04	.28	.38	2.77	.19	.97	3.34	.75	.48	.85	.59	.30	15.94	292	7.06	18.0	10.9	22.52	6.58	6	.38	4.79
Butts	2.92	2.61	.22	.24	2.33	.16	1.19	3.01	.77	.52	.30	.20	1.50	15.97	275	6.88	17.0	13.3	21.09	5.12	6	.36	4.99
Calhoun	1.50	2.00	.30	.28	2.88	.20	1.50	3.23	.77	.52	.23	.37	.25	14.03	255	6.33	15.7	14.0	18.56	4.53	3	.42	4.64
Campbell	3.75	2.02	.14	.18	1.97	.15	1.50	3.40	.74	.61	.44	.48	.44	15.82	274	7.16	16.2	14.6	22.04	6.22	4	.41	4.91
Carroll	2.92	2.75	.19	.16	2.41	.30	1.11	2.52	.63	.39	.33	.25	.20	14.16	233	6.71	14.4	11.4	17.28	3.12	7	.36	5.37
Catoosa	2.00	1.00	.15	.15	2.00	.25	1.25	3.00	1.50	.85	.50	.20	.25	13.10	250	7.00	15.0	15.0	19.75	6.65	1	.40	4.34
Chattooga	3.39	2.54	.20	.23	1.42	.27	1.50	2.79	.89	.50	.45	.44	.58	15.20	231	6.90	16.4	11.5	17.90	2.70	5	.40	5.76
Chattahoochee	2.00	3.50	.15	.20	4.00	.10	1.25	2.50	1.50	.95	1.12	.15	2.00	19.42	300	7.00	20.0	12.0	20.40	.98	1	.28	5.67
Cherokee	3.75	2.47	.24	.40	2.23	.29	1.32	3.74	.92	.61	.54	.36	.13	17.00	255	6.00	15.4	14.1	20.01	3.01	5	.49	5.82
Clarke	2.77	2.52	.19	.23	2.53	.27	1.49	3.01	.76	.51	.50	.35	.67	15.80	294	7.18	17.7	13.6	23.58	7.78	7	.34	4.55
Clay	1.92	2.62	.21	.33	1.75	.30	1.25	2.93	.80	.49	.42	.37	.63	14.02	255	6.58	15.3	12.3	18.69	4.67	3	.38	4.76
Clayton	2.87	2.69	.28	.33	2.93	.26	1.00	3.39	.83	.60	.38	.39	.55	16.59	267	7.20	16.8	11.0	21.18	4.68	5	.42	5.49
Cobb	2.84	4.90	.28	.26	2.30	.24	1.63	3.58	1.08	.62	.40	.47	.77	19.37	318	7.02	19.2	13.0	24.75	5.38	5	.38	5.31
Colquitt	1.75	3.63	.46	.20	3.25	.30	1.00	4.19	1.18	.71	.52	.50	.06	17.75	327	6.88	20.6	13.0	24.68	6.93	4	.43	4.61
Columbia	2.31	2.02	.24	.17	2.02	.16	1.18	2.39	.82	.43	1.15	.32	.63	13.84	226	7.16	15.6	13.4	18.20	4.36	8	.35	5.20
Coweta	2.40	2.95	.19	.19	2.00	.15	1.03	2.61	.47	.40	.36	.30	.10	13.15	217	7.15	13.4	13.0	17.37	4.22	5	.40	5.26
Crawford	1.87	3.06	.20	.45	2.25	.20	.88	2.72	.90	.48	.51	.38	.65	14.55	233	6.50	14.5	11.9	16.75	2.20	4	.39	5.50
Dawson	3.30	2.12	.15	.18	2.25	.20	1.50	2.40	.65	.42	.38	.37		13.92	200	7.09	15.0	11.2	15.84	1.92	2	.40	6.12
Decatur	1.30	2.30	.17	.21	2.47	.54	1.32	3.89	1.32	.75	.35	1.05	.46	16.13	283	6.20	17.4	12.4	19.81	3.68	5	.46	4.94
Dekalb	3.00	4.25	.32	.53	4.15	.46	1.94	4.60	1.40	.81	.69	.56	.53	23.24	390	7.31	23.0	13.8	32.23	8.99	4	.39	5.15
Dodge	1.83	3.50	.12	.16	2.20	.22	.92	4.00	1.15	1.00	.57	.55	.33	16.55	317	6.33	21.3	11.7	22.21	5.66	3	.42	4.44
Dooly	1.67	3.16	.22	.32	2.08	.28	1.17	3.40	.67	.58	.46	.63	.58	15.22	272	6.50	16.0	12.3	19.66	4.44	3	.42	4.87
Dougherty	1.75	2.75	.40	.25	3.68	.45	.88	3.88	1.12	.75	.28	.25	.40	16.84	266	7.00	17.5	15.0	21.21	4.37	2	.49	5.35

Douglas	2.99	3.50	.24	.20	1.81	.26	1.25	3.10	.93	.60	.50	.49	.20	16.07	312	7.02	19.0	11.7	24.19	8.12	5	.33	4.44
Early	2.00	3.00	.15	.25	2.00	.25	1.00	3.20	.65	.75	.25	.50	1.00	15.00	250	7.00	16.0	15.0	19.90	4.90	1	.43	5.04
Effingham	1.17	2.58	.18	.17	3.17	.52	1.43	4.08	1.50	.75	1.25	.35	.50	17.65	333	7.00	20.3	15.0	26.38	8.73	3	.41	4.39
Elbert	2.67	2.89	.24	.24	2.98	.20	1.29	2.90	.74	.42	.35	.39	.44	15.75	268	7.00	17.0	14.2	21.23	5.48	6	.36	4.98
Emanuel	3.00	3.75	.40	.38	2.50	.50	1.32	5.15	2.40	1.15	2.00	.75	.60	23.90	441	7.00	27.5	15.0	35.00	11.10	2	.39	4.49
Fayette	2.42	2.50	.20	.32	1.58	.13	1.05	2.60	.42	.42	.25	.32	.08	12.29	193	7.00	12.0	13.2	15.10	2.81	3	.45	5.55
Floyd	3.66	2.41	.27	.31	2.09	.22	1.62	3.69	1.08	.55	.63	.41	.46	17.40	297	7.25	18.5	12.8	23.88	6.48	6	.41	5.06
Forsyth	3.86	1.84	.19	.23	2.00	.18	1.33	1.99	.96	.38	.32	.23	.84	14.35	214	7.00	12.3	12.5	16.47	2.12	3	.31	5.99
Franklin	5.53	4.50	.18	.20	7.50	1.10	1.25	4.38	1.12	.60	.75	.25	......	27.36	365	7.00	21.8	10.8	28.28	.92	2	.40	6.85
Fulton	1.40	1.50	.25	.25	2.00	.25	1.50	3.60	.60	.75	.25	.10	......	12.45	300	7.75	18.0	12.5	25.50	13.05	1	.40	3.40
Glasscock	1.83	1.66	.13	.28	2.10	.22	1.17	2.06	.45	.37	.42	.47	.45	11.61	185	7.00	10.5	12.3	14.25	2.64	3	.37	5.58
Gordon	3.37	2.39	.24	.19	1.70	.17	1.61	3.71	.90	.58	.53	.27	.69	16.35	282	6.95	17.6	11.8	21.74	5.39	7	.44	5.06
Greene	1.90	1.95	.21	.27	2.16	.16	1.45	2.52	.70	.62	.50	.47	.25	13.16	208	7.02	13.2	12.6	16.28	3.12	5	.40	5.53
Gwinnett	2.52	2.66	.16	.23	2.22	.19	1.10	3.11	.99	.54	.28	.34	.54	14.88	287	7.16	18.8	12.9	22.93	8.05	11	.36	4.34
Hall	3.10	2.74	.13	.24	2.00	.17	1.40	2.32	.75	.32	.24	.25	.08	13.74	221	7.37	12.7	12.5	17.86	4.12	3	.35	5.50
Hancock	2.24	2.12	.29	.21	2.91	.22	.88	1.66	.57	.53	.46	.26	.79	13.14	242	6.69	15.2	11.8	17.72	4.58	4	.23	4.69
Haralson	3.33	5.09	.30	.33	2.25	.25	1.55	4.77	1.25	.77	.25	.58	.63	21.35	377	6.67	23.0	11.7	27.70	6.35	3	.42	4.95
Harris	1.93	2.07	.23	.24	1.91	.19	1.11	2.28	.55	.41	.43	.36	.62	12.33	235	6.79	14.7	12.6	17.92	5.59	7	.32	4.46
Hart	1.93	3.83	.21	.20	2.40	.22	1.50	3.27	.90	.51	.42	.57	.66	16.62	273	6.90	16.7	14.5	21.32	4.70	6	.40	5.20
Heard	4.21	2.95	.22	.18	2.06	.26	1.20	3.60	1.37	.70	.65	.40	.73	18.53	358	7.10	22.1	10.8	27.76	9.23	5	.34	4.51
Henry	2.67	2.90	.28	.22	1.88	.13	1.34	3.22	.88	.48	.22	.25	.46	14.93	284	7.06	17.3	13.5	22.29	7.36	6	.38	4.43
Houston	1.75	2.08	.19	.19	1.85	.15	1.18	2.49	.44	.33	.55	.43	.53	12.16	190	7.23	11.7	12.8	15.22	3.06	6	.44	5.61
Irwin	2.00	3.67	.30	.23	2.33	.28	.97	4.30	2.33	.75	.51	.63	.75	19.05	354	7.17	19.7	20.0	29.20	10.15	3	.40	4.27
Jackson	3.00	2.75	.15	.50	2.50	.40	4.50	3.60	.50	.75	.20	.50	1.25	20.60	300	7.00	18.0	15.0	23.70	3.10	1	.40	5.97
Johnson	2.25	2.56	.18	.25	3.56	.25	.86	4.90	.91	.80	.32	.44	.90	18.18	348	6.50	21.8	11.8	24.32	6.14	4	.47	4.49
Jefferson	1.83	2.00	.18	.20	1.58	.15	.77	2.32	.62	.53	.42	.25	.20	11.05	205	6.83	11.7	11.5	15.28	4.23	3	.38	4.73
Jasper	2.13	2.04	.23	.39	2.11	.28	1.19	2.25	.71	.54	.35	.46	.81	13.49	224	6.98	13.6	12.3	17.25	3.76	5	.33	5.28
Jones	1.96	2.69	.24	.26	1.75	.16	.91	2.57	.79	.54	.49	.47	.61	13.44	244	6.97	15.5	13.0	18.84	5.40	8	.35	4.68
Laurens	1.25	2.75	.11	.31	1.84	.18	.72	2.55	.64	.66	.54	.44	.40	12.39	204	6.94	13.8	12.5	15.89	3.50	4	.42	5.23
Lee	1.33	2.71	.24	.17	1.70	.22	1.25	2.33	.58	.35	.42	.37	.03	11.70	217	6.67	13.0	10.7	15.80	4.10	3	.36	4.75
Liberty	2.00	3.00	.20	.50	1.60	.30	1.00	2.00	.40	.32	.52	.25	.60	12.69	200	7.94	12.0	15.0	17.68	4.99	1	.33	5.44
Lincoln	2.50	4.40	.25	.20	3.00	.25	1.75	2.50	.85	.45	.75	.15	.80	17.85	250	6.90	15.0	10.0	18.75	.90	1	.33	6.54
Lumpkin	1.75	2.50	.12	.38	2.05	.25	1.13	2.50	.58	.20	1.00	.50	.62	13.58	203	7.50	12.0	12.5	16.74	3.16	2	.41	5.95
McDuffie	1.42	3.00	.18	.22	2.50	.20	1.08	2.48	.67	.72	.62	.75	.38	14.22	258	6.75	16.7	12.7	19.45	5.23	3	.32	4.69
Macon	1.79	2.08	.24	.23	2.49	.21	1.07	2.90	.78	.64	.30	.27	.67	13.67	275	6.80	17.0	11.8	20.73	7.06	6	.35	4.24
Madison	3.62	2.37	.20	.16	1.82	.17	1.18	2.56	1.37	.52	.25	.44	.22	14.88	241	7.12	15.2	12.5	19.04	4.16	4	.35	5.39
Marion	2.00	3.00	.57	.18	1.75	.32	1.00	2.00	.70	.40	.22	.38	.50	13.02	283	7.12	17.0	13.5	22.50	9.48	2	.24	3.79
Meriwether	2.00	3.95	.22	.12	1.50	.12	1.00	2.10	.43	.28	.30	.18	.05	12.25	175	7.00	11.0	12.2	13.60	1.35	2	.40	6.23
Miller	1.37	3.25	.28	.40	3.15	.38	1.00	2.60	.88	.95	1.00	.87	1.17	17.30	400	6.50	24.0	11.2	29.28	11.98	2	.22	3.65
Mitchell	2.00	3.25	.22	.32	2.13	.20	1.25	3.65	.98	1.00	.75	.06	.40	16.21	325	6.75	20.0	12.5	24.50	8.29	2	.37	4.22
Milton	2.71	2.18	.22	.21	2.72	.21	1.33	3.48	.90	.46	.35	.36	.15	15.28	297	7.08	17.8	12.0	23.21	7.93	6	.39	4.42
Monroe	2.50	2.91	.20	.36	2.28	.32	1.10	2.69	.68	.69	.39	.58	.36	15.06	250	7.03	16.4	12.0	19.51	4.45	8	.36	5.24
Montgomery	1.50	3.00	.12	.14	2.13	.16	1.10	2.58	.77	.67	.91	.47	.17	13.72	240	6.52	16.8	13.3	17.89	4.17	5	.36	4.79
Morgan	3.00	1.84	.20	.24	2.02	.15	1.19	2.47	.66	.64	.27	.44	.59	12.71	225	7.03	14.0	13.0	17.64	4.93	4	.37	4.84
Muscogee	2.42	2.10	.23	.24	2.65	.29	.84	2.94	.90	.41	.82	.34	.80	14.98	248	6.65	15.2	12.6	18.53	3.55	5	.40	5.27
Newton	3.28	2.67	.16	.24	2.77	.23	1.17	2.97	.80	.53	.50	.33	.68	16.33	264	7.00	16.3	13.7	20.70	4.37	3	.38	5.34
Oconee	2.56	2.00	.21	.18	1.92	.16	1.18	2.49	.70	.52	.30	.45	.39	13.06	244	7.22	18.0	13.5	20.14	7.08	4	.34	4.36
Oglethorpe	2.17	2.57	.23	.16	2.18	.17	1.33	1.98	.41	.42	.37	.24	.47	12.70	201	7.08	12.0	13.5	15.92	3.22	6	.33	5.51
Paulding	5.02	3.60	.23	.27	1.88	.21	1.72	3.49	.88	.51	.33	.37	.60	19.11	281	7.30	16.8	14.2	22.80	3.68	5	.41	5.95
Pickens	4.29	2.53	.21	.22	1.19	.17	1.83	3.46	.88	.47	1.05	.28	.62	17.20	236	7.50	14.3	12.8	19.82	2.62	3	.49	6.51
Pike	2.29	2.81	.28	.25	1.95	.16	1.21	2.57	.60	.45	.30	.40	1.36	14.63	259	7.18	16.3	13.6	20.97	6.34	7	.33	4.79
Polk	2.00	2.00	.30	.20	2.50	.20	1.50	3.50	1.00	.40	.25	.25	.50	14.60	300	7.00	18.0	12.0	23.16	8.56	1	.39	4.15

TABLE 20.—*Average cost of producing an acre of cotton in 1896 on farms showing a PROFIT, by counties*—Continued.

[Wherever a blank occurs in these tables it means that no expense was incurred.]

GEORGIA—Continued.

UPLAND—Continued.

County.	Rent.	Plowing.	Seeds.	Planting seed.	Fertilizers.	Distributing fertilizers.	Chopping and hoeing.	Picking.	Ginning and pressing.	Bagging and ties.	Marketing.	Repairing implements.	Other expenses.	TOTAL COST.	Pounds of lint.	Price per pound.	Bushels of seed.	Price per bushel.	TOTAL RETURN.	PROFIT.	Number of farms reporting.	Cost of picking per 100 pounds.	Cost of production per pound.
																Cents.		Cents.					Cents.
Pulaski	$2.00	$2.89	$0.14	$0.16	$1.97	$0.22	$1.18	$2.88	$0.61	$0.36	$0.69	$0.23	$0.25	$13.58	247	6.95	14.3	11.4	$18.70	$5.12	5	$0.39	4.84
Putnam	2.00	3.00	.20	.25	1.75	.15	1.05	1.90	.70	.65	.50	.25	.25	12.65	200	6.75	12.5	10.0	14.75	2.10	1	.32	5.70
Quitman	1.83	1.75	.13	.10	2.42	.11	.75	2.11	.54	.57	.22	.42	.70	11.65	207	7.00	14.0	12.0	16.27	4.62	3	.34	4.82
Randolph	2.07	2.41	.17	.18	1.96	.17	.94	2.19	.66	.51	.23	.35	.22	12.06	199	6.64	12.6	12.8	14.84	2.78	7	.37	5.25
Richmond	2.50	2.74	.30	.21	2.35	.25	1.25	3.68	.86	.72	.45	.35	.29	15.95	290	7.31	18.0	15.0	23.98	8.03	4	.42	4.57
Rockdale	2.73	2.63	.15	.13	2.14	.17	.70	2.07	.65	.30	.30	.33	.43	12.73	194	7.42	11.7	13.5	15.96	3.23	3	.36	5.75
Schley	2.00	2.75	.20	.19	3.15	.24	.91	3.09	.96	.78	.93	.50	.50	16.20	294	6.94	17.2	12.0	22.98	6.78	4	.35	4.81
Scriven	1.81	3.13	.22	.26	3.56	.34	1.23	4.05	1.12	.74	1.01	.52	.46	18.48	317	6.70	18.6	12.2	23.06	4.58	8	.43	5.11
Spalding	3.00	3.00	.28	.25	2.00	.25	.88	2.55	.62	.39	.37	.38	.75	14.72	250	7.12	15.5	13.8	19.91	5.22	2	.34	5.03
Stewart	3.00	2.72	.29	.23	2.62	.25	.90	2.63	1.00	.65	.56	.56	.85	16.26	267	6.81	17.5	13.8	20.65	4.39	4	.33	5.18
Sumter	2.33	2.08	.16	.19	2.54	.16	1.08	3.19	.75	.47	.43	.43	.92	14.73	276	6.79	16.8	12.2	20.78	6.05	6	.39	4.59
Talbot	2.02	3.07	.25	.28	1.95	.28	.98	2.45	.75	.51	.39	.12	.30	13.35	230	6.85	13.7	12.9	17.57	4.22	6	.36	5.03
Taliaferro	2.07	2.88	.25	.20	2.09	.20	.91	2.33	.54	.50	.27	.14	.30	12.68	231	6.66	14.4	12.9	17.33	4.65	7	.34	4.68
Tattnall	2.25	3.75	.33	.22	2.20	.15	.80	2.44	.77	.35	.70	.20	.50	14.66	212	6.62	14.0	15.0	16.16	1.50	2	.38	5.92
Taylor	1.80	1.55	.18	.25	2.85	.28	1.22	2.46	.88	.52	.54	.31	.97	13.81	267	6.75	16.0	12.6	20.12	6.31	5	.31	4.42
Telfair	3.16	3.08	.18	.32	3.58	.45	1.37	4.75	1.40	.73	.67	.22	.17	20.08	329	6.54	18.3	15.0	24.17	4.09	3	.48	5.27
Terrell	2.29	3.46	.16	.23	2.18	.21	1.06	2.47	.44	.34	.23	.45	.19	13.71	210	6.71	13.0	13.4	15.85	2.14	7	.39	6.70
Thomas	1.88	2.38	.31	.31	2.03	.24	1.29	2.91	.72	.40	.12	.32	.78	13.69	238	6.50	14.8	12.0	17.22	3.53	4	.41	5.00
Troup	2.37	2.70	.29	.38	2.75	.24	1.75	3.12	.67	.59	.48	.81	.70	16.85	269	6.88	16.2	12.8	20.51	3.66	4	.39	5.49
Twiggs	2.00	2.00	.30	.15	2.00	.10	1.75	3.20	.50	.40	.65	.15	.00	13.20	250	7.50	17.5	15.0	21.38	8.18	1	.43	4.23
Upson	3.25	3.12	.20	.21	3.31	.18	1.30	3.07	.85	.48	.58	.38	.22	17.15	279	6.88	16.8	12.6	20.62	3.47	4	.37	5.39
Walker	2.71	3.44	.19	.31	1.99	.22	1.03	3.31	.84	.45	.29	.25	.51	15.57	248	7.12	15.0	13.8	19.75	4.18	4	.44	5.44
Walton	3.79	2.38	.19	.36	2.38	.42	1.75	2.62	.66	.47	.44	.59	.46	16.51	262	7.06	16.0	11.8	20.86	4.35	4	.33	5.58
Warren	2.35	2.81	.28	.19	2.18	.17	1.20	2.29	.65	.62	.18	.30	.51	13.73	224	6.95	15.2	14.5	17.75	4.02	5	.34	5.15
Washington	2.42	2.27	.20	.24	2.20	.21	.77	2.46	.75	.62	.35	.40	.51	13.40	238	6.78	14.8	12.3	17.99	4.59	9	.34	4.87
Webster	2.00	1.90	.36	.50	2.00	.20	1.30	2.00	.42	.35	.15	1.00	.50	12.68	160	7.00	12.0	12.5	12.70	.02	1	.42	6.99
Whitfield	2.66	2.91	.20	.27	1.40	.27	1.42	3.83	1.07	.50	.32	.50	.57	15.92	355	6.50	22.0	11.5	25.71	9.79	3	.36	3.77
Wilcox	1.67	2.56	.15	.27	2.47	.27	.92	3.01	.97	.57	1.08	.20	.55	14.69	250	6.67	15.3	14.0	18.82	4.13	3	.40	5.02
Wilkes	2.05	2.72	.19	.21	2.56	.19	1.35	2.88	.78	.55	.45	.33	.29	14.55	239	6.98	14.8	10.4	18.19	3.64	5	.40	5.44
Wilkinson	1.66	2.23	.15	.27	2.08	.27	.75	2.83	.52	.47	.65	.52	.49	12.89	233	7.17	14.0	14.2	18.67	5.78	3	.40	4.68
Worth	2.06	3.00	.18	.24	2.91	.21	1.25	4.35	1.27	.69	.66	.25	.75	17.82	354	6.56	21.5	13.1	25.83	8.01	4	.41	4.24

SEA-ISLAND.

																Cents.		Cents.					Cents.
Appling	$3.33	$6.67	$0.32	$0.43	$3.72	$0.47	$2.33	$8.33	$2.67	$0.80	$1.94	$0.75	$0.07	$31.83	258	12.17	15.7	20.0	$34 51	$2.68	3	$1.08	11.12
Berrien	2.00	6.00	.50	.50	2.00	.50	.60	5.90	1.50	.90	......	......	......	20.40	200	14.00	10.0	20.0	30 00	9.60	1	.98	9.20
Bullock	2.75	4.00	.50	.44	3.25	.31	.50	4.31	2.43	.63	.50	.38	.18	20.18	156	12.75	11.0	25.0	22.34	2.16	2	.92	11.17
Camden	3.00	.75	.50	.25	5.00	.15	1.00	6.00	1.40	.60	......	......	......	18.65	200	10.00	12.0	20.0	22.40	3.75	1	1.00	8.12
Charlton	3.00	4 50	.30	.27	2.33	.20	1.81	4.08	1.02	.25	.82	.38	.42	19.38	127	14.67	7.3	23.3	20.69	.71	3	1.07	13.92
Clinch	3.00	4 00	.50	.25	2.00	.25	.75	3.00	1.05	.25	.25	.25	.50	16.05	135	12.00	8.0	25.0	18.20	2.15	1	.74	10.41
Coffee	3.50	2.25	.22	.58	2.50	.40	.95	10.00	3.50	.35	1.12	.25	......	25.62	350	15.00	17.5	17.5	55.37	29.75	2	.95	6.44
Echols	3.00	3.00	.25	.20	2.00	.25	1.00	6.00	1.80	.75	.50	.50	.50	19.75	200	12.00	10.0	15.0	25.50	5.75	1	1.00	9.12
Emanuel	2 50	2.50	.15	.25	2.10	.20	.90	4.50	1.50	.45	.50	.50	......	16.05	250	15.00	9.0	20.0	39.30	23.25	1	.60	5.70
Liberty	3 00	2.00	.06	.15	10.00	.50	1.00	6.75	2.45	.60	1.00	......	.75	28.26	275	12.00	15.0	25.0	36.75	8.49	1	.82	8.91
Miller	2.00	2.00	.15	.10	3.25	.07	1.20	7.50	2.75	.66	1.00	.02	.10	20.80	270	11.00	12.0	10.0	30.90	10.10	1	.93	7.26
Pierce	2.00	4.00	.10	1.00	2.50	.50	1.00	5.00	1.00	1.00	1.00	......	......	19.10	175	14.00	6.0	20.0	25.70	6.60	1	.95	10.23
Wayne	2.00	5.50	.22	.18	2.05	.25	1.62	4.63	1.38	.88	.42	.12	......	19.25	166	12.50	9.5	20 0	22.85	3.60	2	.93	10.45

INDIAN TERRITORY.

																Cents.		Cents.					Cents.
Cherokee Nation	$2.86	$2.38	$0.21	$0.21	$0.04	$0.01	$1.61	$5.51	$1.91	$0.83	$0.94	$0.71	$0.36	$17.58	363	6.79	22.0	11.1	$27.05	$9.47	7	$0.51	4.17
Chickasaw Nation	2.38	2.01	.12	.24	......	......	1.49	4.12	1.54	.60	.60	.43	.25	13.78	259	6.49	15.6	10.4	18.31	4.53	21	.53	4.69
Choctaw Nation	2.82	2.61	.14	.21	......	......	1.83	4.58	1.58	.80	.88	.30	.34	16.0[illegible]	293	6.43	19.0	10.3	20.79	4.70	11	.52	4.82
Creek Nation	4.00	1.95	.25	.07	......	......	2.25	8.00	1.75	1.25	.50	.50	......	20.52	500	6.00	36.0	10.0	33.60	13.08	1	.53	3.38
Seminole Nation	2.67	2.50	.15	.25	......	......	.98	5.20	1.92	.67	.67	.08	.33	15.42	278	6.46	17.3	9.3	19.67	4.25	3	.62	4.97

LOUISIANA.

PARISH.																Cents.		Cents.					Cents.
Acadia	$3.50	$1.62	$0.30	$0.65	$1.25	$0.75	$1.25	$6.35	$2.00	$0.75	$0.88	$1.25	......	$20.55	375	6.50	23.0	9.5	$26.57	$6.02	2	$0.56	4.90
Ascension	11.25	3.75	.12	.70	......	......	1.75	6.50	2.25	.90	1.75	1.00	......	29.97	450	6.75	32.0	10.0	33.58	3.61	1	.48	5.95
Avoyelles	4.08	3.08	.25	.34	.46	.09	2.30	6.44	1.70	.90	2.34	.46	$0.82	23.86	453	6.90	28.6	11.2	34.41	10.55	20	.47	4.56
Bienville	1.75	2.25	.10	.17	1.00	.12	1.62	2.70	.68	.48	.51	.38	.52	12.28	198	6.62	11.5	10.0	14.18	1.90	2	.45	5.62
Bossier	2.55	3.45	.23	.26	1.15	.21	1.33	3.94	1.18	.71	.39	1.19	.10	16.69	300	6.40	19.8	9.9	21.25	4.56	5	.44	4.91
Caddo	2.83	2.14	.23	.21	.80	.15	1.79	3.35	.97	.62	.99	.43	.28	14.79	276	6.67	16.7	10.1	20.35	5.56	9	.40	4.75
Calcasieu	2.00	3.00	.30	.10	3.00	.15	2.25	3.50	.75	.50	1.50	.25	.50	17.80	250	6.50	14.0	15.0	18.35	.55	1	.47	6.28
Caldwell	4.00	3.12	.22	.23	......	......	2.62	3.25	1.25	.68	1.62	.43	1.00	18.42	275	6.50	17.5	10.0	19.50	1.08	2	.39	6.06
Cameron	4.00	1.75	.25	.50	......	......	1.44	8.10	2.44	.83	1.75	1.38	......	22.44	450	6.20	26.0	11.6	31.40	8.96	2	.60	4.32
Catahoula	3.10	4.90	.23	.24	......	......	1.64	5.08	1.76	.79	2.07	.40	1.10	21.31	383	6.62	24.4	13.1	28.70	7.39	5	.44	4.73
Claiborne	2.00	2.54	.11	.31	.86	.19	1.44	2.89	.99	.55	.57	.61	.14	13.20	244	6.36	15.7	9.8	16.97	3.77	7	.39	4.78
Concordia	3.79	3.32	.16	.30	......	......	2.10	5.56	1.40	.89	2.76	.55	.61	21.44	431	6.94	26.9	9.4	32.39	10.95	7	.43	4.39
De Soto	2.00	1.29	.16	.21	.52	.06	1.06	2.66	.68	.29	.46	.30	.29	9.98	188	6.47	11.2	10.4	13.28	3.30	7	.47	4.69
East Baton Rouge	3.33	3.26	.40	.26	1.66	.21	1.56	5.40	1.64	.72	.64	.43	.34	19.85	390	6.86	24.6	10.5	29.58	9.73	12	.46	4.43
East Carroll	4.90	2.77	.28	.33	......	......	2.20	5.37	2.00	.90	3.08	.51	.75	23.09	391	7.26	26.2	11.9	31.59	8.50	11	.46	5.11

TABLE 20.—*Average cost of producing an acre of cotton in 1896 on farms showing a* ***PROFIT****, by counties*—Continued.

[Wherever a blank occurs in these tables it means that no expense was incurred.]

LOUISIANA—Continued.

County.	Rent.	Plowing.	Seeds.	Planting seed.	Fertilizers.	Distributing fertilizers.	Chopping and hoeing.	Picking.	Ginning and pressing.	Bagging and ties.	Marketing.	Repairing implements.	Other expenses.	TOTAL COST.	Pounds of lint.	Price per pound.	Bushels of seed.	Price per bushel.	TOTAL RETURN.	PROFIT.	Number of farms reporting.	Cost of picking per 100 pounds.	Cost of production per pound.
PARISH—continued.																*Cents.*		*Cents.*					*Cents.*
East Feliciana	$2.55	$2.17	$0.31	$0.28	$2.49	$0.24	$1.32	$4.44	$1.35	$0.72	$0.57	$0.75	$0.59	$17.78	340	6.72	22.6	10.1	$25.24	$7.46	16	$0.44	4.56
Franklin	2.83	3.04	.29	.26			2.25	3.78	1.31	.85	1.23	.42	.73	16.99	306	6.39	19.0	8.9	21.69	4.70	6	.41	5.00
Grant	3.75	6.00	.19	.28	.25	.19	2.31	4.73	1.98	.96	2.84	.73	.19	24.40	431	6.38	24.8	9.8	29.81	5.41	4	.37	5.10
Iberia	2.37	2.04	.21	.28			1.92	4.02	1.10	1.08	.90	.75	.56	15.23	304	6.83	20.2	12.4	23.69	8.46	4	.44	4.19
Iberville	4.50	2.00	.68	.29	.20	.10	2.04	7.29	2.50	.78	2.42	.69	.40	23.89	510	7.24	29.8	11.7	40.45	16.56	5	.48	4.00
Lafayette	1.67	1.75	.20	.30			1.17	5.17	1.86	1.07	.66	.35	.13	14.33	367	6.42	21.7	9.0	25.48	11.15	3	.47	3.37
Lincoln	1.00	2.00	.25	.05	1.00	.10	.35	2.10	.45	.50	.30	.25	.10	8.45	233	6.00	15.0	15.0	16.23	7.78	1	.30	2.66
Livingston	2.70	3.41	.35	.48			1.33	3.40	1.49	.57	.42	.37	.50	15.02	299	7.08	17.0	10.0	22.90	7.88	3	.38	4.45
Madison	3.67	3.60	.28	.17	.80	.08	1.40	4.50	1.50	.65	1.80	.66	1.00	20.11	339	7.33	22.7	11.7	28.31	8.20	3	.44	5.15
Morehouse	3.43	3.05	.17	.26	.64	.08	1.42	3.23	1.32	.70	.63	.18	.18	15.29	303	6.49	20.0	8.9	21.49	6.20	7	.36	4.46
Natchitoches	3.72	6.50	.31	.23	.83	.17	1.42	6.00	1.58	.87	1.50	.83		23.96	442	6.50	27.5	9.3	31.16	7.20	3	.45	4.84
Ouachita	4.00	3.00	.45	.20	1.50	.25	1.50	5.50	1.62	.78	1.88	.62	.88	22.18	400	6.75	27.0	9.0	29.40	7.22	2	.46	4.94
Point Coupee	4.67	2.82	.25	.33			2.55	6.83	2.33	.97	2.18	.25	.77	23.95	452	6.92	31.0	9.7	34.53	10.58	3	.50	4.63
Rapides	3.35	2.40	.22	.17	.42	.04	1.79	6.18	1.72	.81	.64	.34	.50	18.61	458	6.89	31.4	11.6	35.44	16.83	10	.45	3.27
Red River	4.00	4.25	.25	.23	.75	.25	2.12	4.75	1.00	.62	1.75	.25	1.38	21.60	340	6.88	22.5	10.5	25.76	4.16	2	.47	5.66
Richland	3.33	2.50	.09	.38			1.13	2.50	.90	.76	.42	.52	.50	13.03	233	7.00	15.0	9.0	17.62	4.59	3	.36	5.01
Sabine	3.52	3.38	.15	.20	.75	.14	2.24	5.00	1.65	.81	1.21	.08	.34	19.47	316	6.30	22.5	10.3	22.13	2.66	4	.53	5.43
St. Helena	2.75	3.87	.15	.20	2.09	.25	1.46	4.07	1.46	.74	.72	.56	.19	18.51	300	6.59	17.9	9.8	21.24	2.73	8	.45	5.59
St. Landry	3.45	2.52	.30	.44			2.29	4.58	1.37	.83	.61	.94	.68	18.01	345	6.42	20.2	10.3	24.28	6.27	10	.44	4.62
St. Martin	2.05	1.50	.15	.28			1.67	5.00	1.67	.81	2.43	.65	.59	16.80	367	7.17	26.3	9.5	28.47	11.67	3	.45	3.90
St. Tammany	4.45	.75	.15	.25	2.50	.10	.50	3.50	.75	.30	.25	.10		13.60	250	7.12	15.0	15.0	20.05	6.45	1	.47	4.54
Tangipahoa	2.79	3.64	.14	.32	2.17	.30	1.40	5.50	1.84	.77	.25	.37	.54	20.03	362	6.93	22.0	11.1	27.48	7.45	7	.51	4.86
Tensas	4.40	2.99	.23	.24	.31	.05	2.03	5.29	1.45	.87	2.18	.64	.79	21.47	411	6.96	25.9	11.2	31.59	10.12	18	.43	4.52
Union	2.15	2.94	.12	.16	2.34	.40	.98	2.86	1.08	.48	.47	.75	.49	15.22	263	6.25	16.0	10.0	18.16	2.94	5	.36	5.18
Vermilion	2.50	3.62	.18	.24			1.06	8.18	2.10	1.18	1.28	.64	.68	21.66	456	6.80	30.3	9.2	33.84	12.18	4	.60	4.14
Vernon	2.00	1.00	.20	.20	3.75	.50	1.30	5.00	.99	1.00	2.00	.25	.10	18.29	400	6.50	25.0	10.0	28.50	10.21	1	.42	3.95
Washington	2.25	3.75	.09	.22	1.75	.17	1.62	4.50	1.38	.45	.38	.38	1.12	18.06	300	6.75	17.5	11.6	22.12	4.06	2	.50	5.34
Webster	1.90	2.50	.20	.22	1.92	.23	1.44	4.70	1.45	.72	1.00	.52	.45	17.25	345	6.70	22.8	11.0	25.72	8.47	5	.45	4.27
West Baton Rouge	5.12	2.09	.28	.18	.16	.06	2.32	6.68	1.92	.96	2.22	.39	.52	22.90	435	7.44	25.5	9.9	34.84	11.94	4	.51	4.68
West Carroll	3.00	2.75	.20	.38			1.75	4.40	1.65	.77	.82	.25		15.97	300	6.50	21.5	11.5	21.99	6.02	2	.49	4.50
West Feliciana	2.70	2.40	.29	.40	.60	.05	1.85	3.48	2.14	.63	.30	.60	.18	15.62	262	6.65	16.5	16.4	20.18	4.56	5	.41	4.93
Winn	2.50	4.00	.15	.28	2.12	.37	1.62	3.95	1.36	.78	.70	.69	.35	18.87	314	6.53	17.0	10.0	22.36	3.49	4	.42	5.47

MISSISSIPPI.

																Cents.		Cents.					Cents.
Adams	$6.00	$6.00	$0.50	$0.75	$3.00	$0.50	$2.00	$7.00	$2.25	$1.25	$1.00	$0.50	$2.00	$32.75	500	7.25	28.0	10.0	$39.05	$6.30	1	$0.47	5.99
Alcorn	2.30	2.76	.13	.23	1.10	.10	1.16	2.56	1.03	.43	.47	.20	.44	12.91	222	6.62	13.4	9.6	15.99	3.08	5	.38	5.24
Amite	2.00	2.25	.12	.42	1.00	.15	1.12	2.80	1.00	.38	.38	.38	.25	12.25	258	7.12	13.5	10.0	19.71	7.46	2	.36	4.22
Attala	2.62	3.37	.15	.35	.50	.06	1.44	2.91	.86	.41	.55	.34	.98	14.54	233	6.81	14.4	9.2	17.41	2.87	4	.41	5.62
Benton	2.12	2.26	.21	.40	1.88	.62	1.00	3.41	1.24	.48	.44	.26	.69	15.01	253	6.25	15.8	10.9	17.28	2.27	4	.45	5.25
Bolivar	4.50	3.63	.25	.25	......	......	1.62	6.10	1.35	.78	1.62	.38	......	20.48	362	7.25	22.5	12.5	20.00	8.52	2	.56	4.88
Calhoun	2.50	3.33	.25	.48	......	......	2.17	3.53	1.42	.67	.95	.42	.83	16.55	317	6.53	18.0	9.3	22.46	5.91	3	.37	4.09
Carroll	3.00	2.19	.26	.30	1.25	.12	1.12	4.48	1.25	.78	.62	.39	.38	16.14	325	6.56	20.5	10.2	23.29	7.15	4	.46	4.32
Chickasaw	3.17	2.04	.20	.28	.33	.04	1.29	3.37	1.17	.47	.68	.22	.32	13.58	248	6.46	16.5	9.6	17.52	3.94	6	.45	4.84
Choctaw	2.50	1.38	.12	.18	1.13	.12	1.19	3.13	.88	.42	.62	.50	.75	12.92	275	6.75	17.0	10.0	20.20	7.28	2	.38	4.08
Claiborne	2.90	2.75	.15	.30	......	......	1.50	4.60	1.35	.95	.38	.62	.38	15.88	310	7.00	20.0	9.5	23.60	7.72	2	.49	4.51
Clarke	2.25	2.50	.12	.33	2.13	.20	.75	2.80	.90	.52	.35	.18	.08	13.11	271	6.50	15.5	12.5	19.55	6.44	2	.34	4.12
Clay	2.60	2.33	.23	.20	......	......	.93	2.90	1.25	.66	.64	.44	.82	13.00	260	6.54	17.8	9.2	18.24	5.24	5	.37	4.37
Coahoma	5.41	4.42	.32	.42	......	......	1.25	6.66	1.82	.86	1.52	.40	.27	23.35	425	6.92	29.8	9.6	32.16	8.81	6	.52	4.82
Copiah	2.08	2.34	.21	.18	1.94	.21	1.42	3.44	1.09	.63	.64	.66	.31	15.15	259	6.83	16.6	9.1	19.18	4.03	8	.44	5.27
Covington	3.17	2.50	.13	.18	2.08	.23	1.79	4.67	1.57	.63	1.25	.33	.67	19.20	321	6.67	20.0	10.8	23.58	4.38	3	.48	5.31
De Soto	3.87	3.50	.48	.20	2.87	.88	2.01	4.92	1.45	.74	1.78	.56	.51	23.77	375	6.83	27.5	10.4	28.29	4.52	4	.44	5.58
Franklin	2.50	3.70	.21	.31	1.25	.31	1.38	2.90	1.24	.79	.90	.62	.49	16.60	262	6.88	16.2	8.2	19.26	2.66	4	.37	5.83
Grenada	2.25	2.00	.18	.35	......	......	1.37	5.00	1.33	.80	.45	.38	......	14.11	334	6.75	20.0	8.0	24.73	10.62	2	.50	3.75
Green	3.00	4.20	1.50	.30	2.65	.50	1.50	4.00	1.75	1.00	.25	......	1.75	22.40	410	7.25	30.0	12.5	33.48	11.08	1	.33	4.55
Hinds	2.39	3.27	.15	.21	1.29	.38	1.39	4.54	1.44	.63	.45	.58	.21	16.93	320	6.54	22.2	8.4	22.20	5.27	6	.47	4.71
Holmes	4.83	2.83	.18	.38	2.90	1.17	1.67	5.17	1.47	1.08	.53	.60	.27	22.18	367	6.83	27.0	8.6	27.15	4.97	3	.47	5.41
Issaquena	4.85	3.25	.35	.22	......	......	1.72	5.90	2.05	1.38	2.38	1.00	......	23.10	388	6.50	23.5	9.5	27.34	4.24	2	.51	5.38
Itawamba	3.06	2.25	.19	.24	1.55	.18	1.29	2.55	1.13	.47	.57	.15	.12	13.75	225	6.88	13.8	10.0	16.91	3.16	4	.38	5.50
Jasper	2.00	4.00	.15	.11	2.00	.22	1.75	3.00	1.25	.42	1.00	.88	.80	17.58	258	6.75	14.5	15.0	19.54	1.96	2	.39	5.97
Jefferson	2.73	2.46	.26	.26	.50	.02	1.11	2.90	1.01	.61	.47	.37	.41	13.11	232	6.75	16.5	9.1	17.46	4.35	6	.42	5.00
Jones	2.83	5.17	.17	.25	4.07	.33	1.67	4.66	1.20	.68	1.50	.42	.20	23.15	406	6.83	25.3	13.3	31.33	8.18	3	.38	4.87
Kemper	2.20	3.18	.26	.24	.94	.20	1.40	2.89	1.14	.64	1.02	.28	.20	14.59	249	6.88	15.0	11.0	18.77	4.18	10	.39	5,20
Lafayotte	2.08	2.79	.18	.22	1.45	.18	1.22	2.89	.97	.50	.44	.37	.37	13.57	230	6.67	14.0	10.2	16.79	3.22	6	.42	5.28
Lauderdale	3.40	2.67	.30	.27	1.67	.15	1.33	3.60	1.23	.62	.52	.60	.90	17.26	294	6.75	18.7	11.8	22.25	4.99	3	.41	5.12
Lawrence	2.12	4.00	.16	.30	1.50	.24	1.88	2.81	1.10	.40	.88	.26	.09	15.74	239	6.88	16.0	9.2	18.00	2.26	4	.39	5.97
Leake	2.50	3.08	.20	.32	1.08	.22	1.08	2.97	1.25	.55	.72	.33	.67	14.97	261	6.50	15.7	9.3	18.32	3.35	3	.38	5.18
Lee	3.58	2.75	.24	.29	......	......	1.20	3.21	1.21	.46	.33	.51	1.36	15.14	263	6.70	15.8	10.5	19.37	4.23	5	.41	5.13
Leflore	6.00	2.85	.35	.22	......	......	1.80	4.68	1.12	.80	1.73	.70	2.00	22.25	350	6.75	21.5	12.5	26.35	4.10	2	.45	5.59
Lincoln	3.20	3.10	.19	.27	1.75	.24	1.52	3.63	1.26	.63	.55	.43	.33	17.10	298	7.04	20.1	10.5	23.13	6.03	5	.41	5.03
Lowndes	1.75	1.75	.28	.38	.50	.12	1.12	1.75	1.00	.40	.38	1.00	.75	11.18	225	6.75	12.0	12.5	16.63	5.45	2	.26	4.30
Madison	2.10	1.56	.13	.16	1.60	.09	.98	3.05	1.22	.48	.39	.29	.49	12.54	203	6.80	15.2	8.5	15.16	2.62	5	.50	5.54
Marion	3.19	2.08	.12	.27	2.00	.33	.92	4.33	1.55	.50	.58	.25	1.00	17.12	271	6.87	17.3	10.8	20.54	3.42	3	.53	5.63
Marshall	2.35	2.55	.21	.29	......	......	1.51	4.12	1.16	.55	.75	.30	.39	14.18	300	6.75	20.4	10.5	22.84	8.66	5	.46	4.01
Monroe	2.34	2.18	.20	.23	1.28	.13	1.44	2.72	.99	.55	.42	.71	.45	13.64	216	6.96	13.8	10.0	16.44	2.80	6	.42	5.68
Montgomery	2.75	3.25	.18	.32	1.00	.50	1.75	6.50	2.00	.95	.75	1.00	.75	21.70	475	6.75	28.5	10.0	34.43	12.73	2	.46	3.97
Neshoba	3.25	2.69	.14	.16	1.22	.12	.99	2.73	1.01	.29	.78	.40	.12	13.90	216	6.75	13.2	10.6	16.16	2.26	4	.42	5.79
Newton	3.92	3.69	.11	.28	2.32	.26	2.00	4.89	1.78	.65	.81	.29	.50	21.50	362	7.12	22.8	11.2	28.47	6.97	4	.45	5.23
Noxubee	2.50	2.50	.20	.25	......	......	1.00	2.40	.75	.80	.25	.35	......	11.00	250	7.00	16.0	10.0	19.10	8.10	1	.32	3.76
Oktibbeha	2.90	2.67	.27	.21	2.10	.05	1.02	3.35	.81	.56	.45	.43	.27	15.09	248	6.76	17.6	10.0	18.52	3.43	5	.45	5.38
Panola	2.63	3.00	.16	.24	.30	.05	1.36	2.96	.87	.41	.20	.23	.31	12.72	239	6.32	14.7	9.0	16.50	3.78	7	.41	4.77
Parry	2.33	2.67	.30	.23	1.92	.15	1.18	4.33	1.00	.54	.40	.35	.09	15.49	278	6.67	17.3	17.5	21.75	6.26	3	.52	4.48

TABLE 20.—*Average cost of producing an acre of cotton in 1896 on farms showing a* ***PROFIT****, by counties*—Continued.

[Wherever a blank occurs in these tables it means that no expense was incurred.]

MISSISSIPPI—Continued.

County.	Rent.	Plowing.	Seeds.	Planting seed.	Fertilizers.	Distributing fertilizers.	Chopping and hoeing.	Picking.	Ginning and pressing.	Bagging and ties.	Marketing.	Repairing implements.	Other expenses.	TOTAL COST.	Pounds of lint.	Price per pound.	Bushels of seed.	Price per bushel.	TOTAL RETURN.	PROFIT.	Number of farms reporting.	Cost of picking per 100 pounds.	Cost of production per pound.
																Cents.		*Cents.*					*Cents.*
Pike	$2.00	$3.67	$0.14	$0.36	$2.12	$0.37	$1.17	$3.87	$1.30	$0.54	$0.32	$0.33	$0.17	$16.36	270	7.00	13.8	10.9	$20.32	$3.96	6	$0.48	5.50
Pontotoc	2.46	3.21	.22	.33	1.00	.25	1.44	2.98	.99	.48	.36	.46	.63	14.81	214	6.84	13.5	9.5	15.86	1.05	4	.46	6.32
Prentiss	2.67	1.92	.27	.28	.50	.13	1.33	2.62	.80	.36	.39	.23	.23	11.67	212	6.62	12.7	10.0	15.38	3.71	3	.41	4.91
Quitman	5.50	3.50	.19	.33			1.67	5.50	1.58	.92	3.17	.33	.42	23.11	403	6.92	25.3	8.8	29.79	6.68	3	.45	5.18
Rankin	2.17	2.66	.15	.30	1.83	.38	2.20	3.67	1.17	.70	.70	.67	.33	16.93	267	6.92	16.0	10.8	20.10	3.17	3	.46	5.69
Scott	2.60	3.80	.13	.18	1.92	.18	1.05	4.65	1.54	.71	.31	.42	.12	17.61	325	6.60	20.8	10.0	23.55	5.94	5	.48	4.78
Sharkey	5.17	1.25	.14	.12			2.03	4.53	1.33	.69	1.58	.37	1.70	18.91	330	6.92	20.7	11.1	25.10	6.19	3	.46	5.03
Simpson	1.67	3.79	.13	.23	2.17	.32	1.78	3.83	1.33	.67	1.20	.53	.53	18.18	289	7.04	17.7	10.8	21.79	3.61	3	.44	5.63
Smith	2.94	2.38	.12	.21	1.72	.19	1.06	3.65	1.35	.49	1.08	.42	.45	16.06	259	6.69	16.2	11.0	19.20	3.14	4	.47	5.51
Sunflower	6.00	2.50	.35	.10			2.00	4.00	1.20	.45	.30	.40		17.30	300	7.25	19.5	10.0	23.70	6.40	1	.44	5.12
Tallahatchie	4.17	2.17	.25	.21			1.67	4.26	1.13	.60	.28	.50	.33	15.57	294	7.00	17.7	9.3	22.30	6.73	3	.48	4.74
Tate	2.50	2.69	.21	.24	.50	.12	1.44	3.08	.92	.49	.75	.06	.52	13.52	229	6.38	14.2	10.0	16.01	2.49	4	.45	5.28
Tippah	2.00	2.31	.19	.22	.38	.05	1.13	2.21	.79	.28	.24	.29	.22	10.31	190	6.75	11.0	10.5	14.06	3.75	4	.39	4.82
Tunica	3.20	2.30	.25	.20			1.50	4.00	1.50	1.00	2.65	.25		16.85	260	7.25	16.0	10.0	20.45	3.60	1	.51	5.87
Union	2.87	2.58	.20	.23	.79	.17	1.38	2.89	.93	.42	.36	.44	.40	13.66	244	6.77	14.2	10.2	17.98	4.32	6	.39	5.00
Warren	6.00	3.25	.25	.25			2.05	7.50	1.35	.85	3.75	.50	.50	26.25	450	7.50	31.0	11.3	37.25	11.00	1	.56	5.05
Washington	5.36	2.56	.33	.14	.43	.01	2.14	5.54	1.47	.80	1.09	.69	.61	21.17	400	7.14	27.7	10.5	31.46	10.29	7	.46	4.57
Wayne	2.25	3.62	.22	.18	1.64	.26	1.44	2.55	.71	.32	.45	.38	.49	14.51	209	7.03	13.0	11.1	16.17	1.66	4	.41	6.25
Webster	3.34	2.53	.13	.23	.33	.10	1.50	4.25	1.12	.87	.53	.67	.20	15.80	361	6.75	22.7	11.7	26.95	11.15	3	.39	3.64
Wilkinson	3.08	4.01	.24	.36	1.88	.29	1.62	3.55	1.19	.82	.56	.34		17.34	300	6.75	18.2	9.6	22.06	4.72	4	.39	5.20
Winston	2.25	3.75	.22	.18	.58	.08	1.38	2.97	1.12	.85	.80	.22	.60	15.00	275	6.50	13.8	9.0	15.88	.88	2	.36	5.00
Yalobusha	2.50	1.65	.13	.27	.40	.10	1.00	3.08	1.40	.61	.47	.21	.45	12.27	243	6.50	17.3	8.8	17.41	5.14	5	.42	4.42
Yazoo	4.22	3.23	.16	.22			1.68	4.19	.95	.65	.85	.41	.29	16.85	268	7.61	17.6	10.0	22.29	5.44	7	.52	5.63
LONG STAPLE COTTON.																							
Claiborne	4.00	2.92	.40	.33	.33	.07	1.83	6.67	1.67	.92	1.25	.56	.25	21.20	375	10.83	29.7	12.3	44.76	23.25	3	.59	4.68
Washington	5.00	1.25	.10	.75			5.25	6.00	.75	1.00	4.00	1.00		25.10	300	10.00	25.0	10.0	32.50	7.40	1	.67	7.53

MISSOURI.

															Cents.		Cents.					Cents.
Dunklin	$3.25	$2.62	$0.20	$0.22	$0.25	$0.10	$1.00	$5.00	$1.38	$0.55	$0.50	$0.12	$0.38	$15.57	325	6.50	20.5	10.0	$23.55	$7.98	2	$0.51	4.16
Howell	4.50	1.50	.25	.25	4.75	.25	1.50	2.50	1.50	1.00	1.00	1.00	......	20.00	333	6.25	20.0	25.0	25.81	5.81	1	.25	4.50
New Madrid	3.00	2.00	.20	.15	......	......	2.25	5.00	1.00	.75	.75	.25	......	15.35	300	6.00	22.0	8.0	19.76	4.41	1	.56	4.53
Oregon	2.00	2.50	.20	.25	......	......	2.00	4.00	1.00	.50	.50	.50	.40	13.85	250	6.50	16.0	10.0	17.85	4.00	1	.53	4.90
Ozark	2.00	1.00	.30	1.00	......	......	2.00	3.20	1.00	1.00	.60	......	......	12.10	265	5.00	16.0	10.0	14.85	2.75	1	.40	3.96
Pemiscot	4.00	1.00	.10	.35	......	......	2.50	12.00	2.25	1.25	1.50	.25	.40	25.60	550	6.38	33.0	10.0	38.39	12.79	1	.73	4.05
Taney	3.00	2.00	.30	1.00	......	......	.50	4.50	1.50	1.00	.75	.25	.80	15.60	200	7.00	12.5	15.0	15.88	.28	1	.75	6.86

NORTH CAROLINA.

															Cents.		Cents.					Cents.
Anson	$2.61	$2.73	$0.36	$0.34	$2.14	$0.22	$1.37	$2.68	$0.84	$0.61	$0.52	$0.57	$0.59	$15.58	270	6.95	17.7	12.1	$20.98	$5.40	7	$0.33	4.98
Beaufort	3.20	2.60	.31	.21	3.25	.24	1.66	3.78	1.38	.92	.54	.51	1.10	19.70	342	7.00	22.8	13.8	26.95	7.25	5	.37	4.84
Bertie	3.00	4.00	.15	.25	2.00	.50	2.00	2.50	1.25	1.00	1.50	.50	.50	19.15	300	6.50	16.0	10.0	21.10	1.95	1	.28	5.85
Bladen	3.69	3.55	.25	.43	3.23	.25	.56	3.07	1.07	.64	1.21	.29	.32	18.56	300	6.72	19.0	13.7	22.78	4.22	9	.34	5.32
Cabarrus	7.08	3.33	.21	.50	2.17	.22	1.17	4.66	1.33	.57	.67	.50	.70	23.11	393	7.25	24.7	13.3	31.71	8.60	3	.40	5.04
Camden	2.00	1.00	.20	.25	2.00	.50	4.00	5.00	2.00	1.00	1.25	......	1.20	20.40	400	7.00	25.0	10.0	30.50	10.10	1	.42	4.48
Carteret	4.75	1.75	.30	.17	2.00	.18	1.75	4.15	.80	1.00	1.00	.17	.30	18.32	330	7.00	14.5	12.2	24.88	6.56	2	.42	5.02
Catawba	3.00	1.80	.20	.20	1.13	.12	.75	2.32	.65	.35	.62	.18	.30	11.62	195	7.62	12.0	13.8	16.53	4.91	2	.40	5.11
Chatham	3.17	3.00	.22	.49	1.87	.19	1.03	3.44	.72	.79	.41	.34	.26	15.63	266	6.68	18.8	14.0	20.50	4.87	5	.39	4.89
Cleveland	4.06	2.96	.24	.39	2.36	.22	1.42	2.96	1.03	.48	.34	.28	.27	17.01	281	7.48	17.4	12.9	23.21	6.20	8	.35	5.25
Columbus	3.25	3.20	.23	.23	2.20	.18	.84	2.37	1.37	.92	.48	.14	.12	15.53	273	7.30	17.1	18.2	22.93	7.40	5	.29	4.55
Craven	5.67	3.46	.45	.40	5.62	.65	1.35	4.67	1.58	.88	.47	.46	.30	25.96	421	7.17	27.0	14.5	34.44	8.48	6	.37	5.24
Cumberland	2.37	3.00	.20	.14	2.12	.09	1.05	2.36	.58	.39	.21	.21	.45	13.17	212	7.06	13.6	13.6	16.81	3.64	4	.37	5.34
Davidson	7.21	3.00	.15	.47	1.28	.20	1.75	4.40	.90	.65	.71	.25	.06	21.03	316	7.00	20.0	10.5	24.23	3.20	2	.46	5.99
Davie	2.00	2.50	.15	.25	2.00	.25	1.00	2.00	.50	.30	.50	.50	.35	12.30	200	7.00	12.0	12.0	15.44	3.14	1	.33	5.43
Duplin	4.80	3.31	.22	.19	2.84	.14	1.29	3.89	1.23	.64	.25	.38	.12	19.30	334	6.80	20.1	14.1	25.84	6.54	8	.39	4.93
Durham	4.88	2.75	.18	.62	2.00	.18	1.00	3.00	.88	.42	.37	.22	.55	17.05	300	6.75	18.0	11.2	21.45	4.40	2	.33	5.01
Edgecombe	3.50	1.75	.15	.42	2.50	.43	1.59	2.90	.90	.70	.30	.83	......	15.97	300	6.33	23.0	12.3	22.06	6.09	3	.32	4.38
Franklin	3.46	3.55	.24	.29	2.75	.28	1.56	2.62	.93	.55	.41	.40	.20	17.24	272	7.20	17.3	12.1	21.65	4.41	5	.32	5.57
Gaston	3.99	2.72	.23	.39	1.69	.19	1.33	2.88	.75	.33	.62	.64	.21	15.97	279	7.12	15.9	13.8	22.15	6.18	6	.34	4.94
Gates	3.62	2.62	.23	.39	2.38	.24	1.34	2.70	1.16	.47	.44	.19	.68	16.46	256	6.81	15.5	12.1	19.47	3.01	4	.35	5.70
Greene	3.50	1.75	.25	.30	4.06	.29	.80	3.94	1.41	.54	.22	.38	.85	18.29	346	6.75	21.9	12.5	25.90	7.61	4	.38	4.49
Halifax	2.21	3.11	.26	.37	3.57	.32	.80	2.77	1.20	.91	.64	.50	.27	16.93	320	6.71	19.6	11.9	23.95	7.02	7	.29	4.56
Harnett	2.50	4.00	.20	.38	2.25	.18	1.38	2.82	.95	.65	.62	.10	.50	16.53	275	7.25	18.8	11.5	22.01	5.48	2	.34	5.22
Hertford	3.33	2.50	.21	.20	2.38	.25	.95	2.93	.86	.74	.83	.35	.41	15.94	264	6.98	16.5	12.3	20.44	4.50	6	.37	5.27
Iredell	2.75	2.90	.18	.25	2.12	.34	1.33	3.47	1.44	.61	.50	.34	.19	16.42	262	6.75	15.9	12.2	19.46	3.04	4	.44	5.53
Johnston	3.06	3.26	.48	.31	2.68	.19	1.24	3.62	1.36	.52	.43	.19	.28	17.62	335	7.44	20.9	12.6	27.75	10.13	7	.36	4.47
Jones	4.18	2.25	.22	.58	4.00	.37	1.00	3.10	.88	.68	.28	.62	......	18.16	300	6.50	13.5	10.0	20.60	2.44	2	.34	5.60
Lenoir	3.77	2.64	.55	.18	2.91	.24	1.04	3.52	1.14	.59	.45	.26	.44	17.73	297	7.00	18.2	12.1	23.06	5.33	7	.40	5.23
Lincoln	4.02	3.92	.26	.28	2.00	.30	1.50	4.87	1.02	.57	.50	.33	.36	19.93	340	7.60	24.0	11.8	28.77	8.84	3	.48	5.03
Martin	3.00	2.83	.20	.23	3.50	.33	.83	2.17	.98	.75	.85	.25	......	15.92	261	6.33	16.0	13.2	18.59	2.67	3	.28	5.29
Mecklenburg	4.11	2.83	.20	.17	2.55	.30	1.04	3.40	.97	.44	.40	.48	1.10	17.99	300	7.15	18.7	15.6	24.31	6.32	6	.38	5.02
Montgomery	4.16	2.89	.24	.22	2.10	.29	1.23	3.08	1.29	.70	.40	.60	.06	17.26	286	6.97	19.6	11.0	22.17	4.91	5	.36	5.28
Moore	3.60	3.22	.20	.23	2.39	.20	.89	3.00	.92	.69	.52	.34	.18	16.38	261	6.75	16.8	13.2	19.74	3.36	10	.38	5.43

TABLE 20.—*Average cost of producing an acre of cotton in 1896 on farms showing a* ***PROFIT***, *by counties*—Continued.

[Wherever a blank occurs in these tables it means that no expense was incurred.]

NORTH CAROLINA—Continued.

County.	Rent.	Plowing.	Seeds.	Planting seed.	Fertilizers.	Distributing fertilizers.	Chopping and hoeing.	Picking.	Ginning and pressing.	Bagging and ties.	Marketing.	Repairing implements.	Other expenses.	TOTAL COST.	Pounds of lint.	Price per pound.	Bushels of seed.	Price per bushel.	TOTAL RETURN.	PROFIT.	Number of farms reporting.	Cost of picking per 100 pounds.	Cost of production per pound.
																Cents.		Cents.					Cents.
Nash	$4.14	$3.64	$0.23	$0.39	$3.08	$0.25	$1.11	$2.95	$1.11	$0.81	$0.46	$0.47	$0.10	$18.74	315	6.73	19.6	11.9	$23.61	$4.87	7	$0.31	5.21
Northampton	2.50	2.00	.22	.20	2.25	.20	.75	2.25	1.10	.40	.13	.10	.30	12.40	237	6.50	14.0	12.5	17.16	4.76	1	.32	4.49
Onslow	5.50	1.75	.75	.27	2.25	1.00	1.87	4.65	2.12	.68	.75	.88	.50	22.97	396	6.50	25.0	15.0	20.51	6.54	2	.39	4.85
Orange	5.00	3.75	.25	.74	2.12	.36	1.87	3.31	1.29	.54	.75	.38	.28	20.64	279	7.12	19.0	12.5	22.28	1.64	4	.40	6.55
Pamlico	4.15	2.75	.20	.15	2.25	.20	1.45	4.80	1.80	1.25	.62	.23	......	19.85	375	6.38	27.0	10.2	26.83	6.98	2	.43	4.56
Pasquotank	4.65	1.88	.23	.42	4.97	.47	.81	4.28	1.70	.78	1.38	.34	.32	22.26	347	7.04	24.3	10.6	26.90	4.64	5	.41	5.67
Perquimans	5.95	2.80	.31	.30	4.70	.29	1.67	4.77	1.54	.86	1.40	.39	.60	25.58	403	6.92	25.6	11.9	31.20	5.62	5	.39	5.59
Pitt	4.50	4.00	1.63	.30	4.00	.25	1.50	2.50	2.00	.85	......	.50	......	22.03	375	6.75	19.0	14.0	27.97	5.94	1	.22	5.17
Polk	3.05	2.19	.44	.39	2.30	.22	1.75	2.88	1.42	.74	.75	.20	.12	16.45	244	7.12	14.2	13.8	19.54	3.09	4	.39	5.94
Randolph	3.70	1.88	.18	.22	2.00	.20	1.32	2.40	.80	.56	.23	.30	.62	14.41	200	7.25	15.0	12.2	16.33	1.92	2	.40	6.29
Richmond	2.74	2.65	.24	.16	4.20	.20	1.10	3.27	.94	.68	.61	.29	.14	17.22	276	6.67	17.2	12.8	20.52	3.30	6	.39	5.44
Robeson	3.60	2.60	.19	.25	3.45	.17	.89	2.88	.74	.48	.32	.23	.12	15.92	283	7.00	16.6	13.5	22.15	6.23	5	.34	4.83
Rowan	5.17	3.30	.21	.23	2.20	.27	.96	3.66	1.06	.45	.57	.35	.54	18.37	289	7.00	17.6	13.3	22.71	4.34	5	.35	5.55
Rutherford	3.96	2.58	.19	.30	1.80	.22	1.67	3.42	.83	.35	.55	.18	.33	16.38	238	7.02	14.3	13.3	18.64	2.26	3	.48	6.08
Sampson	3.00	2.83	.25	.48	3.48	.40	.83	3.02	1.57	.53	.50	.44	.20	17.53	293	7.17	16.7	13.2	23.14	5.61	3	.34	5.23
Stanly	3.26	3.46	.21	.25	2.39	.29	1.83	3.48	1.24	.54	.41	.64	.03	18.03	305	7.06	18.4	12.9	23.81	5.78	7	.38	5.13
Tyrrell	4.16	2.67	.25	.45	4.16	.47	1.17	4.47	1.53	1.08	1.42	.33	.47	22.63	383	6.96	25.7	10.7	29.46	6.83	3	.39	5.19
Union	3.08	3.23	.25	.27	2.24	.20	1.40	3.60	1.02	.43	.48	.49	.19	16.88	297	7.12	19.3	13.3	23.79	6.91	11	.40	4.82
Vance	1.75	5.00	.25	1.00	2.00	.25	1.25	2.75	1.45	.80	.15	.75	1.00	18.40	300	7.00	15.0	12.5	22.88	4.48	1	.31	5.51
Wake	3.90	3.28	.22	.36	2.79	.20	1.54	3.18	1.04	.55	.61	.40	.64	18.71	308	7.28	19.1	12.5	24.79	6.08	10	.34	5.30
Warren	3.00	2.72	.31	.34	2.39	.21	1.06	2.93	1.13	.68	.46	.42	.22	15.87	281	7.07	17.9	12.0	22.02	6.15	8	.35	4.88
Washington	6.00	6.00	.25	.30	2.00	.20	3.50	5.25	2.25	.90	1.10	.20	......	27.95	500	6.00	30.0	20.0	36.00	8.05	1	.35	4.39
Wayne	4.05	3.06	.19	.25	2.83	.21	1.10	3.59	1.02	.66	.56	.23	.66	18.41	312	6.98	17.9	12.8	24.06	5.65	8	.38	5.17
Wilson	3.38	2.75	.19	.22	2.77	.18	1.23	2.83	.82	.43	.21	.14	.46	15.61	278	6.88	16.7	11.5	20.95	5.34	6	.34	4.92

SOUTH CAROLINA.

UPLAND.

																Cents.		Cents	$				Cents.
Abbeville	$2.25	$3.25	$0.30	$0.21	$2.05	$0.18	$1.17	$2.11	$0.75	$0.50	$0.75	$0.38	$0.12	$14.02	208	7.50	13.0	15.5	17.40	$3.38	2	$0.34	5.77
Aiken	2.35	3.28	.19	.31	2.40	.30	1.14	3.34	1.14	.81	.70	.52	.02	16.50	288	7.22	16.2	14.5	23.34	6.84	5	.39	4.91
Anderson	2.50	3.37	.19	.21	3.47	.16	1.33	3.50	1.05	.45	.42	.33	.33	17.31	333	7.00	18.7	15.7	26.23	8.92	3	.35	4.32
Barnwell	2.40	2.27	.20	.18	2.60	.17	.91	3.30	1.01	.61	.50	.38	.38	14.91	260	6.75	15.6	13.9	19.42	4.51	5	.42	4.90
Beaufort	1.50	2.15	.38	.64	3.25	.37	.22	6.56	1.22	.85	1.75	.08	.04	19.01	437	7.44	28.0	17.5	36.75	17.74	2	.50	3.23
Chester	2.70	2.28	.29	.09	2.61	.21	1.00	3.23	.99	.65	.36	.39	.32	15.12	275	7.18	17.5	15.2	22.26	7.14	6	.39	4.53
Chesterfield	2.45	3.92	.30	.27	2.83	.35	1.43	3.88	.85	.70	.58	.58	.92	19.06	345	6.92	22.3	11.7	26.20	7.14	3	.37	4.77
Cherokee	2.00	2.50	.25	.20	1.25	.20	.80	2.50	.25	.15	.25	.20	.15	10.70	245	7.50	15.0	13.0	18.82	8.12	1	.37	3.89
Clarendon	2.40	4.85	.24	.25	3.60	.17	1.00	4.69	1.22	.62	1.00	.55	.32	20.91	347	6.95	21.4	13.4	27.22	6.31	5	.45	5.20
Colleton	1.80	2.55	.26	.28	2.15	.23	.62	2.41	.94	.57	.17	.59	.70	13.27	210	6.85	13.3	12.4	16.06	2.79	5	.38	5.53
Darlington	2.72	2.90	.28	.22	3.84	.21	1.11	3.88	.86	.79	.32	.22	1.02	18.37	312	6.66	19.7	14.0	23.58	5.21	9	.41	5.00
Edgefield	2.36	2.10	.25	.15	1.99	.29	.90	2.87	.82	.62	.89	.50	.36	14.10	244	7.13	15.3	13.6	19.34	5.24	7	.39	4.93
Fairfield	2.00	2.56	.31	.14	1.64	.13	1.06	3.38	99	.74	.44	.40	.84	14.63	275	6.81	15.8	19.2	21.36	6.73	4	.41	4.22
Florence	2.70	2.57	.22	.24	3.98	.20	.79	4.30	1.61	.76	.32	.60	.89	19.18	365	7.07	22.7	14.5	29.39	10.21	11	.39	4.35
Georgetown	2.00	2.50	.30	.15	2.50	.12	1.00	3.00	.62	.40	.50	.10	......	13.19	240	6.50	18.0	15.0	18.30	5.11	1	.42	4.37
Greenville	3.40	2.81	.25	.28	3.62	.26	1.49	3.84	1.32	.52	.46	.48	.60	19.33	331	6.94	20.4	15.1	25.87	6.54	8	.39	4.91
Hampton	1.90	2.35	.23	.27	5.25	.28	.66	5.45	1.30	.84	.95	.52	.30	20.30	410	6.70	22.4	13.0	30.37	10.07	5	.44	4.24
Horry	3.30	2.77	.31	.32	2.88	.18	.75	3.47	1.07	.95	.85	.19	.24	17.28	305	6.70	18.2	12.5	22.54	5.26	5	.38	4.92
Kershaw	3.21	2.39	.31	.11	1.38	.14	1.20	3.00	.72	1.06	.50	.20	.10	14.32	270	7.12	16.2	15.0	21.62	7.30	2	.37	4.40
Lancaster	2.89	3.43	.27	.26	2.85	.20	1.33	4.14	1.41	.90	.45	.88	1.13	20.14	374	7.00	24.7	12.3	29.39	9.25	3	.37	4.57
Laurens	2.79	2.07	.29	.25	2.25	.19	1.03	3.21	.79	.49	.33	.58	.31	14.58	297	6.63	18.2	15.3	22.11	7.53	7	.36	3.97
Lexington	2.38	1.73	.26	.24	1.96	.26	1.03	2.28	.75	.52	.42	.24	.29	12.36	186	7.04	11.7	14.7	14.82	2.46	6	.41	5.72
Marion	3.98	2.71	.19	.18	4.21	.18	.88	3.87	.82	.58	.27	.40	.25	18.62	343	6.92	21.0	15.4	27.09	8.47	6	.38	4.49
Marlboro	5.38	3.35	.24	.23	6.44	.30	1.09	5.63	1.29	.94	.29	.51	.93	26.62	445	6.98	29.0	15.3	35.76	9.14	6	.42	4.98
Newberry	2.98	1.85	.25	.32	1.72	.14	.94	3.15	.69	.42	.19	.37	.59	13.61	233	6.90	15.2	15.0	18.30	4.69	5	.45	4.86
Oconee	3.25	1.20	.20	.20	2.00	.15	1.25	2.00	.65	.40	.25	.20	......	11.75	200	6.50	12.0	15.0	14.80	3.05	1	.33	4.98
Orangeburg	2.43	2.64	.29	.24	5.49	.34	1.09	3.96	1.17	.72	.26	.54	.14	19.31	360	7.00	21.9	15.0	28.55	9.24	7	.37	4.45
Pickens	3.74	2.77	.24	.23	2.37	.14	1.55	3.02	1.01	.40	.82	.42	.40	17.11	266	7.00	15.7	15.2	20.54	3.43	6	.38	5.53
Richland	1.94	3.82	.19	.24	1.71	.16	1.20	2.35	.62	.48	.41	.41	.32	13.85	200	6.94	11.8	14.9	15.57	1.72	4	.39	6.04
Saluda	2.50	.50	.25	.10	1.50	.10	.50	2.40	.50	.25	.50	.10	.50	9.70	200	6.75	13.0	12.5	15.12	5.42	1	.40	4.04
Spartanburg	3.84	2.71	.25	.28	2.11	.26	1.42	2.88	.91	.36	.22	.39	.64	16.27	243	7.16	14.2	15.3	19.52	3.25	6	.40	5.80
Sumter	2.59	2.75	.29	.25	3.40	.15	.84	3.82	.75	.48	.86	.22	.68	17.08	313	6.98	19.0	14.1	24.55	7.47	7	.41	4.60
Union	4.44	2.35	.26	.20	2.43	.19	1.08	3.14	.80	.37	.39	.33	.28	16.26	261	7.04	16.8	12.8	20.53	4.27	9	.40	5.41
Williamsburg	1.80	2.69	.18	.27	2.36	.13	1.22	3.00	1.20	.75	1.80	.22	.20	15.82	270	6.90	17.8	13.6	20.96	5.14	5	.37	4.96
York	2.70	2.55	.31	.18	2.40	.19	.89	3.75	.79	.73	.19	.67	.49	15.84	295	6.95	20.6	13.4	23.17	7.33	5	.42	4.43

SEA-ISLAND.

																Cents.		Cents.					Cents.
Beaufort	$1.83	$3.00	$0.58	$0.48	$5.67	$0.37	$3.30	$5.83	$3.99	$0.55	$1.25	$0.42	$0.44	$27.71	168	21.00	9.7	40.0	$40.27	$12.56	3	$1.16	14.18
Berkley	3.47	3.05	.55	.63	9.04	.42	5.73	9.78	6.29	.71	2.86	.42	3.09	46.04	235	29.71	16.1	26.9	73.73	27.69	7	1.39	17.75
Charleston	3.37	1.44	.54	.31	6.12	.15	3.95	7.75	4.56	.54	1.35	.81	1.54	32.43	210	27.75	17.0	28.2	62.39	29.96	4	1.23	13.16

TABLE 20.—*Average cost of producing an acre of cotton in 1896 on farms showing a **PROFIT**, by counties*—Continued.

[Wherever a blank occurs in these tables it means that no expense was incurred.]

OKLAHOMA TERRITORY.

County.	Rent.	Plowing.	Seeds.	Planting seed.	Fertilizers.	Distributing fertilizers.	Chopping and hoeing.	Picking.	Ginning and pressing.	Bagging and ties.	Marketing.	Repairing implements.	Other expenses.	TOTAL COST.	Pounds of lint.	Price per pound.	Bushels of seed.	Price per bushel.	TOTAL RETURN.	PROFIT.	Number of farms reporting.	Cost of picking per 100 pounds.	Cost of production per pound.
																Cents.		*Cents.*					*Cents.*
Blaine	$2.50	$1.50	$0.15	$0.20			$0.50	$1.50	$0.25	$0.15	$0.40			$7.15	100	7.00	6.0	10.0	$7.60	$0.45	1	$0.50	6.55
Canadian	1.67	1.42	.18	.38	$0.33	$0.02	2.47	3.00	.88	.75	.62	$0.30	$0.50	12.52	172	7.47	12.0	19.0	15.01	2.50	3	.58	5.95
D	2.00	.75	.05	.30			1.00	3.75	2.00	1.00	1.00			11.85	170	7.00	12.0	12.5	13.40	1.55	1	.74	6.09
Greer	1.83	1.17	.11	.22			1.17	3.46	1.33	.75	.58	.91		11.53	213	6.46	13.3	17.5	15.94	4.41	3	.54	4.32
Kingfisher	2.25	1.00	.16	.50			1.38	3.12	1.88	.78	1.62	.02		12.71	208	7.38	12.5	12.0	16.93	4.22	2	.50	5.39
Lincoln	2.00	1.13	.08	.14			1.06	4.00	1.21	.53	.70	.11	.20	11.16	227	6.75	13.5	7.8	16.18	5.02	4	.59	4.45
Logan	1.63	1.29	.13	.23			1.53	3.42	1.03	.42	.58	.14	.62	11.02	203	6.58	13.7	11.6	15.16	4.14	6	.56	4.65
Oklahoma	1.83	.72	.11	.32			1.67	4.63	1.50	.52	.77	.08	.41	12.56	306	6.42	19.0	12.5	22.43	9.87	3	.50	3.33
Pawnee	2.00	1.00	.20	.33			1.00	2.50	.83	.33	.67			8.86	167	7.00	11.0	20.0	13.89	5.03	1	.50	3.99
Pottawatomie	1.58	1.28	.16	.20			.68	3.12	.80	.36	.45	.18		8.81	207	6.21	13.0	10.7	14.16	5.35	3	.50	3.58
Woods	1.00	.75	.05	.20			1.00	2.50	2.75	1.25	2.00		1.00	12.50	300	7.00	30.0	10.0	38.00	25.50	1	.17	1.90

TENNESSEE.

County.	Rent.	Plowing.	Seeds.	Planting seed.	Fertilizers.	Distributing fertilizers.	Chopping and hoeing.	Picking.	Ginning and pressing.	Bagging and ties.	Marketing.	Repairing implements.	Other expenses.	TOTAL COST.	Pounds of lint.	Price per pound.	Bushels of seed.	Price per bushel.	TOTAL RETURN.	PROFIT.	Number of farms reporting.	Cost of picking per 100 pounds.	Cost of production per pound.
																Cents.		*Cents.*					*Cents.*
Bradley	$2.00	$1.42	$0.22	$0.23	$1.83	$0.22	$1.33	$5.33	$1.35	$0.98	$0.51	$0.18	$0.17	$15.77	383	7.00	23.0	11.7	$30.22	$14.45	3	$0.46	3.41
Carroll	3.33	2.87	.21	.36	.50	.33	1.17	3.68	1.06	.70	.42	.28	.38	15.29	262	6.38	17.3	11.7	18.77	3.48	6	.47	5.06
Chester	3.12	2.44	.16	.19			.99	2.71	1.04	.48	.29	.19	.68	12.29	210	6.62	14.2	9.5	15.25	2.96	4	.43	5.21
Crockett	3.38	3.00	.26	.44			1.19	4.19	1.22	.72	.46	.46	1.12	16.44	291	6.53	18.0	10.0	20.79	4.35	4	.48	5.03
Decatur	4.00	1.00	.20	.20			1.50	3.00	1.00	.45	.50	.10		11.95	230	7.00	14.0	7.5	17.15	5.20	1	.43	4.74
Dyer	3.62	2.14	.29	.32			1.50	4.12	1.19	.72	.80	.16	.65	15.51	266	6.66	17.0	11.2	19.76	4.25	4	.52	5.12
Fayette	2.50	2.70	.23	.30	.02	.02	1.46	2.22	.72	.39	.33	.33	.34	11.56	178	7.04	11.0	9.7	13.66	2.10	6	.42	5.89
Gibson	3.46	2.84	.32	.42	.11	.04	1.64	4.11	1.34	.66	.60	.38	.53	16.45	283	6.57	19.7	11.1	20.87	4.42	7	.48	5.04
Giles	3.28	2.69	.26	.30			1.25	3.65	1.09	.58	.59	.30	.86	14.85	286	6.38	18.0	12.9	20.53	5.68	4	.43	4.38
Hamilton	3.00	4.50	.15	.08	1.50	.10	.75	3.75	1.10	.60	.25	.25	.10	16.13	250	7.00	15.0	15.0	19.75	3.62	1	.50	5.55
Hardeman	2.50	2.29	.30	.32	.38	.12	1.62	3.77	1.22	.74	.38	.42	.43	14.49	265	6.46	18.7	9.7	18.75	4.26	6	.47	4.78
Hardin	3.33	2.92	.19	.32	.17	.08	1.25	3.47	1.11	.59	.06	.27	.52	14.28	260	6.46	15.8	8.7	18.04	3.76	6	.44	4.96
Haywood	2.00	1.50	.15	.50			2.00	1.60	.50	.30	.12	.75	.12	9.54	125	7.00	8.0	10.0	9.55	.01	1	.43	6.99
Henderson	2.61	2.87	.20	.32	.46	.37	1.41	3.53	1.16	.55	.52	.31	.17	14.48	269	6.45	17.3	10.5	19.05	4.57	6	.44	4.71

Henry	3.22	2.70	.20	.30	.62	.50	1.10	2.70	1.08	.55	.55	.55	.88	14.95	238	6.50	13.5	12.5	17.03	2.08	2	.38	5.57
Lake	5.00	2.67	.23	.28			2.00	6.83	2.10	1.10	2.00	.38	.84	23.43	439	6.58	29.0	10.0	31.63	8.20	3	.52	4.68
Lauderdale	3.50	3.38	.22	.35	.62	.10	1.25	3.05	1.75	.50	.38	.20		15.30	250	6.38	17.5	10.0	17.68	2.38	2	.41	5.42
Lawrence	3.76	2.50	.29	.20			2.10	3.20	1.02	.52	.58	.75		14.92	256	6.65	16.0	10.0	18.93	4.01	2	.42	5.20
Lincoln	3.00	4.02	.50	.50	.62	.16	.78	2.80	1.20	.65	.58	1.00	.25	16.06	298	6.75	18.0	16.2	22.98	6.92	2	.31	4.41
McMinn	1.50	2.00	.15	.10	1.50	.15	1.00	2.40	1.00	.50	.25	.10	.30	10.95	170	6.50	11.0	15.0	12.70	1.75	1	.47	5.47
McNairy	3.97	2.45	.17	.16	.30	.10	1.27	3.04	1.15	.52	.59	.39	.40	14.51	259	6.60	15.2	9.2	18.73	4.22	5	.39	5.06
Madison	2.25	3.25	.10	.28	.50	.12	.75	2.25	.84	.49	.56	.45	.36	12.20	162	7.00	10.0	10.0	12.38	.18	2	.46	6.91
Marion	2.50	3.50	.35	.50			2.40	4.60	1.50	.40	.25	.25	.15	16.40	275	7.00	17.0	13.0	21.46	5.06	1	.56	5.16
Marshall	3.00	5.00	.25	.50			1.00	4.50	1.25	.75	1.00	1.00		18.25	270	6.62	13.5	12.5	19.56	1.31	1	.56	6.13
Maury	3.50	1.50	.30	.13			1.35	3.10	1.30	.92	.62	.85	.25	13.82	238	7.50	17.5	8.5	19.32	5.50	2	.43	5.18
Obion	3.50	1.75	.18	.29	.12	.08	1.37	3.64	1.29	.67	.33	.27	.46	13.95	242	6.48	16	10.6	17.39	3.44	4	.50	5.06
Shelby	2.50	4.25	.35	.25			2.50	3.50	.70	.70	.32	.50	1.30	16.87	232	6.75	16	11	17.57	.70	2	.50	6.51
Tipton	3.25	3.56	.26	.35	.38	.12	1.75	4.10	1.31	.69	.60	.44	.25	17.06	300	6.62	20.5	12.2	23.44	6.38	4	.46	4.85
Wayne	2.00	1.25	.25	.50	1.50	.50	1.00	3.75	1.28	.75	.25	.25	.12	13.40	250	7.40	20	10	20.50	7.10	1	.50	4.56
Weakley	3.00	2.00	.15	.38			1.00	4.00	1.25	.75	.25	.62	.25	13.65	258	6.50	18	12.5	18.98	5.33	2	.52	4.42

TEXAS.

																Cents.		*Cents.*					*Cents.*
Anderson	$3.00	$2.13	$0.10	$0.25			$1.50	$3.70	$1.52	$0.52	$1.50	$0.20	$0.45	$14.87	268	6.50	16.0	10.0	$18.65	$3.78	2	$0.46	4.95
Angelina	2.75	2.00	.18	.20			2.13	3.70	1.20	.62	.40	.62	.75	14.55	300	6.50	17.5	10.0	21.25	6.70	2	.41	4.27
Aransas	3.00	4.00	.05	.75			1.50	4.80	1.00	.75	1.00	.75	1.00	18.60	300	6.00	16.0	10.0	19.60	1.00	1	.53	5.67
Atascosa	2.74	2.06	.22	.32			.88	2.37	.76	.58	.19	.08		10.20	231	6.38	15.5	12.4	16.74	6.54	4	.34	3.58
Austin	4.12	3.25	.28	.24	$0.75	$0.02	.81	5.25	1.84	.86	.81	.18	.68	19.09	350	6.69	21.8	10.5	25.66	6.57	4	.50	4.80
Bastrop	3.50	2.28	.30	.34			.56	2.97	1.78	.71	.48	.25	.30	13.45	221	6.89	15.5	12.2	17.13	3.68	4	.45	5.23
Bee	3.00	1.50	.20	.25			1.00	3.20	1.25	.65	.75	.15		11.95	250	7.00	15.0	15.0	19.75	7.80	1	.43	3.88
Bell	2.57	2.01	.14	.31			.77	3.24	1.27	.46	.33	.54	.60	13.24	223	6.78	14.6	11.9	16.95	3.71	8	.48	5.16
Bexar	3.20	1.50	.24	.37			.75	3.25	1.40	.63	.70	.19	.40	12.63	223	6.63	14.4	21.2	17.71	5.08	5	.49	4.29
Blanco	2.75	2.00	.12	.31			.88	2.46	.83	.36	.55	.18	.43	10.87	175	6.78	10.9	12.6	13.07	2.20	8	.47	5.43
Bosque	3.00	3.25	.18	.37			.25	5.25	1.20	.48	.12	.12	.80	15.02	266	7.00	16.0	12.5	20.62	5.60	2	.66	4.89
Bowie	2.34	2.92	.17	.25			.75	2.49	.83	.33	.45	.45	.50	11.48	207	6.67	13.0	13.2	14.91	3.43	3	.40	4.72
Brazoria	3.50	4.37	.39	.58			2.37	4.20	1.46	.58	.75	.31	.25	18.76	325	7.25	21.0	17.8	26.81	8.05	4	.43	4.62
Brazos	5.25	4.52	.39	.37			1.25	6.49	1.81	.77	.69	.44	1.06	23.04	406	7.25	26.2	13.9	33.55	10.51	4	.53	4.78
Brown	2.85	2.05	.14	.32			.90	3.56	1.18	.64	.38	.27	.18	12.47	213	6.88	13.6	11.2	16.14	3.67	5	.56	5.14
Burleson	3.00	1.00	.30	.30			3.00	4.50	1.00	.40	.25	.50		14.25	250	6.50	15.0	12.5	18.12	3.87	1	.60	4.95
Burnet	2.64	1.88	.10	.34			.64	2.26	.64	.38	.21	.21	.37	9.67	159	6.80	10.0	12.2	11.91	2.24	8	.47	5.31
Caldwell	3.84	2.67	.12	.28			.80	2.94	.98	.57	.43	.13		12.76	222	6.83	13.7	19.2	17.53	4.77	3	.44	4.56
Callahan	3.37	1.50	.09	.30			.69	4.14	1.39	.68	.31	.25	.22	12.94	275	6.88	16.2	10.9	20.46	7.52	4	.50	4.06
Camp	2.25	2.92	.20	.27		.08	1.06	3.00	.99	.37	.52	.17	.18	12.01	218	6.10	12.4	12.3	14.84	2.83	5	.46	4.81
Cass	1.25	1.75	.10	.05			1.20	1.20	.45	.20	.15	.20		6.55	100	6.00	7.0	10.0	6.70	.15	1	.40	5.85
Cherokee	2.50	4.13	.10	.29			.62	3.50	1.12	.38	.32		.10	13.06	250	6.75	15.0	10.0	18.38	5.32	2	.47	4.62
Clay	2.00	1.63	.09	.32			.32	2.35	.08	.35	.10	.05		7.89	150	6.88	9.0	15.0	11.85	3.96	2	.52	4.36
Coke	2.00	.90	.10	.60			1.00	1.25	.50	.20	.35	.30		7.20	100	6.50	6.5	12.5	7.31	.11	1	.42	6.39
Coleman	2.19	1.80	.10	.29			.67	4.02	1.05	.38	.20	.13	.50	11.33	194	6.50	12.7	10.0	13.71	2.38	3	.69	5.19
Collin	3.68	2.16	.12	.28			1.07	4.11	1.34	.48	.32	.51	.09	14.16	244	6.83	14.6	11.1	18.31	4.15	7	.56	5.14
Colorado	5.00	3.50	.30	.50			2.40	6.00	1.45	.55	1.00	.50	.75	21.95	368	7.00	23.0	12.5	28.64	6.69	1	.54	5.18
Comal	3.36	2.11	.29	.44	.32	.18	1.22	3.89	1.14	.53	.58	.46	.14	14.66	260	6.57	17.4	10.8	18.95	4.29	7	.50	4.92

TABLE 20.—*Average cost of producing an acre of cotton in 1896 on farms showing a PROFIT, by counties*—Continued.

[Wherever a blank occurs in these tables it means that no expense was incurred.]

TEXAS—Continued.

County.	Rent.	Plowing.	Seeds.	Planting seed.	Fertilizers.	Distributing fertilizers.	Chopping and hoeing.	Picking.	Ginning and pressing.	Bagging and ties.	Marketing.	Repairing implements.	Other expenses.	TOTAL COST.	Pounds of lint.	Price per pound.	Bushels of seed.	Price per bushel.	TOTAL RETURN.	PROFIT.	Number of farms reporting.	Cost of picking per 100 pounds.	Cost of production per pound.
																Cents.		*Cents.*					*Cents.*
Comanche	$3.08	$2.50	$0.09	$0.27			$0.96	$3.58	$1.28	$0.48	$0.40	$0.31	$0.37	$13.32	243	6.68	14.9	10.4	$17.62	$4.30	6	$0.49	4.84
Cooke	2.67	1.83	.10	.28			1.22	3.77	1.30	.47	.88	.20	.62	13.34	233	6.34	14.2	12.2	16.50	3.16	6	.54	4.98
Coryell	3.88	1.44	.11	.39			1.06	3.70	1.03	.39	.26	.29	.25	12.80	222	6.69	14.0	10.6	16.42	3.62	4	.56	5.10
Cottle	2.00	1.50	.25	.25			.75	5.00	1.50	1.00	3.00	.50		15.75	325	6.25	20.0	12.5	22.81	7.06	1	.51	4.08
Dallas	3.17	2.08	.15	.37			1.08	2.90	1.00	.34	.24	.25	.75	12.33	233	6.67	14.3	12.9	17.41	5.08	3	.41	4.50
Delta	4.00	2.63	.12	.22			1.10	4.61	1.25	.38	.32	.34	.46	15.43	280	6.44	17.0	11.5	20.01	4.58	4	.55	4.81
Denton	3.03	3.31	.13	.21		$0.10	.88	3.42	1.21	.53	.24	.37	.50	13.93	240	6.70	15.8	11.1	17.65	3.72	5	.48	5.07
Dewitt	3.44	2.66	.24	.42	$0.06	.06	.73	4.16	1.29	.79	.73	.44	.86	15.86	294	6.44	16.1	12.9	20.94	5.06	8	.47	4.69
Eastland	2.49	2.55	.10	.36			.91	3.06	.97	.46	.46	.27	.28	11.91	190	6.58	11.8	11.9	13.90	1.99	9	.54	5.53
Ellis	3.91	1.97	.11	.28			1.15	3.88	1.15	.49	.22	.38	.13	13.67	249	6.61	14.5	12.2	18.23	4.56	13	.52	4.78
Erath	2.66	2.07	.10	.22			.92	2.67	.65	.32	.22	.20	.33	10.36	168	6.58	10.0	10.0	12.12	1.76	3	.53	5.57
Falls	3.04	2.00	.18	.21	.42	.02	.99	2.92	.87	.35	.30	.23	.10	11.63	206	6.58	12.2	15.9	15.59	3.96	6	.47	4.70
Fannin	3.46	3.29	.12	.19			.96	3.83	1.17	.47	.31	.20	.88	14.88	242	6.98	15.5	13.3	18.88	4.00	6	.53	5.30
Fayette	4.43	2.08	.22	.27	.07	.07	1.32	4.23	1.61	.68	.68	.37	.55	16.58	294	6.86	18.9	13.4	22.62	6.04	7	.48	4.78
Fort Bend	4.25	3.31	.18	.26			1.42	7.63	2.40	.98	.71	.41	.31	21.86	425	7.12	27.8	11.5	33.30	11.44	4	.60	4.39
Franklin	2.50	5.00	.20	.20			1.00	5.00	1.25	.50	.50	.20		16.35	250	6.00	15.0	10.0	16.50	.15	1	.67	5.94
Freestone	2.00	2.50	.12	.35			1.00	1.60	.90	.50	.19	.06		9.22	133	6.75	8.0	15.0	10.18	.96	1	.40	6.03
Gillespie	2.72	1.39	.16	.45	.39	.04	1.32	3.56	1.53	.58	.71	.27	.40	13.52	259	6.82	16.4	10.1	19.40	5.88	7	.46	4.58
Goliad	3.50	.75	.20	.24			.75	2.16	.82	.33	.25	.15		9.15	180	6.50	11.0	12.0	13.02	3.87	1	.40	4.34
Gonzales	3.30	1.73	.10	.26			.68	3.80	1.25	.52	.58	.32	.75	13.29	253	7.00	16.8	9.9	19.52	6.23	5	.50	4.60
Grayson	3.67	3.18	.12	.18			1.50	4.10	1.17	.36	.17	.50	.33	15.28	233	6.42	13.7	12.8	16.76	1.48	3	.59	5.81
Gregg	2.21	2.00	.15	.28	.80	.20	1.55	3.32	1.27	.50	.32	.39	.27	13.26	228	7.05	14.4	10.5	17.69	4.43	5	.49	5.15
Grimes	3.50	2.94	.19	.29	.25	.05	.94	4.17	1.66	.46	.22	.56	.82	16.05	282	6.66	19.8	10.2	20.92	4.87	4	.49	4.98
Guadalupe	3.31	1.86	.08	.28	.03	.06	.71	3.00	1.16	.47	.23	.24	.50	11.93	222	6.81	13.5	13.3	16.85	4.92	8	.45	4.57
Hale	3.75	2.50	.10	.10			.75	4.00	1.00	.45	1.00			13.65	250	6.00	17.0	10.0	16.70	3.05	1	.53	4.78
Hall	1.44	1.75	.17	.28			.83	3.30	1.18	.56	.72	.55		10.78	192	5.92	12.0	14.5	13.01	2.23	3	.57	4.71
Hamilton	2.50	1.00	.13	.15			.50	3.00	.67	.25	.17	.15	1.00	9.52	185	6.50	12.0	10.0	13.22	3.70	1	.54	4.50
Hardeman	2.00	1.50	.10	.15			.25	2.00	.60	.30	.25	.30		7.45	125	6.50	8.0	12.5	9.12	1.67	1	.53	5.16
Harris	3.25	2.54	.33	.30	1.09	.48	.88	6.84	1.94	.98	1.46	1.11	.92	22.12	408	7.25	26.2	17.2	34.00	11.88	6	.56	4.32
Harrison	1.50	2.75	.15	.26	.50	.02	1.35	2.42	.73	.25	.35	.27	.34	10.89	170	6.45	10.0	9.9	11.94	1.05	5	.47	5.82

Hays	2.90	2.24	.13	.34			1.05	2.27	.93	.51	.46	.06	.25	11.14	178	6.82	11.0	12.5	13.64	2.50	5	.43	5.49
Henderson	4.13	3.56	.19	.24			1.56	4.10	1.10	.46	.56	.91	.38	17.19	267	6.38	16.2	10.0	18.30	1.11	4	.51	5.83
Hill	3.30	2.44	.15	.24			1.04	2.84	1.05	.42	.25	.27	.11	12.11	213	6.63	11.9	10.5	15.24	3.13	6	.44	5.10
Hood	2.09	1.69	.13	.13			.73	3.25	.93	.33	.05	.13	.07	9.53	203	6.67	12.3	10.8	14.69	5.16	3	.53	4.04
Hopkins	3.00	2.53	.12	.15			1.56	2.92	1.12	.54	.58	.44	.62	13.58	208	7.21	13.8	11.8	16.53	2.95	4	.47	5.75
Houston	2.33	2.08	.15	.22	.67	.17	.83	3.73	1.45	.77	.61	.32	.33	13.66	297	6.33	18.0	10.8	20.46	6.80	3	.42	3.94
Hunt	3.42	2.83	.13	.26			.72	2.92	1.25	.42	.53	.61	.33	13.42	211	6.79	12.7	13.5	16.00	2.58	6	.46	5.55
Jack	2.20	1.19	.09	.34			.53	1.68	.54	.30	.28	.29	.51	7.94	134	6.60	8.6	14.9	9.95	2.01	5	.42	4.97
Jasper	4.00	3.50	.11	.10	2.33	.22	1.50	7.50	1.88	1.00	2.00	.62		24.76	402	7.50	26.0	13.2	33.28	8.52	2	.62	5.31
Johnson	3.56	1.78	.13	.32			1.11	3.59	1.47	.58	.39	.49	.64	14.06	233	6.69	14.8	11.0	17.23	3.17	8	.51	5.34
Jones	1.00	1.25	.05	.20			.50	3.00	.70	.35	.05	.25	.22	7.57	160	6.00	11.0	12.0	10.92	3.35	1	.62	3.91
Karnes	3.00	3.00	.10	.30			.75	3.15	1.10	.35	1.00	.25		13.00	220	6.50	14.5	10.0	15.75	2.75	1	.48	5.25
Kaufman	3.44	2.84	.14	.25	.12	.06	.89	4.31	1.26	.74	.31	.46	.27	15.09	266	6.62	17.5	10.4	19.18	4.09	8	.54	4.99
Kendall	3.00	2.25	.20	.42	1.67	.23	1.18	4.37	1.79	.62	1.00	.17	.60	17.50	295	6.75	17.7	15.0	22.39	4.89	3	.49	5.03
Kerr	2.75	1.38	.24	.50			1.50	2.50	.89	.38	.25	.25		10.64	166	7.25	10.5	15.0	13.61	2.97	2	.50	5.46
Lamar	3.00	2.04	.13	.15			1.12	3.10	1.05	.38	.35	.27	.48	12.07	192	6.54	11.7	10.5	13.79	1.73	6	.54	5.65
Lampasas	2.25	1.00	.10	.38			.50	3.00	1.38	.45	.25	.12	.50	9.93	212	6.50	13.0	12.5	15.18	5.25	2	.47	3.92
Lavaca	3.69	1.81	.19	.28			.85	4.38	1.21	.60	.62	.34	.57	14.54	244	6.38	15.5	11.2	17.28	2.74	4	.60	5.25
Lee	3.25	3.00	.12	.25			.75	1.58	.83	.42	.12	.10		10.42	183	7.00	11.0	8.2	13.70	3.28	2	.29	5.20
Leon	3.84	3.67	.13	.25			.87	3.90	1.30	.58	.50	.10	.42	15.56	294	6.50	17.3	9.3	20.49	4.93	3	.44	4.75
Liberty	5.00	1.00	.25	.50			1.50	5.00	1.50	1.25	1.00	1.00	1.00	19.00	300	7.50	22.0	5.0	23.60	4.60	1	.56	5.97
Limestone	3.35	2.16	.18	.23			.80	3.32	1.19	.48	.50	.32	.92	13.45	222	6.72	15.2	12.4	16.80	3.35	10	.50	5.21
Live Oak	3.25	2.87	.12	.40			.40	2.20	.90	.38	.92	.08	.50	12.02	188	7.00	11.5	11.0	13.88	1.86	2	.39	5.72
Llano	2.17	2.42	.13	.50			1.25	4.14	1.13	.66	.78	.18	.43	13.79	243	6.29	14.0	11.7	16.99	3.20	3	.57	5.00
McCulloch	2.30	1.65	.11	.29			.70	2.09	.78	.30	.28	.24	.60	9.34	140	7.00	9.2	10.5	10.74	1.40	5	.50	5.98
McLennan	3.40	2.18	.15	.29			.95	3.22	1.38	.51	.32	.27	.28	12.95	214	6.53	15.3	13.4	16.09	3.14	10	.50	5.09
Madison	3.00	3.75	.05	.38			1.50	3.25	1.00	.50	1.00	.50	.12	15.05	250	6.50	16.0	10.0	17.85	2.80	1	.43	5.38
Marion	2.00	1.67	.22	.22			.80	2.76	1.13	.30	.25	.07	.16	9.58	202	6.13	10.0	10.3	13.50	3.92	3	.46	4.23
Matagorda	4.00	2.30	.13	.08			1.38	9.25	2.38	1.12	3.50	.10	2.37	26.61	500	6.88	33.5	12.0	38.40	11.79	2	.62	4.52
Medina	2.17	1.59	.15	.34			1.21	2.68	1.03	.55	.28	.13	.55	10.68	213	6.44	13.6	14.9	15.58	4.90	7	.42	4.06
Menard	3.00	3.00	.08	.42			.90	4.33	1.48	.88	.22	.10		14.41	464	6.88	24.5	10.0	34.20	19.79	2	.31	2.58
Milam	3.67	2.43	.12	.33			1.00	4.46	1.19	.52	.41	.22	.71	15.06	292	6.30	18.2	10.6	20.63	5.57	6	.51	4.50
Mills	2.32	2.33	.09	.22			.70	2.13	.71	.25	.12	.03		8.90	135	7.08	8.3	13.3	10.65	1.75	3	.67	5.77
Montague	2.17	2.17	.15	.20			1.32	3.66	.70	.43	.13	.33	.47	11.73	225	6.50	14.7	12.5	16.04	4.31	3	.54	4.40
Montgomery	3.67	2.52	.25	.20			1.52	3.48	1.05	.60	.87	.60	.50	15.26	250	6.87	16.3	11.0	18.52	3.26	3	.46	5.39
Morris	2.50	2.00	.10	.10			.90	2.00	.75	.25		.25		8.85	175	6.50	10.0	10.0	12.38	3.52	1	.38	4.49
Nacogdoches	1.81	2.00	.10	.27			.92	2.46	.80	.42	.58	.25	.17	9.78	157	6.17	9.3	10.0	10.58	.80	3	.52	5.64
Navarro	3.30	2.25	.20	.19			1.00	2.53	.99	.45	.24	.22		11.37	180	6.87	11.3	10.8	13.56	2.19	5	.47	5.64
Newton	3.50	5.00	.18	.28	2.10	.10	1.75	3.00	1.16	.75	.50	.62	.10	19.04	275	6.75	20.0	12.5	21.03	1.99	2	.36	6.01
Nueces	1.50	2.00	.20	.50			.75	4.50	1.30	.70	.25	.15	.10	11.95	250	7.00	10.0	20.0	19.50	7.55	1	.60	3.98
Palo Pinto	4.38	4.00	.10	.25			.75	3.75	1.25	.50	.25	.25	1.20	16.68	250	7.00	15.0	12.5	19.38	2.70	1	.50	5.92
Panola	2.67	4.34	.15	.33	.83	.33	1.67	4.83	1.38	.62	1.00	.33	.67	19.15	317	6.00	18.0	9.8	20.78	1.63	3	.51	5.48
Parker	2.93	2.06	.11	.22	.20	.20	.92	2.28	.85	.45	.65	.34	.47	11.68	168	7.00	10.4	12.9	13.10	1.42	5	.45	6.15
Polk	3.50	2.50	.12	.38	1.00	.12	.75	6.25	2.25	.90	.75	.33	.25	19.10	400	7.00	32.5	11.2	31.69	12.59	2	.52	3.86
Rains	3.00	1.50	.12	.20			1.17	4.16	1.52	.70	.58	.28	.67	13.90	283	6.58	16.7	11.7	20.46	6.56	3	.49	4.22
Red River	3.50	2.90	.20	.26			1.30	2.78	.80	.37	.23	.25	.40	12.99	193	7.20	12.2	13.3	15.54	2.55	5	.48	5.89
Refugio	2.50	1.00	.10	.25			2.75	4.50	1.15	.65	2.00	1.00	.08	15.98	267	6.75	16.0	10.0	19.62	3.64	1	.56	5.39
Robertson	3.13	3.12	.20	.14			1.12	3.55	1.29	.45	.50	.15	.54	14.19	225	6.56	13.0	12.2	16.31	2.12	4	.53	5.60
Rockwell	3.50	2.08	.14	.28			1.25	3.94	1.19	.55	.43	.47	.25	14.08	246	6.62	14.8	12.5	18.12	4.04	6	.53	4.97
Rusk	3.00	2.00	.22	.30	1.25	.12	1.40	6.00	2.13	.60	.75	.30	1.25	19.32	375	6.00	24.0	9.0	24.11	4.79	2	.53	4.58

TABLE 20.—*Average cost of producing an acre of cotton in 1896 on farms showing a **PROFIT**, by counties*—Continued.

[Wherever a blank occurs in these tables it means that no expense was incurred.]

TEXAS—Continued.

County.	Rent.	Plowing.	Seeds.	Planting seed.	Fertilizers.	Distributing fertilizers.	Chopping and hoeing.	Picking.	Ginning and pressing.	Bagging and ties.	Marketing.	Repairing implements.	Other expenses.	TOTAL COST.	Pounds of lint.	Price per pound.	Bushels of seed.	Price per bushel.	TOTAL RETURN.	PROFIT.	Number of farms reporting.	Cost of picking per 100 pounds.	Cost of production per pound.
																Cents.		Cents.					Cents.
Sabine	$2.67	$2.33	$0.09	$0.22			$0.75	$3.06	$0.95	$0.68	$0.79	$0.21	$0.62	$12.37	233	6.50	15.3	10.7	$16.82	$4.45	3	$0.44	4.61
San Augustino	3.00	3.62	.19	.45	$0.62	$0.38	1.44	5.69	1.90	.79	1.61	.28	.02	19.99	371	5.50	23.2	9.2	22.19	2.20	4	.51	4.81
San Jacinto	4.00	2.60	.18	.45			1.50	5.00	1.37	.75	2.33	.75	.04	18.97	390	6.50	22.5	7.5	26.19	7.22	2	.43	4.43
San Patricio	2.25	1.25	.18	.32			.62	2.80	1.20	.55	1.25	.05	.35	10.82	233	7.00	13.5	18.8	18.60	7.78	2	.40	3.55
San Saba	3.00	.75	.10	.25			1.00	3.25	1.00	.50	.50	.40	.50	11.25	250	6.00	16.0	10.0	16.60	5.35	1	.43	3.86
Shackelford	2.50	3.00	.12	.38			1.25	5.62	2.38	.70	1.50	.75	1.25	19.45	375	6.75	24.0	12.5	28.00	8.55	2	.50	4.39
Shelby	3.00	1.62	.14	.20	1.00	.25	.75	2.25	1.00	.38	.38	.30	.37	11.64	216	6.88	14.0	11.0	16.41	4.77	2	.35	4.68
Smith	2.42	2.63	.17	.35			1.44	2.92	1.00	.40	.34	.35	.35	12.37	206	6.50	13.0	10.1	14.65	2.28	4	.47	5.37
Somerville	2.33	1.09	.12	.28			.88	3.50	1.03	.55	.26	.50		10.54	191	6.50	12.5	10.0	13.96	3.42	2	.61	4.86
Stephens	3.82	3.33	.10	.27	.67	.08	1.00	4.34	1.25	.62	.58	.50		16.56	278	6.92	16.3	10.0	21.07	4.51	3	.52	5.37
Tarrant	2.91	2.00	.15	.42			1.07	2.56	.80	.33	.27	.37		10.88	166	6.25	10.0	13.3	11.70	.82	3	.51	5.75
Taylor	2.00	2.17	.09	.30			1.08	3.23	1.15	.46	.08	.13	.33	11.02	208	6.67	12.7	10.8	14.82	3.80	3	.52	4.64
Titus	2.69	2.19	.15	.28			.94	3.20	.89	.30	.19	.21	.32	11.36	196	6.38	12.0	10.6	13.98	2.62	4	.54	5.15
Travis	3.75	1.88	.11	.30			.65	2.90	.90	.42	.22	.64	.50	12.27	198	6.90	15.1	10.1	15.19	2.92	4	.49	5.43
Trinity	2.98	2.62	.12	.18			1.12	3.40	1.38	.50	.58	.42	.38	13.68	300	6.75	16.5	10.0	22.34	8.66	2	.38	4.01
Trio	1.50	1.00	.12	.10			.50	1.20	.55	.35	.10			5.42	125	7.00	7.0	20.0	10.15	4.73	1	.32	3.22
Tyler	3.00	3.33	.15	.16	1.58	.32	.75	3.40	1.20	.63	.92	.33	.35	16.12	283	6.83	17.3	12.5	21.61	5.49	3	.40	4.93
Upshur	2.00	2.00	.15	.25			.50	3.75	1.00	.75			.25	10.65	250	6.00	15.5	12.5	16.94	6.29	1	.50	3.48
Valverde	2.50	3.00	.25	.50			1.00	4.00	1.25	.75	.75	.50		14.00	250	7.00	15.0	10.0	19.00	5.00	1	.53	5.00
Van Zandt	3.11	2.76	.10	.27			1.45	3.84	1.31	.54	.69	.36	1.06	15.49	300	6.22	20.0	10.0	20.55	5.06	4	.43	4.50
Victoria	3.00	2.43	.17	.27			1.33	4.57	1.26	.57	.68	.20	.34	14.82	272	6.52	16.3	10.6	19.47	4.65	5	.56	4.81
Walker	2.00	4.00	.15	.50			1.00	3.75	1.00	.75		1.00	1.00	15.15	250	7.00	16.0	10.0	19.10	3.95	1	.50	5.42
Waller	3.25	3.25	.27	.25	.20	.20	1.40	4.45	1.29	.56	.39	.54	1.48	17.53	286	6.95	18.2	10.0	21.64	4.11	5	.52	5.49
Washington	4.75	4.50	.22	.35		.25	1.88	7.00	2.25	.88	.25	.60		22.93	468	7.31	29.5	12.5	37.79	14.86	2	.50	4.11
Wharton	3.92	2.12	.26	.37			1.69	5.58	1.50	.86	.88	.56	.90	18.64	371	6.58	22.5	13.2	27.29	8.65	6	.50	4.22
Wichita	1.91	.75	.10	.28			.72	2.35	.73	.38	.25	.75	.62	8.84	129	7.00	8.0	15.0	10.23	1.39	2	.61	5.92
Wilbargor	1.75	2.00	.11	.32			.72	2.85	.93	.48	.75	.75	.10	10.76	158	7.00	10.0	25.0	13.60	2.84	2	.60	5.23
Williamson	3.38	2.44	.06	.24			1.00	3.50	1.20	.51	.32	.05	.04	12.74	223	6.94	14.0	11.9	17.14	4.40	4	.52	4.97
Wilson	2.75	1.38	.22	.36			.64	2.83	.98	.52	.22	.42	.19	10.51	208	6.62	13.2	13.1	15.53	5.02	4	.45	4.22

Wise	3.00	1.67	.15	.22	......	......	.53	3.83	1.48	.45	.23	.22	.57	12.35	248	6.92	16.3	13.8	19.44	7.09	3	.51	4.07
Wood	2.33	3.16	.25	.20	.17	.08	.75	2.92	.93	.47	.37	.55	.65	12.83	223	6.17	13.7	10.0	15.05	2.22	3	.44	5.14
Young	2.25	1.13	.12	.22	......	......	1.00	3.00	.95	.38	.18	.22	.43	9.88	182	7.00	10.5	15.0	14.35	4.47	2	.55	4.56

VIRGINIA.

																Cents.		Cents.					Cents.
Brunswick	$2.83	$1.48	$0.19	$0.19	$1.33	$0.09	$0.97	$2.46	$1.03	$0.42	$1.55	$0.33	......	$12.87	243	7.00	13.7	10.8	$18.09	$5.22	3	$0.34	4.68
Greenesville	1.75	2.44	.21	.63	2.36	.22	.62	3.05	.88	.60	.77	.25	$0.28	14.06	271	6.88	18.2	12.5	20.96	6.90	4	.38	4.35
Mecklenburg	3.25	2.38	.32	.29	2.75	.25	.95	1.90	1.00	.44	.75	.25	.55	15.08	200	7.00	12.0	12.5	15.50	.42	2	.32	6.79
Nansemond	2.50	7.00	.30	.60	......	......	1.00	4.00	1.65	1.75	.20	.25	......	19.25	500	7.00	25.0	15.0	38.75	19.50	1	.27	3.10
Southampton	2.50	3.38	.32	.43	2.82	.22	.60	3.25	1.26	.99	1.89	.46	.89	19.01	306	6.69	20.0	14.9	23.52	4.51	4	.35	5.24

TABLE 21.—*Average cost of producing an acre of cotton in 1896 on farms showing a* ***LOSS****, by counties.*

[Wherever a blank occurs in these tables it means that no expense was incurred.]

ALABAMA.

County.	Rent.	Plowing.	Seed.	Planting seed.	Fertilizers.	Distributing fertilizers.	Chopping and hoeing.	Picking.	Ginning and pressing.	Bagging and ties.	Marketing.	Repairing implements.	Other expenses.	TOTAL COST.	Pounds of lint.	Price per pound.	Bushels of seed.	Price per bushel.	TOTAL RETURN.	Loss.	Number of farms reporting.	Cost of picking per 100 pounds.	Cost of production per pound.
																Cents.		Cents.					Cents.
Autauga	$2.00	$3.75	$0.25	$0.15	$3.50	$0.50	$2.00	$2.40	$1.50	$0.75	$0.75	$0.50	$0.40	$18.45	2.00	6.75	14.0	15.5	$15.67	$2.78	1	$0.40	8.14
Barbour	1.63	2.00	.25	.14	2.00	.12	1.50	1.60	.40	.45	.32	.25	.40	11.06	1.34	6.88	8.0	12.5	10.08	.98	2	.40	7.51
Bibb	2.67	3.00	.28	.32	2.33	.30	1.83	3.00	.88	.50	.53	.34	.90	16.88	1.97	6.67	14.0	12.4	14.81	2.07	3	.51	7.69
Blount	2.75	2.50	.18	.32	1.65	.32	1.25	1.50	.45	.32	.38	.18	.14	11.94	1.33	6.75	8.0	10.0	9.86	2.08	2	.38	8.38
Bullock	2.00	1.75	.30	.10	2.00	.10	.50	.50	.45	.25	.40	.50	......	8.85	1.00	6.50	6.0	13.0	7.28	1.57	1	.17	8.07
Butler	2.00	2.00	.15	.13	3.12	.30	1.00	2.00	1.00	.25	.50	.25	.70	13.40	1.70	6.50	12.0	13.8	12.70	.70	2	.39	6.91
Calhoun	2.50	4.00	.25	.25	1.20	.20	1.00	2.00	.60	.40	.15	.30	.80	13.65	1.50	6.50	10.0	12.5	11.00	2.65	1	.44	8.27
Cherokee	2.83	3.74	.23	.18	1.60	.15	1.35	2.26	.61	.43	.47	.30	.68	14.83	1.78	6.80	14.0	13.5	13.54	1.29	5	.42	7.50
Chilton	2.00	3.00	.30	.25	2.50	.25	1.50	1.75	1.00	.60	.20	.25	......	13.60	1.66	6.75	12.0	15.0	13.00	.60	1	.35	7.11
Choctaw	2.00	4.00	.10	.10	2.00	.25	1.00	2.00	.50	.35	1.50	1.00	......	14.80	1.66	6.50	10.0	10.0	11.79	3.01	1	.40	8.31
Clay	2.50	3.92	.32	.40	2.60	.47	1.33	2.13	.60	.62	.46	.46	.92	16.73	1.81	6.85	11.3	12.5	13.74	2.99	3	.39	8.46
Cleburne	3.50	4.00	.25	.50	1.50	.25	2.00	2.50	.70	.25	.20	......	......	15.65	2.00	7.00	12.0	10.0	15.20	.45	1	.42	7.22
Coffee	1.91	4.13	.19	.17	3.09	.26	1.13	2.67	.76	.41	.66	.57	.20	16.15	1.65	6.65	9.8	15.0	12.66	3.49	5	.54	8.90
Colbert	2.25	3.40	.30	.20	2.38	.38	1.25	3.25	1.39	.60	.62	.50	1.40	17.92	2.08	6.75	12.5	13.8	15.72	2.20	2	.52	7.79
Conecuh	1.38	3.38	.20	.26	2.25	.14	1.35	2.40	1.38	.95	.87	.87	.07	15.50	2.00	6.12	13.0	12.5	13.88	1.62	2	.40	6.94
Coosa	4.00	5.00	.25	.25	2.50	.25	1.50	3.25	.85	.37	.50	.75	......	19.47	2.50	6.50	16.0	12.5	18.25	1.22	1	.43	6.99
Covington	1.44	3.80	.19	.25	2.82	.25	.94	2.39	1.26	.45	.48	.27	.37	14.91	1.64	6.61	10.5	15.1	12.33	2.58	4	.49	8.12
Crenshaw	1.50	2.50	.25	.10	2.00	.50	1.25	3.75	.75	.35	.25	.20	1.60	15.00	2.00	6.50	12.0	12.5	14.50	.50	1	.62	6.75
Cullman	2.50	3.75	.25	.15	1.25	.15	1.50	2.50	.62	.30	.35	.25	......	13.57	1.67	7.00	10.0	15.0	13.19	.38	1	.50	7.23
Dale	2.00	2.92	.18	.20	2.75	.23	1.16	2.50	1.12	.40	.62	.62	.06	14.76	1.61	6.67	11.7	15.0	12.51	2.25	3	.52	8.07
Escambia	1.00	3.03	.25	.25	2.25	.25	1.50	2.00	1.50	.90	2.00	......	......	14.93	1.50	6.00	12.0	12.5	10.50	4.43	1	.44	8.95
Etowah	2.78	4.67	.17	.23	1.95	.25	1.33	2.73	1.05	.53	.75	.42	.83	17.69	2.33	6.33	13.0	10.0	16.05	1.64	3	.39	7.03
Fayette	2.56	1.75	.25	.40	2.50	.50	1.25	3.00	1.75	.85	1.00	.75	.30	16.80	2.00	6.50	12.0	10.0	14.20	2.60	1	.50	7.80
Franklin	4.50	6.00	.30	.25	2.50	.25	1.00	4.00	1.50	.75	.30	.50	1.00	22.85	3.00	6.50	20.0	10.0	21.50	1.35	1	.44	6.95
Greene	1.75	4.00	.25	.38	2.12	.32	3.50	2.00	.75	.68	.58	.75	1.12	18.20	166	6.75	10.5	11.2	12.34	5.86	2	.40	10.25
Henry	2.00	3.00	.15	.15	2.25	.13	.50	2.60	.52	.30	.33	.25	.24	12.42	120	6.75	7.0	15.0	9.15	3.27	1	.72	9.48
Jackson	1.72	2.25	.20	.20	1.25	.25	1.50	2.00	.55	.35	.10	.13	.80	11.30	150	6.00	10.0	10.0	10.00	1.30	1	.44	6.87
Jefferson	2.50	2.25	.25	.25	1.07	.15	1.00	3.00	.91	.12	.25	.10	......	11.85	144	6.62	12.0	12.5	11.03	.82	1	.09	7.19
Lawrence	2.25	2.38	.20	.32	1.95	.35	2.00	2.05	.89	.56	.28	.50	.08	13.81	150	6.50	9.0	10.0	10.61	3.20	2	.46	8.61
Lee	1.50	2.50	.25	.25	2.50	.25	1.00	1.50	.35	.20	.10	.10	.10	10.60	125	7.00	8.0	12.0	9.71	.89	1	.40	7.71
Macon	2.00	4.00	.20	.20	2.00	.25	2.00	2.40	.75	.35	.50	1.00	1.00	16.65	200	6.50	11.0	15.0	14.65	2.00	1	.40	7.50
Madison	2.50	3.20	.28	.38	1.00	.12	2.15	2.50	.61	.34	.22	.68	......	13.98	186	6.75	10.0	11.2	13.77	.21	2	.45	6.91
Marion	2.25	4.50	.20	.15	1.20	.20	.62	2.75	.71	.42	.55	.58	......	14.13	175	7.00	11.0	10.0	13.35	.78	2	.52	7.45

County																							
Marshall	2.19	4.76	.16	.31	.88	.25	1.69	2.35	.72	.34	.36	.81	1.02	15.84	173	6.31	11.5	10.4	12.00	3.84	4	.45	8.46
Morgan	2.00	4.00	.40	.25	1.00	.25	2.00	3.00	2.00	1.00	.50	.50	.50	17.40	200	6.00	12.0	15.0	13.80	3.60	1	.50	7.80
Pickens	2.50	4.00	.20	.42	2.17	.33	1.25	2.25	.95	.53	1.17	.45	.68	16.90	205	6.50	12.3	10.8	14.54	2.36	3	.37	7.60
Pike	2.17	2.17	.25	.20	2.10	.22	1.33	2.27	.72	.38	.61	.58	.03	13.03	167	6.67	10.7	12.5	12.33	.70	3	.45	7.00
Randolph	2.00	6.00	.25	.25	3.00	.50	3.00	2.50	1.00	.35	.50	.50	......	19.85	234	7.50	15.0	15.0	19.80	.05	1	.36	7.52
Russell	1.50	3.00	.25	.20	1.00	.20	1.50	1.50	.55	.35	.10	.25	......	10.40	120	7.00	7.0	15.0	9.45	.95	1	.42	7.79
St. Clair	2.50	4.00	.30	.25	1.50	.75	1.50	2.00	.75	.33	.17	.25	.50	14.80	166	6.75	10.0	15.0	12.70	2.10	1	.40	8.01
Sumter	2.00	2.63	.20	.30	1.00	.05	1.00	1.52	.40	.50	.28	.10	.50	10.48	132	6.88	8.0	11.8	10.00	.48	2	.38	7.23
Tallapoosa	2.50	3.00	.15	.10	2.50	.25	1.00	5.00	1.25	.60	1.00	.25	1.00	18.60	250	6.75	16.0	10.0	18.48	.12	1	.67	6.80
Tuscaloosa	2.50	3.00	.25	.25	2.50	.10	1.00	1.92	.70	.30	.25	.50	.20	13.47	183	6.00	11.0	12.5	12.36	1.11	1	.35	6.61
Wilcox	2.00	3.00	.25	.25	2.00	.50	1.50	4.00	1.50	1.00	......	1.00	......	17.00	250	6.00	15.0	12.0	16.80	.20	1	.53	6.08

ARKANSAS.

County															Cents.		Cents.					Cents.
Arkansas	$3.25	$4.27	$0.25	$0.32	......	......	$1.15	$2.18	$1.75	$0.75	$1.12	$0.38	......	$15.42	162	6.50	9.0	12.5	$11.90	$3.52	2	$0.45	8.83
Ashley	3.50	3.50	.15	.18	......	......	1.90	1.78	.52	.66	.50	.18	$0.42	13.29	158	6.38	9.6	10.0	10.03	2.26	2	.38	7.80
Baxter	3.25	2.75	.22	.25	......	......	1.25	2.25	1.37	.68	3.00	1.00	.25	16.27	145	6.00	8.5	10.0	9.55	6.72	2	.52	10.63
Bradley	1.84	3.83	.15	.42	$2.00	$0.17	1.08	2.00	.63	.39	.58	.43	.22	13.74	167	6.04	10.3	10.0	10.74	3.00	3	.40	7.61
Calhoun	2.12	3.50	.15	.38	1.62	.38	1.25	2.55	1.10	.50	.62	.71	......	14.88	186	6.38	12.0	10.0	12.74	2.14	2	.46	7.35
Carroll	4.00	1.00	.20	.30	......	......	1.00	2.00	.45	.30	.50	......	......	9.75	100	7.00	6.0	10.0	7.60	2.15	1	.67	9.15
Chicot	3.00	3.25	.15	.25	......	......	2.25	1.75	.25	.25	.30	.40	......	11.85	140	7.75	7.0	12.5	11.72	.13	1	.42	7.84
Clark	3.33	5.00	.25	.47	.33	.17	1.33	2.87	.76	.40	.67	.75	.42	16.75	192	6.33	11.7	11.7	13.52	3.23	3	.50	8.01
Cleburne	3.02	3.06	.18	.37	1.00	.50	1.75	2.50	1.00	.45	.55	.48	.18	15.04	183	6.26	11.8	13.5	12.68	2.36	4	.46	7.35
Cleveland	2.75	4.50	.25	.62	......	......	1.50	1.50	.40	.19	.25	.40	......	12.36	105	5.50	5.8	15.0	6.63	5.73	2	.48	10.94
Columbia	2.00	3.00	.10	.25	3.00	.50	1.00	2.40	.90	.40	.50	.50	.40	14.95	200	6.25	18.0	10.0	14.30	.65	1	.40	6.58
Conway	2.00	2.75	.23	.10	......	......	2.50	1.70	1.00	.22	.20	.75	.75	12.20	129	5.88	8.0	11.2	8.50	3.70	2	.44	8.76
Craighead	2.50	3.00	.15	.10	......	......	3.10	2.50	.65	.30	.50	.30	......	13.10	160	6.00	11.0	10.0	10.70	2.40	1	.52	7.50
Crawford	2.00	7.00	.15	.50	......	......	1.50	4.00	1.20	.30	.75	.25	.75	18.40	250	6.50	15.0	10.0	17.75	.65	1	.53	6.76
Cross	3.25	3.63	.28	.20	......	......	1.00	3.35	.99	.78	.37	.62	1.12	15.59	238	5.50	15.0	8.5	14.15	1.44	2	.47	6.01
Desha	3.50	4.00	.15	.50	......	......	.80	4.00	1.00	1.00	1.00	.50	.25	16.70	200	6.50	15.0	8.0	14.20	2.50	1	.67	7.75
Drew	2.34	3.33	.15	.20	.67	.25	.92	2.27	1.28	.68	.55	.33	.50	13.47	172	6.25	11.3	10.0	11.93	1.54	3	.44	7.17
Faulkner	3.00	2.00	.25	.50	......	......	1.00	2.00	.50	.18	.05	.10	.50	10.08	125	7.00	8.0	15.0	9.95	.13	1	.53	7.10
Franklin	2.00	3.00	.25	.15	.50	.25	1.00	1.75	.75	.50	.05	.05	.25	10.50	140	6.00	7.0	10.0	9.10	1.40	1	.42	7.00
Fulton	4.98	4.00	.15	.25	......	......	2.50	3.50	1.14	.40	.80	.25	......	17.97	230	6.50	14.0	10.0	16.35	1.62	1	.51	7.20
Greene	6.00	6.00	.30	.50	......	......	2.25	7.50	2.00	.60	.50	1.00	......	26.65	333	7.00	24.0	10.0	25.71	.94	1	.75	7.28
Hempstead	2.50	6.00	.25	.25	......	......	2.25	6.40	.50	.75	.25	.25	1.00	20.40	167	7.00	10.0	10.0	12.69	7.71	1	1.28	11.62
Hot Spring	3.00	4.00	.25	.50	......	......	1.00	3.00	.50	.75	......	.25	......	13.25	100	6.25	6.0	15.0	7.15	6.10	1	1.00	12.35
Howard	2.25	4.58	.17	.30	......	......	1.40	2.28	.82	.44	.80	.50	.42	13.96	149	6.35	10.4	10.0	10.43	3.53	5	.51	8.67
Independence	1.75	3.43	.15	.21	......	......	1.63	1.95	.52	.27	.30	.25	......	10.46	125	6.00	8.0	10.0	8.30	2.16	2	.52	7.73
Izard	2.86	2.94	.14	.17	.50	.25	2.00	2.00	.85	.52	.39	.30	.37	13.29	143	6.38	9.0	10.0	9.94	3.35	4	.47	8.66
Jackson	2.00	2.50	.16	.34	......	......	1.50	3.00	2.50	1.00	.50	.50	......	14.00	167	7.00	10.0	8.3	12.52	1.48	1	.60	7.89
Jefferson	3.50	2.00	.20	.40	......	......	1.62	1.45	.52	.65	.22	.18	.30	11.04	129	6.68	12.5	9.2	10.00	1.04	2	.37	7.67
Lawrence	2.50	2.45	.10	.20	.12	.25	1.63	2.30	.62	.25	.38	.38	.60	11.78	125	6.50	8.0	10.0	9.08	2.70	2	.61	8.78
Lee	3.75	3.05	.25	.22	......	......	3.25	1.80	.50	.28	.12	.08	.97	14.27	150	6.88	10.4	9.2	11.31	2.96	2	.40	8.88
Lincoln	3.17	2.40	.20	.23	.67	.07	1.28	1.42	.49	.44	.42	.26	......	11.05	110	6.87	6.7	10.0	8.18	2.87	3	.43	9.44
Little River	2.50	3.00	.20	.50	......	......	.75	1.50	.50	.80	1.00	1.00	......	11.75	100	8.00	6.0	12.5	8.75	3.00	1	.50	11.00
Logan	3.00	4.33	.20	.50	.83	.67	1.59	3.07	.95	.48	.38	.45	.20	16.65	188	6.33	14.0	10.0	13.58	3.07	3	.54	8.11
Lonoke	3.00	3.62	.29	.31	......	......	1.88	1.91	.93	.35	.41	.20	......	12.90	131	6.00	8.6	10.9	8.79	4.11	4	.49	9.13

TABLE 21.—*Average cost of producing an acre of cotton in 1896 on farms showing a LOSS, by counties*—Continued.

[Wherever a blank occurs in these tables it means that no expense was incurred.]

ARKANSAS—Continued.

County.	Rent.	Plowing.	Seed.	Planting seed.	Fertilizers.	Distributing fertilizers.	Chopping and hoeing.	Picking.	Ginning and pressing.	Bagging and ties.	Marketing.	Repairing implements.	Other expenses.	TOTAL COST.	Pounds of lint.	Price per pound.	Bushels of seed.	Price per bushel.	TOTAL RETURN.	Loss.	Number of farms reporting.	Cost of picking per 100 pounds.	Cost of production per pound.
																Cents.		*Cents.*					*Cents.*
Miller	$2.50	$2.75	$0.15	$0.50	......	......	$1.50	$2.00	$0.70	$0.30	$1.00	$0.10	$0.10	$11.60	167	6.00	10.0	10.0	$11.02	$0.58	1	$0.40	6.35
Mississippi	5.00	2.00	.25	.50	$4.00	$0.25	2.00	4.00	1.50	.60	1.75	.25	......	22.10	250	7.25	15.0	15.0	20.38	1.72	1	.53	7.94
Monroe	4.17	3.16	.26	.27	......	......	2.00	2.00	1.30	.40	.42	.30	.03	14.31	153	6.30	9.7	9.1	10.24	4.07	3	.44	8.78
Montgomery	2.50	5.00	.20	.15	1.50	.20	.75	2.50	2.00	.85	2.50	.75	......	18.90	200	6.50	12.0	12.5	14.50	4.40	1	.42	8.70
Nevada	4.00	3.50	.15	.50	2.00	.65	.75	2.00	.65	.35	.80	1.25	......	16.60	221	6.00	14.0	12.5	15.01	1.59	1	.30	6.72
Newton	4.00	3.00	.10	.16	......	......	1.75	3.00	1.00	.85	1.00	......	......	14.86	200	6.50	12.0	10.0	14.20	.66	1	.50	6.83
Ouachita	3.43	5.00	.15	.15	......	......	1.50	2.40	.85	.36	.25	.15	.10	14.34	200	6.25	12.0	10.0	13.70	.64	1	.40	6.57
Perry	2.75	2.75	.20	.20	......	......	2.25	2.98	1.33	.62	.62	1.25	......	14.95	208	6.25	12.5	9.5	14.27	.68	2	.48	6.62
Phillips	4.00	2.25	.50	.50	......	......	2.50	3.75	2.00	.50	1.50	.75	......	18.25	225	7.00	17.0	10.0	17.45	.80	1	.56	7.36
Pike	2.23	3.10	.18	.21	......	......	1.68	1.41	.54	.17	.32	.22	.01	10.07	121	7.05	7.2	10.6	9.22	.85	4	.39	7.69
Poinsett	3.00	8.00	.20	.50	......	......	3.00	3.60	2.00	1.00	......	......	......	21.30	300	6.00	20.0	10.0	20.00	1.30	1	.40	6.43
Polk	2.25	2.62	.32	.26	......	......	3.00	3.50	1.06	.68	.88	.68	.20	15.45	233	5.75	14.0	12.5	15.23	.22	2	.50	5.68
Pope	2.19	4.05	.26	.28	......	......	1.88	3.00	.92	.44	.50	.56	......	14.08	174	6.41	11.2	10.1	12.14	1.94	4	.58	7.44
Prairie	2.67	3.25	.20	.38	......	......	1.41	2.20	1.07	.38	.42	.37	......	12.35	166	6.33	9.3	10.8	11.48	.87	3	.44	6.83
Pulaski	5.00	1.50	.25	.95	......	......	1.50	3.20	.70	.50	.40	.25	2.00	16.25	200	6.75	12.0	13.3	15.10	1.15	1	.53	7.33
Scott	3.50	4.08	.13	.18	......	......	2.17	3.67	.98	.58	.52	.50	.23	16.54	207	5.58	12.3	11.6	12.90	3.64	3	.59	7.30
Searcy	2.50	3.50	.10	.25	......	......	1.50	3.25	.75	.25	1.00	.10	......	13.20	183	6.10	12.0	10.0	12.36	.84	1	.59	6.56
Sebastian	2.00	2.50	.19	.32	......	......	1.89	2.37	1.18	.27	.28	.37	......	11.37	130	6.25	7.5	11.2	9.01	2.36	2	.61	8.10
Sevier	2.50	7.50	.15	.15	......	......	2.25	2.40	.60	.40	.50	......	......	16.45	200	6.70	15.0	10.0	14.90	1.55	1	.40	7.48
Sharp	3.00	8.00	.20	.20	......	......	1.00	3.20	1.21	.35	1.00	......	......	18.16	240	6.00	16.0	10.0	16.00	2.16	1	.44	6.90
Stone	2.50	1.50	.20	.50	......	......	2.00	1.50	.20	.20	.50	.50	......	9.60	100	6.60	5.0	10.0	7.10	2.50	1	.50	9.10
Union	1.75	3.12	.18	.18	1.45	.25	1.12	2.88	1.10	.45	.62	.20	.20	13.50	190	6.00	12.5	11.2	12.84	.66	2	.51	6.37
Van Buren	2.00	3.50	.18	.23	......	......	1.65	2.33	1.20	.38	.50	.60	.55	13.12	178	6.00	10.7	10.0	12.17	.98	3	.44	6.77
Washington	2.00	2.75	.50	.50	......	......	1.40	2.00	3.00	.50	.25	1.50	......	14.40	200	6.00	12.0	12.5	13.50	.90	1	.33	6.45
White	2.50	3.00	.10	.35	......	......	2.00	1.50	.42	.20	......	.20	......	10.27	100	6.00	6.0	12.5	6.75	3.52	1	.50	9.52
Woodruff	4.58	3.75	.25	.29	......	......	1.16	3.10	1.02	.47	.20	.17	.75	15.74	167	6.58	10.0	11.8	12.12	3.62	3	.62	8.72
Yell	2.66	3.67	.20	.28	......	......	1.08	2.27	.70	.42	.38	.70	.67	13.03	148	6.17	9.0	11.7	10.14	2.89	3	.51	8.09

FLORIDA.

UPLAND.

																Cents.		Cents.					Cents.
Holmes	$1.84	$2.83	$0.13	$0.23	$2.42	$0.23	$0.83	$1.92	$0.52	$0.35	$0.75	$0.75	$0.18	$12.98	155	6.33	8.7	14.2	$11.04	$1.94	3	$0.41	7.58
Jackson	1.25	4.00	.16	.35	2.25	.35	.94	2.29	.77	.59	.34	.36	.41	14.06	173	6.56	11.4	10.6	12.62	1.44	4	.44	7.47
Jefferson	1.50	4.50	.20	.50	.85	.30	1.20	2.00	1.25	.25	.50	......	......	13.05	167	6.00	10.5	12.5	11.33	1.72	1	.40	7.03
Lake	3.00	1.04	.25	.12	......	......	1.50	2.00	.50	.20	.50	.25	2.00	11.36	137	6.75	8.0	11.5	10.17	1.19	1	.49	7.62
Walton	1.50	4.00	.15	.15	1.25	.25	.50	1.50	.67	.30	2.85	.25	......	13.37	167	6.38	12.0	15.0	12.45	.92	1	.30	6.93
Washington	1.17	2.50	.13	.42	2.00	.32	1.42	2.47	.83	.53	.70	.35	.33	13.17	164	6.42	9.7	10.5	11.47	1.70	3	.50	7.41

SEA-ISLAND.

																Cents.		Cents.					Cents.
Baker	$2.50	$5.50	$0.25	$0.25	$3.00	$0.25	$1.50	$4.00	$0.60	$0.35	$2.00	$0.50	$1.00	$21.70	133	9.50	8.0	20.0	$14.24	$7.46	1	$1.00	15.11
Bradford	2.00	4.00	.15	1.00	......	......	4.00	4.00	1.00	.50	.25	.10	......	17.00	100	15.00	10.0	12.5	16.25	.75	1	1.33	15.75
Calhoun	2.00	.50	.50	.20	2.50	.25	.50	3.60	.75	.25	.25	......	......	11.30	73	11.00	7.0	25.0	9.78	1.52	1	1.64	13.08
Citrus	2.00	5.00	.50	.25	4.20	.50	3.00	5.00	1.25	1.00	2.00	1.00	.20	25.90	100	13.00	5.0	25.0	14.25	11.65	1	1.67	24.65
Columbia	1.40	5.00	.20	1.00	1.80	.50	3.00	5.00	.15	.20	1.50	1.00	1.00	21.75	125	13.00	8.0	15.0	17.45	4.30	1	1.33	16.44
Hamilton	2.00	2.17	.29	.53	3.00	.37	1.00	2.58	1.25	.87	1.33	.83	1.00	17.22	89	12.67	7.3	15.7	12.71	4.51	3	.97	18.06
Holmes	2.00	2.00	.50	.20	1.25	.10	2.00	2.00	1.00	.22	1.50	.10	......	12.87	100	12.00	6.0	12.0	12.72	.15	1	.67	12.15
Lafayette	1.67	2.50	.42	.58	1.83	.50	1.00	3.67	1.25	.58	.50	1.00	.27	15.77	100	12.67	6.3	25.0	14.25	1.52	3	1.22	14.20
Levy	1.83	5.50	.26	.50	1.92	.75	.66	5.17	1.08	.34	1.46	.62	.57	20.66	108	14.17	7.3	30.3	17.64	3.02	3	1.60	17.08
Putnam	1.50	3.00	.25	.25	2.25	.25	2.00	3.00	1.20	.30	1.00	.50	1.25	16.75	100	14.50	6.0	25.0	16.00	.75	1	1.00	15.25
Suwanee	1.25	4.50	.13	.11	.75	.05	1.13	2.50	.62	.18	.38	.25	.05	11.90	73	12.50	5.2	22.0	10.30	1.60	2	1.14	14.73
Taylor	1.83	4.33	.66	.58	2.67	.58	1.42	3.58	1.04	.68	1.17	.42	.09	19.05	100	15.17	6.3	20.0	16.47	2.58	3	1.10	17.79

GEORGIA.

UPLAND.

																Cents.		Cents.					Cents.
Baker	$1.00	$2.50	$0.20	$0.15	$2.00	$0.10	$1.20	$2.00	$0.50	$0.25	$0.25	......	$0.10	$10.25	130	6.50	10.0	15.0	$0.95	$0.30	1	$0.51	6.73
Banks	3.50	2.80	.20	.10	2.50	.25	2.00	3.00	.75	.75	.25	$0.50	......	16.60	200	6.50	12.0	14.0	14.68	1.92	1	.50	7.46
Calhoun	1.25	4.35	.25	.35	2.50	.10	1.20	2.00	.40	.28	.25	.25	.50	13.68	160	7.50	12.0	10.5	13.26	.42	1	.42	7.76
Chattooga	2.50	7.50	.30	.50	2.00	.50	1.50	5.00	1.50	.75	.50	1.00	.50	24.05	330	6.00	20.0	12.0	22.20	1.85	1	.51	6.56
Cherokee	2.00	1.25	.15	.25	1.47	.25	2.25	1.72	.45	.16	.20	.15	.30	10.60	120	7.00	7.0	12.5	9.28	1.32	1	.48	8.10
Clay	2.00	3.40	.25	.22	1.50	.18	1.20	2.00	.42	.32	.30	.50	......	12.29	166	6.50	10.0	12.5	12.04	.25	1	.40	6.65
Cobb	2.50	6.25	.25	.25	2.50	.25	1.50	2.40	.75	.30	.25	.10	.80	18.10	200	7.25	12.0	12.5	16.00	2.10	1	.40	8.30
Coweta	2.57	3.80	.32	.41	2.10	.14	1.40	2.06	.44	.29	.31	.45	.76	15.05	180	6.90	11.0	12.1	13.69	1.36	5	.38	7.62
Crawford	1.75	2.70	.28	.25	2.30	.20	.50	1.66	.35	.20	.52	1.00	.50	12.21	134	6.75	8.0	15.0	10.13	2.08	2	.41	8.22
Decatur	2.00	2.95	.20	.12	3.30	.25	1.00	2.40	.60	.30	.60	.15	.60	14.47	200	6.00	13.0	15.0	13.95	.52	1	.40	6.26
Dekalb	3.00	5.25	.30	.10	3.00	.10	.75	3.00	1.20	.60	.50	.50	1.00	19.30	250	7.00	15.0	10.0	19.00	.30	1	.40	7.12

TABLE 21.—*Average cost of producing an acre of cotton in 1896 on farms showing a LOSS, by counties*—Continued.

[Wherever a blank occurs in these tables it means that no expense was incurred.]

GEORGIA—Continued.

UPLAND—Continued.

County.	Rent.	Plowing.	Seed.	Planting seed.	Fertilizers.	Distributing fertilizers.	Chopping and hoeing.	Picking.	Ginning and pressing.	Bagging and ties.	Marketing.	Repairing implements.	Other expenses.	TOTAL COST.	Pounds of lint.	Price per pound.	Bushels of seed.	Price per bushel.	TOTAL RETURN.	Loss.	Number of farms reporting.	Cost of picking per 100 pounds.	Cost of production per pound.
																Cents.		Cents.					Cents.
Emanuel	$1.50	$3.65	$0.20	$0.20	$2.25	$0.20	$1.25	$1.91	$0.52	$0.34	$0.28	$0.25	$0.25	$12.80	174	6.00	12.0	12.5	$11.86	$0.94	2	$0.37	6.49
Floyd	3.50	3.41	.27	.24	1.75	.27	1.33	2.57	.74	.35	.42	.42	.80	16.07	207	6.92	13.7	10.7	15.68	.39	3	.41	7.06
Forsyth	2.97	3.50	.14	.42	2.32	.30	1.25	2.20	.55	.30	.25	.35	.40	14.95	184	6.75	11.0	11.2	13.59	1.36	2	.40	7.46
Franklin	2.75	4.50	.25	.28	1.40	.25	1.75	2.90	.98	.52	.12	.63	.80	17.13	190	6.50	10.0	12.5	13.65	3.48	2	.51	8.36
Greene	2.00	6.00	.25	.10	1.50	.10	1.40	1.50	.33	.33	.25	.50	.10	14.36	165	7.00	10.0	12.5	12.80	1.56	1	.30	7.95
Gwinnett	2.00	4.00	.15	.25	2.00	.15	.50	3.00	1.50	.25	.50	.30	2.00	16.60	200	7.00	12.0	15.0	15.80	.80	1	.50	7.40
Hall	1.58	3.41	.27	.30	1.42	.17	1.43	1.92	.45	.27	.15	.25	.80	12.42	150	7.08	9.0	13.2	11.78	.64	3	.43	7.49
Hancock	2.00	5.00	.25	.30	2.50	.20	1.50	2.00	1.00	.70				15.45	180	6.50	13.0	13.0	13.39	2.06	1	.37	7.64
Haralson	3.38	3.17	.23	.27	2.28	.40	1.58	3.17	.57	.56	.25	.67	1.33	17.86	197	6.98	13.3	13.3	15.59	2.27	3	.54	8.17
Hart	3.70	4.00	.25	.50	2.10	.25	1.50	2.80	1.00	.65	.50	1.00	1.50	19.75	235	7.50	14.0	15.0	19.72	.03	1	.40	7.51
Johnson	2.00	2.00	.12	.12	5.00	.10	.50	2.50	1.00	1.00	.25	.50	1.00	16.09	175	7.00	10.0	12.0	13.45	2.64	1	.48	8.51
Jefferson	1.50	1.45	.28	.20	1.50	.15	1.10	1.60	.40	.85	.90	.77	.25	10.95	134	6.88	9.0	13.2	10.41	.54	2	.40	7.29
Jasper	2.53	3.00	.25	.13	2.00	.17	1.43	2.00	.53	.34	.48	.75	.75	14.36	189	6.33	11.7	13.7	13.47	.89	3	.35	6.75
Laurens	1.75	3.82	.28	.18	2.00	.35	1.37	2.80	.78	.97	.38	.50		15.18	183	6.50	13.0	12.2	13.50	1.68	2	.51	7.43
Lowndes	2.50	7.00	.50	.15	2.50	.50	1.50	3.75	1.10	.50	.50	1.00	.80	22.30	250	7.00	15.0	15.0	19.75	2.55	1	.50	8.02
Madison	2.00	2.00	.15	.25	1.50	.25	1.00	1.80	.55	.30	.30	.50	1.25	11.85	150	7.00	8.0	12.0	11.46	.39	1	.40	7.26
Mitchell	3.00	5.00	.25	.25	2.50	.10	2.00	2.00	.50	.25	.35	.25	.00	16.45	167	6.50	11.0	15.0	12.50	3.95	1	.40	8.86
Milton	3.00	4.00	.15	.50	2.00	.25	1.50	2.40	.60	.60	.10	.50	1.00	16.60	216	7.00	13.0	10.0	16.42	.18	1	.37	7.08
Montgomery	2.00	3.00	.15	1.00	1.50	.50	1.00	2.00	.35	.25	.25	.00	.00	12.00	150	6.50	10.0	15.0	11.25	.75	1	.44	7.00
Morgan	2.50	4.00	.25	.18	1.90	.10	1.10	2.12	.54	.57	1.25	.50	.67	15.68	166	7.00	11.0	14.2	13.23	2.45	2	.43	8.50
Muscogee	2.00	5.00	.30	.50	2.00	.20	1.50	1.50	.50	.30	.30	.50	1.00	15.60	150	7.50	10.0	12.0	12.45	3.15	1	.33	9.60
Newton	2.62	3.08	.20	.38	2.25	.25	.75	2.28	.42	.38	.22	.38	.40	13.61	152	6.50	8.0	16.2	11.25	2.36	2	.50	8.10
Paulding	2.00	1.75	.35	.50	2.00	.50	2.00	3.00	2.25	.75	.50	2.50	1.00	19.10	250	7.00	15.0	10.0	19.00	.10	1	.40	7.04
Pickens	5.87	3.62	.28	.38	1.95	.22	1.50	3.62	1.48	.65	.38	.22	.50	20.67	262	6.50	15.5	13.8	19.25	1.42	2	.46	7.07
Pulaski	2.00	4.00	.25	.30	2.50	.20	1.00	3.50	.50	.45	.30	.50	.85	16.35	235	6.25	12.0	11.0	16.01	.34	1	.50	6.40
Randolph	1.25	2.00	.25	.20	2.25	.15	1.00	2.00	.50	.35	.20	.30	1.00	11.45	160	6.00	10.0	12.5	10.85	.60	1	.42	6.38
Spalding	2.00	4.00	.15	.15	2.25	.15	1.50	2.00	.50	.25	.20	1.00	.00	14.15	167	7.00	10.0	15.0	13.19	.96	1	.40	7.57
Stewart	3.00	3.75	.15	.25	2.00	.10	1.25	2.00	.60	.30	1.00	.50	.00	14.90	200	6.50	12.0	12.5	14.50	.40	1	.33	6.70
Talbot	3.00	4.09	.10	.10	1.50	.10	.50	2.00	.40	.40	.42	.25	.50	13.27	165	6.50	12.0	10.0	11.92	1.35	1	.40	7.32
Terrell	2.00	4.00	.15	.25	2.00	.25	1.50	2.00	.40	.25	.75	.00	.80	14.35	167	7.00	8.0	12.0	12.65	1.70	1	.40	8.02

Thomas	2.00	3.50	.50	.50	3.00	.50	1.00	3.00	2.50	.75	1.00	1.00	.40	19.65	250	6.50	17.0	12.0	18.29	1.36	1	.40	7.04
Troup	2.25	3.50	.30	.19	2.00	.10	1.65	2.00	.42	.25	.18	.18	.80	13.82	167	7.00	10.0	12.2	12.91	.91	2	.40	7.54
Twiggs	1.50	2.00	.20	.25	2.00	.25	1.00	3.20	1.50	1.00	2.00	.25	1.00	16.15	200	7.00	12.0	15.0	15.80	.35	1	.53	7.18
Upson	2.50	3.50	.15	.10	1.25	.14	1.80	1.50	.34	.30	.41	.75	1.10	13.84	166	7.25	11.0	13.0	13.46	.38	1	.30	7.48
Walker	2.50	2.75	.20	.30	2.75	.32	1.50	3.25	1.25	.95	.75	1.00	1.18	18.70	225	7.00	13.5	12.5	17.40	1.30	2	.48	7.56
Whitfield	3.17	2.54	.22	.20	1.98	.28	2.28	2.60	.80	.68	.58	.42	.58	16.33	189	7.00	11.7	12.5	14.67	1.66	3	.46	7.87

SEA-ISLAND.

																Cents.		*Cents.*					*Cents.*
Lowndes	$2.00	$4.50	$0.22	$0.18	$1.58	$0.10	$1.00	$3.37	$2.20	$0.84	$0.38	$0.75	$0.32	$17.44	112	12.0	6.0	16.0	$14.46	$2.98	2	$1.00	14.71
Pierce	2.00	3.00	1.00	1.00	3.75	.25	2.00	5.00	1.25	.51	1.02	.25	......	21.02	168	11.0	7.0	25.0	20.23	.79	1	.99	11.47
Tattnall	2.50	5.50	.62	.38	4.50	.52	.80	7.75	2.00	.42	1.25	.38	.53	27.15	200	11.0	10.5	17.5	23.85	3.30	2	1.29	12.66

INDIAN TERRITORY.

																Cents.		*Cents.*					*Cents.*
Chickasaw Nation	$2.61	$2.78	$0.17	$0.31	......	......	$1.54	$2.62	$1.15	$0.48	$0.70	$0.39	$0.29	$13.04	163	6.28	10.7	9.8	$11.32	$1.72	9	$0.54	7.36
Choctaw Nation	2.75	2.50	.21	.36	......	......	1.60	2.30	.88	.54	.35	.39	.17	12.05	135	6.25	9.5	13.0	9.54	2.51	6	.57	8.01

LOUISIANA.

																Cents.		*Cents.*					*Cents.*
Avoyelles	$3.50	$5.50	$0.28	$0.22	$1.05	$0.22	$2.15	$4.60	$1.10	$0.73	$1.63	$0.62	$0.12	$21.72	262	6.25	17.5	11.2	$18.06	$3.66	2	$0.59	7.54
Bienville	2.16	2.70	.15	.29	......	......	1.45	1.66	.59	.29	.27	.30	.24	10.10	110	6.90	7.6	10.0	8.36	1.74	5	.50	8.49
Bossier	2.38	2.88	.18	.27	1.38	.30	1.61	1.88	.88	.33	.45	.35	.12	13.01	150	5.94	9.2	13.2	10.03	2.98	4	.42	7.86
Caddo	2.00	2.00	.10	.18	......	......	1.25	2.50	1.50	1.00	.75	.25	.80	12.33	166	5.75	10.0	10.0	10.54	1.79	1	.50	6.83
Caldwell	3.28	5.00	.28	.40	.37	.07	2.40	3.15	1.08	.58	1.03	.69	.56	18.89	196	6.38	14.0	9.3	13.77	5.12	6	.54	8.97
Catahoula	3.08	2.00	.18	.25	......	......	1.62	3.50	1.22	.65	1.38	.55	.38	14.81	185	6.38	12.5	12.2	13.23	1.58	2	.63	7.18
Claiborne	1.95	3.40	.18	.29	.47	.06	1.48	1.88	.49	.37	.29	.27	.08	11.21	139	6.04	8.4	10.0	9.26	1.95	6	.45	7.46
De Soto	1.89	2.39	.23	.24	1.21	.21	1.56	1.76	.56	.32	.46	.29	.10	11.22	126	6.45	8.4	10.4	9.04	2.18	7	.47	8.21
E. Baton Rouge	3.00	2.75	.10	.10	3.00	.25	1.50	2.80	.70	1.00	2.00	......	......	17.20	225	6.50	16.0	10.0	16.22	.98	1	.41	6.93
E. Feliciana	1.00	3.00	.25	.25	1.00	.25	2.00	6.00	1.50	.75	.50	.50	1.50	18.50	200	7.50	15.0	10.0	16.50	2.00	1	1.00	8.50
Franklin	3.17	2.67	.20	.30	......	......	.83	2.47	.98	.78	1.00	.50	.47	13.37	169	6.08	11.1	9.0	11.26	2.11	3	.49	7.32
Grant	3.50	5.00	.40	.10	......	......	2.50	4.00	1.00	.50	3.25	.50	......	20.75	250	6.25	15.0	10.0	17.12	3.63	1	.53	7.70
Iberia	3.50	1.00	.50	.25	......	......	2.00	5.00	2.50	1.00	3.50	.50	1.50	21.25	250	7.00	15.0	16.6	19.99	1.26	1	.67	7.50
Lincoln	2.00	2.67	.13	.22	......	......	.95	2.03	.33	.22	.27	.13	.37	9.32	133	5.67	9.3	10.0	8.47	.85	3	.51	6.31
Livingston	4.00	5.00	.15	1.00	2.00	.75	2.00	6.00	1.70	.75	1.50	1.00	......	25.85	400	6.00	28.0	6.0	25.68	.17	1	.50	6.04
Madison	3.16	2.05	.45	.08	......	......	1.65	2.02	.58	.53	1.25	1.00	......	12.77	135	7.75	12.0	10.0	11.66	1.11	1	.50	8.57
Morehouse	3.50	2.75	.37	.38	1.50	.25	1.75	5.50	1.75	1.25	2.00	.25	.40	21.65	270	6.88	17.0	10.0	20.35	1.30	2	.68	7.39
Natchitoches	3.00	2.50	.10	.10	2.50	.10	.50	1.80	.85	.25	.30	.20	......	12.20	150	6.00	10.0	10.0	10.00	2.20	1	.40	7.47
Ouachita	3.58	2.00	.20	.17	1.25	.10	1.25	2.00	.90	.35	.55	.20	.75	13.30	165	6.25	13.5	10.0	11.82	1.48	2	.40	7.24
Rapides	1.50	1.00	.15	.50	1.50	.25	2.00	1.50	.45	.25	1.50	.50	.12	11.22	100	7.25	6.0	10.0	7.85	3.37	1	.50	10.62

TABLE 21.—*Average cost of producing an acre of cotton in 1896 on farms showing a* ***LOSS****, by counties*—Continued.

[Wherever a blank occurs in these tables it means that no expense was incurred.]

LOUISIANA—Continued.

County.	Rent.	Plowing.	Seed.	Planting seed.	Fertilizers.	Distributing fertilizers.	Chopping and hoeing.	Picking.	Ginning and pressing.	Bagging and ties.	Marketing.	Repairing implements.	Other expenses.	TOTAL COST.	Pounds of lint.	Price per pound.	Bushels of seed.	Price per bushel.	TOTAL RETURN.	Loss.	Number of farms reporting.	Cost of picking per 100 pounds.	Cost of production per pound.
																Cents.		*Cents.*					*Cents.*
Red River	$5.00	$6.25	$0.10	$0.25	$1.00	$0.50	$1.50	$3.75	$1.15	$0.65	$2.50	$0.75	$0.50	$23.90	292	6.00	18.5	10.0	$19.34	$4.56	2	$0.43	7.55
Richland	3.00	3.50	.25	.20	1.00	.25	.75	1.65	1.50	.30	......	.25	......	12.65	160	7.00	10.0	8.0	12.00	.65	1	.34	7.41
Sabine	2.65	4.75	.16	.34	.62	.06	1.39	2.65	.80	.38	1.02	.58	.01	15.41	192	6.31	12.0	10.0	13.35	2.06	4	.46	7.40
St. Helena	2.50	3.00	.50	.25	2.00	.25	1.50	2.00	.75	.30	1.00	.20	.30	14.55	200	6.00	10.0	10.0	13.00	1.55	1	.33	6.78
St. Landry	2.72	4.67	.31	.53	2.00	.50	1.33	5.33	2.00	.87	.83	1.50	.22	22.81	300	6.17	18.0	10.0	20.05	2.76	3	.59	7.00
Tangipahoa	2.50	4.50	.15	.15	2.00	.15	1.50	4.00	2.00	.80	.50	1.00	.80	20.05	275	6.50	16.0	10.0	19.48	.57	1	.48	6.71
Union	2.00	2.15	.15	.18	.75	.05	1.15	1.50	.39	.22	.32	.50	.65	10.01	106	6.75	6.0	12.5	7.84	2.17	2	.47	8.74
Vernon	3.00	6.00	.25	.30	2.50	.50	2.00	4.00	1.20	.85	3.00	......	......	23.60	300	6.50	18.0	10.0	21.30	2.30	1	.44	7.27
Washington	2.75	2.25	.20	.10	2.75	.40	1.75	4.25	1.65	.60	2.00	.16	.12	18.98	258	6.38	17.5	10.0	18.00	.98	2	.55	6.68
Webster	1.25	2.75	.20	.18	1.00	.25	1.38	1.50	.32	.18	.27	.30	.12	9.70	100	6.25	8.0	10.0	7.05	2.65	2	.50	8.90
West Carroll	3.00	3.00	.25	.38	......	......	1.75	1.42	.50	.28	.87	.12	.25	11.82	112	7.25	7.0	11.2	8.98	2.84	2	.42	9.85
Winn	1.90	2.95	.11	.25	2.50	.50	2.10	3.00	.97	.66	.87	.37	.37	16.55	179	6.30	11.4	9.6	12.30	4.25	5	.56	8.63

MISSISSIPPI.

County.	Rent.	Plowing.	Seed.	Planting seed.	Fertilizers.	Distributing fertilizers.	Chopping and hoeing.	Picking.	Ginning and pressing.	Bagging and ties.	Marketing.	Repairing implements.	Other expenses.	TOTAL COST.	Pounds of lint.	Price per pound.	Bushels of seed.	Price per bushel.	TOTAL RETURN.	Loss.	Number of farms reporting.	Cost of picking per 100 pounds.	Cost of production per pound.
																Cents.		*Cents.*					*Cents.*
Alcorn	$2.50	$3.50	$0.30	$0.50	$2.25	$0.50	$2.25	$4.00	$1.10	$1.00	$1.00	$1.00	......	$19.90	266	6.50	16.0	15.0	$19.69	$0.21	1	$0.50	6.58
Amite	2.00	2.25	.10	.10	1.50	.10	2.25	2.00	.73	.37	.60	.50	$0.25	12.75	166	7.00	8.0	10.0	12.42	.33	1	.40	7.20
Attala	2.00	3.25	.30	.25	2.50	.38	1.75	3.00	1.12	.87	.50	.68	.25	16.85	220	6.12	15.0	10.0	14.88	1.97	2	.45	6.98
Benton	2.00	2.00	.15	.50	......	......	1.50	1.50	.50	.25	.25	......	.10	8.75	130	6.00	8.0	10.0	8.60	.15	1	.38	6.12
Bolivar	6.00	4.50	.25	.25	......	......	1.00	5.00	1.75	.90	2.25	1.00	......	22.90	350	6.00	20.0	7.5	22.50	.40	1	.48	6.11
Calhoun	2.96	3.75	.22	.50	......	......	.62	2.33	.77	.65	1.25	1.25	1.00	15.30	170	6.50	10.5	10.0	12.11	3.19	2	.46	8.38
Carroll	1.75	4.00	.15	.50	......	1.50	1.50	4.00	1.50	.80	1.00	1.00	1.00	18.70	200	6.50	12.0	10.0	14.20	4.50	1	.67	8.75
Choctaw	2.50	1.80	.20	.20	2.75	.20	1.00	2.50	.50	.25	.10	.25	.25	12.50	167	6.50	10.0	10.0	11.86	.64	1	.50	6.89
Clarke	2.00	2.63	.22	.20	2.25	.20	.92	2.45	1.25	.60	.40	.81	......	13.93	200	6.25	12.5	10.0	13.75	.18	2	.41	6.34
Clay	2.00	1.50	.20	.20	.50	.50	.50	3.00	.50	.50	.50	.50	......	10.40	100	6.75	8.0	10.0	7.55	2.85	1	1.00	9.60
Coahoma	6.00	1.50	.50	1.00	......	......	4.00	8.00	1.50	1.00	2.25	2.00	......	27.75	300	6.00	18.0	10.0	19.80	7.95	1	.89	8.65
Covington	2.50	1.50	.10	.10	1.75	.25	2.00	1.50	.80	.25	.50	1.00	......	12.25	150	7.00	10.0	10.0	11.50	.75	1	.33	7.50
De Soto	2.25	2.25	.30	.25	......	......	.88	1.48	.35	.18	.12	.62	.62	9.30	108	6.94	6.0	10.0	8.05	1.25	2	.46	8.06
Grenada	2.50	4.00	.10	.25	......	......	1.75	1.80	.90	.50	1.00	.50	1.00	14.30	200	6.00	12.0	10.0	13.20	1.10	1	.30	6.55

Hinds	2.00	3.25	.25	.25			2.25	8.00	1.30	.70	.50	.50		19.00	250	7.00	15.0	8.0	18.70	.30	1	1.07	7.12
Jasper	1.87	5.50	.15	.20	6.10	.45	.88	4.43	1.16	.46	.80	.60	.40	23.00	278	6.44	15.8	10.0	19.62	3.38	2	.53	7.71
Kemper	2.16	4.00	.60	.30	2.00	.28	1.17	3.23	.87	.57	.75	1.17	.43	17.53	192	6.67	12.0	10.0	13.95	3.58	3	.56	8.51
Lafayette	2.50	2.25	.18	.25			1.50	1.80	.65	.32	.50	.25	.70	10.90	150	6.12	9.5	10.0	10.16	.74	2	.40	6.63
Lauderdale	2.50	4.00	.30	.10	1.85	.15	1.50	1.75	.50	.25	.20	.25	1.00	14.35	167	6.80	10.0	15.0	12.86	1.49	1	.35	7.69
Leake	2.67	3.59	.23	.10	3.12	.33	1.08	2.20	.72	.37	.63	.33	.52	15.89	169	6.97	10.3	10.0	12.84	3.05	3	.43	8.79
Lee	3.25	3.75	.25	.45	1.50	.50	2.50	3.50	1.01	.63	.88	.50	.50	19.22	225	6.25	13.5	10.0	15.35	3.87	2	.52	7.94
Leflore	6.00	4.50	.25	.15			3.00	4.50	1.50	1.00	3.50	.50		24.90	300	7.25	18.0	11.0	23.73	1.17	1	.50	7.64
Madison	2.00	.75	.11	.12	1.50	.25	1.40	1.89	.50	.40	.65	.55	1.35	11.47	140	6.88	9.0	10.0	10.53	.94	1	.45	7.55
Monroe	3.00	1.50	.20	.25			1.50	1.80	.62	.25	.25	1.00	.75	11.12	150	6.25	9.0	10.0	10.28	.84	1	.40	6.81
Montgomery	2.50	4.00	.25	.25			2.00	3.00	.90	.50	.50	.50	1.00	15.40	200	6.25	12.0	10.0	13.70	1.70	1	.50	7.10
Neshoba	2.00	2.50	.15	.10	1.25	.10	1.20	2.00	.65	.25	.75	.25	.50	11.70	125	7.00	10.0	10.0	9.75	1.95	1	.53	8.56
Newton	2.50	3.50	.20	.25	2.00	.15	1.50	2.56	.80	.90	.25	.25	.50	15.36	213	6.50	13.0	10.0	15.14	.22	1	.40	6.60
Oktibbeha	1.25	1.50	.15	.25	1.25	.25	.50	1.50	.45	.25	.50	.25	.50	8.60	100	6.00	6.0	10.0	6.60	2.00	1	.50	8.00
Pike	3.75	3.00	.30	.25	2.00	.25	1.50	3.75	1.10	.40	1.50	.25		18.05	225	6.50	20.0	10.0	16.62	1.43	1	.56	7.13
Scott	3.00	5.00	.15	.15	1.50	.15	3.00	3.00	2.00	.80	.75	.25	.25	20.00	250	6.75	15.0	10.0	18.38	1.62	1	.40	7.40
Simpson	2.00	2.00	.20	.25	1.85	.25	1.00	1.60	.70	.75	.50	.15		11.25	130	6.50	8.0	10.0	9.25	2.00	1	.41	8.04
Sunflower	6.00	3.75	.30	.30			1.50	4.00	1.00	.45	1.62	.50		19.42	250	6.00	18.0	12.0	17.16	2.26	1	.53	6.90
Tippah	2.00	3.00	.25	.50			1.00	1.60	.55	.20	.20		.20	9.50	125	6.50	8.0	10.0	8.92	.58	1	.43	6.96
Tishomingo	2.50	2.00	.30	.25			1.50	2.40	.75	.40	.40	.25	3.25	14.00	200	6.00	12.0	10.0	13.20	.80	1	.40	6.40
Union	2.67	3.67	.23	.40	1.27	.42	2.25	3.25	1.43	.68	.63	.37	.75	18.02	197	6.42	14.0	11.7	14.36	3.66	3	.55	8.32
Wayne	1.50	5.00	.25	.20	3.50	.25	1.75	2.80	1.00	.35	2.00	.20	.40	19.20	230	7.50	15.0	12.5	19.12	.08	1	.41	7.53
Winston	2.25	4.22	.25	.38	1.19	.25	.94	2.87	.79	.46	.69	.44	.15	14.88	198	6.44	12.0	10.1	13.88	1.00	4	.48	6.90
Yalobusha	2.88	4.25	.25	.25			2.50	2.85	1.45	.70	.50	.62	.05	16.30	225	5.62	14.0	9.0	13.80	2.50	2	.42	6.68

MISSOURI.

																Cents.		Cents.					Cents.
Dunklin	$3.00	$6.25	$0.20	$0.50			$2.00	$6.00	$1.50	$0.75	$1.50	$0.50		$22.20	300	6.50	21.0	10.0	$21.60	$0.60	1	$0.67	6.70
Ozark	2.50	1.00	.15	.75	$2.00	$0.50	2.50	2.50	.85	.35	.45	.10	$0.40	14.05	160	6.00	10.0	10.0	10.60	3.45	1	.52	8.16
Stone	2.50	2.00	.15	.50			1.00	2.00	1.00	1.50	1.50	.50		12.65	130	8.00	10.0	12.5	11.65	1.00	1	.51	8.77

NORTH CAROLINA.

																Cents.		Cents.					Cents.
Beaufort	$4.25	$3.75	$0.20	$0.25	$2.50	$0.25	$1.00	$2.40	$0.70	$1.00	$0.20			$16.50	200	7.00	15.0	10.0	$15.50	$1.00	1	$0.40	7.50
Bertie	2.50	3.00	.25	.25	3.00	.20	1.50	1.35	.60	.30	.30	$0.60	$0.30	14.15	165	6.50	10.0	12.0	11.92	2.23	1	.27	7.85
Bladen	4.27	3.00	.15	.20	3.37	.25	1.75	1.80	.50	.25	.25	.10	.40	16.29	167	7.00	10.0	12.0	12.89	3.40	1	.36	9.04
Cabarrus	3.50	2.50	.20	.40	2.10	.20	2.00	3.50	.75	.50		.75		16.40	200	7.00	14.0	15.0	16.10	.30	1	.58	7.15
Carteret	4.85	2.75	.40	.25	6.00	.30	.50	2.80	1.00	.50	.40	.10		19.85	250	7.00	16.0	12.5	19.50	.35	1	.37	7.14
Catawba	5.28	3.00	.25	.25	2.25	.25	1.50	2.80	1.00	.35	.50	.75	.60	18.78	235	6.75	15.0	15.0	18.11	.67	1	.40	7.03
Chatham	3.02	2.96	.48	.23	3.38	.27	1.45	2.52	.86	.67	.62	.28	.38	17.12	200	7.40	12.0	13.7	16.43	.69	5	.42	7.74
Cleveland	4.00	5.00	.25	.15	1.90	.15	1.50	2.40	2.00	.75	.50	.30		18.90	200	7.00	12.0	12.0	15.44	3.46	1	.40	8.73
Cumberland	1.00	6.00	.50	.50	6.00	.50	2.00	2.60	.87	.50	.50			20.97	250	7.00	15.0	15.0	19.75	1.22	1	.35	7.49
Durham	2.00	5.00	.25	.50	1.70	.20	1.00	2.00	.62	.25	.55	.25	.50	14.82	165	7.12	10.0	15.0	13.25	1.57	1	.40	8.07
Edgecombe	4.00	2.00	.30	.25	2.50	.15	1.50	1.50	.50	.40	.40	.25	.15	13.90	165	6.00	12.0	15.0	11.70	2.20	1	.30	7.33
Franklin	2.75	2.88	.35	.25	1.82	.45	1.50	1.50	.50	.55	.08	.62	.30	13.55	147	6.75	9.2	11.2	10.97	2.58	2	.34	8.52

TABLE 21.—*Average cost of producing an acre of cotton in 1896 on farms showing a LOSS, by counties*—Continued.

[Wherever a blank occurs in these tables it means that no expense was incurred.]

NORTH CAROLINA—Continued.

County.	Rent.	Plowing.	Seed.	Planting seed.	Fertilizers.	Distributing fertilizers.	Chopping and hoeing.	Picking.	Ginning and pressing.	Bagging and ties.	Marketing.	Repairing implements.	Other expenses.	TOTAL COST.	Pounds of lint.	Price per pound.	Bushels of seed.	Price per bushel.	TOTAL RETURN.	Loss.	Number of farms reporting.	Cost of picking per 100 pounds.	Cost of production per pound.
																Cents.		Cents.					Cents.
Gates	$5.00	$1.50	$0.25	$0.25	$1.25	$0.25	$2.50	$5.00	$1.00	$1.00	$1.00	$1.00		$20.00	300	6.00	18.0	10.0	$19.80	$0.20	1	$0.56	6.07
Greene	3.90	4.00	.15	.25	2.20	.25	2.00	3.00	.75	.38	.25	.25	$2.00	19.38	250	6.50	15.0	12.5	18.12	1.26	1	.40	7.00
Halifax	2.50	3.50	.25	.25	3.00	.25	.50	1.80	1.60	.80	1.25	.50	.35	16.55	225	6.25	14.0	10.0	15.46	1.09	1	.27	6.73
Hertford	3.25	3.00	.25	.25	4.50	.60	1.40	3.20	.90	.45	1.50	.50		19.80	234	7.12	15.0	11.0	18.31	1.49	1	.46	7.76
Iredell	3.70	1.50	.15	.20	1.00	.15	1.70	2.00	.60	.20	.25	.20		11.65	154	6.50	8.0	15.0	11.21	.44	1	.43	6.79
Lincoln	5.00	3.50	.25	.25	1.75	.25	2.00	6.00	1.00	.80	1.60	.50	.60	22.90	270	7.00	17.0	14.0	21.28	1.62	1	.74	7.60
Mecklenburg	8.00	2.00	.25	.25	1.25	.25	.50	4.00	1.20	.55	.50	.50	.60	19.85	225	7.00	11.5	14.0	17.36	2.49	1	.59	8.11
Montgomery	3.75	5.00	.25	.35	1.25	.30	1.50	1.75	.75	.50			.25	15.65	200	6.75	12.0	12.5	15.00	.65	1	.29	7.08
Onslow	4.00	4.37	.13	.37	6.25	1.25	1.50	3.00	1.00	.45	1.50	.25		24.07	250	6.80	15.0	10.0	18.50	5.57	1	.40	9.03
Orange	3.25	4.00	.25	.75	1.75	.25	1.00	4.00	.65	.75	.50	.50		17.65	167	7.25	10.0	12.5	13.36	4.29	1	.80	9.82
Pamlico	3.70	3.00	.30	.15			4.00	2.40	.85	.85	1.75	.10		17.10	214	6.50	12.0	15.0	15.71	1.39	1	.37	7.15
Pender	4.00	3.00	.20	.15	2.50	1.00	.50	1.75	.62	.25	.25	.50	.40	15.12	125	7.00	7.0	12.5	9.62	5.50	1	.47	11.39
Pitt	7.00	3.00	.25	.25	4.00	.25	2.00	3.60	.93	.68	.25	.25		22.46	300	6.25	15.0	13.0	20.70	1.76	1	.40	6.84
Polk	3.70	3.50	.25	.25	2.00	.25	1.75	4.50	.75	.50	.75	.50		18.70	200	7.50	14.0	12.5	16.75	1.95	1	.75	8.48
Rowan	4.58	2.50	.22	.25	2.25	.25	2.00	1.85	.85	.55	.50	.62	.67	17.09	155	7.00	10.5	11.2	12.06	5.03	2	.40	10.26
Rutherford	4.00	3.75	.24	.20	2.00	.20	1.80	1.75	1.57	.20	.30	.50		16.51	166	7.00	10.0	12.0	12.82	3.69	1	.35	9.22
Stanley	2.00	6.00	.25	1.00	2.00	.50	3.00	4.50	1.05	1.25	1.00	.75	.25	23.55	300	7.00	18.0	12.0	23.16	.39	1	.50	7.13
Tyrrell	6.50	4.38	.25	.50	6.25	.62	3.00	5.90	2.05	1.12	1.00	.38	.13	32.08	450	6.00	27.0	10.0	29.70	2.38	2	.44	6.53
Union	1.50	2.00	.10	.20			.75	1.20	.36	.25	.25	.25		6.86	100	6.00	6.0	10.0	6.60	.26	1	.40	6.23
Vance	3.00	2.00	.40	.25	2.50	.20	.40	2.00	.50	.40	.60	.40		12.65	135	6.00	10.0	20.0	10.10	2.55	1	.49	7.89

OKLAHOMA TERRITORY.

County.	Rent.	Plowing.	Seed.	Planting seed.	Fertilizers.	Distributing fertilizers.	Chopping and hoeing.	Picking.	Ginning and pressing.	Bagging and ties.	Marketing.	Repairing implements.	Other expenses.	TOTAL COST.	Pounds of lint.	Price per pound.	Bushels of seed.	Price per bushel.	TOTAL RETURN.	Loss.	Number of farms reporting.	Cost of picking per 100 pounds.	Cost of production per pound.
																Cents.		Cents.					Cents.
Greer	$1.83	$3.25	$0.15	$0.23			$1.92	$2.30	$1.24	$0.50	$0.67	$0.25	$0.33	$12.67	133	6.50	7.8	10.8	$9.55	$3.12	3	$0.58	8.89
Lincoln	2.00	3.00	.15	.50			3.50	4.00	1.50	1.50	.75	1.00		17.90	200	7.50	12.0	15.0	16.80	1.10	1	.67	8.05
Logan	2.00	1.00	.10	.50			1.10	2.00	.50	.25	.50	.25	.75	8.95	125	6.50	8.0	8.0	8.76	.19	1	.53	6.65
Pottawatomie	2.50	1.25	.10	.25			1.25	4.00	.80	1.00	1.00	.75	.50	13.40	200	6.00	15.0	9.0	13.35	.05	1	.67	6.02

SOUTH CAROLINA.

																Cents.		Cents.					Cents.
Chester	$2.65	$4.60	$0.25	$0.30	$5.50	$0.15	$0.90	$2.10	$0.25	$0.40	$1.50	$0.60		$19.20	230	6.70	17.0	13.0	$17.62	$1.58	1	$0.30	7.39
Greenville	3.00	7.00	.25	.30	2.50	.20	1.50	2.80	1.00	.40	.50	1.50		20.95	234	7.25	15.0	15.0	19.21	1.74	1	.40	7.99
Oconee	3.00	2.00	.23	.25	2.25	.30	1.20	1.80	.45	.30	.25	.50		12.53	150	6.00	9.0	15.0	10.35	2.18	1	.40	7.45
Pickens	3.00	3.00	.30	.30	1.80	.10	1.75	2.00	.58	.17	.25	.40	$0.30	13.95	166	7.00	9.5	15.0	13.04	.91	1	.40	7.55
Richland	4.56	4.00	.36	.40	3.00	1.00	1.00	2.80	.75	.30	.50	.25	1.00	19.92	225	7.00	14.0	18.0	18.27	1.65	1	.41	7.73
Sumter	3.00	3.50	.20	.20	4.50	.25	1.25	3.00	.90	.40	.50	.10	.50	18.30	250	6.25	15.0	15.0	17.88	.42	1	.40	6.42
Union	4.43	3.20	.30	.20	2.00	.13	.75	2.00	.79	.25	.25	.15		14.45	166	7.00	10.0	15.0	13.12	1.33	1	.40	7.80
Williamsburg	2.00	5.00	.30	.25	3.00	.50	.80	2.25	.30	.30	.00	.10	.25	15.05	175	6.50	11.0	12.0	12.70	2.35	1	.43	7.85

TENNESSEE.

																Cents.		Cents.					Cents.
Benton	$2.50	$5.00	$0.10	$0.25			$1.00	$3.00	$0.70	$0.40				$12.95	167	6.00	10.0	10.0	$11.02	$1.93	1	$0.61	7.16
Carroll	2.98	2.50	.85	.25	$0.38	$0.50	1.25	3.50	.95	.50	$0.62	$0.25	$1.00	15.53	195	6.12	13.0	11.2	13.38	2.15	2	.60	7.22
Chester	4.00	3.50	.15	.50			1.00	1.50	.50	.25		.25		11.65	100	6.50	6.0	7.0	6.92	4.73	1	.50	11.23
Crockett	3.50	4.00	.20	.50			2.00	4.00	1.00	.75	.50	1.50		17.95	228	7.00	16.0	10.0	17.56	.39	1	.58	7.17
Davidson	2.00	3.35	.15	.10	2.40	.10	1.00	1.90	1.40	.30	.75	.75	.65	14.85	175	7.00	10.0	10.0	13.25	1.60	1	.36	7.91
Dyer	4.00	1.50	.25	.50			2.00	5.00	1.15	.60	1.00	.75		16.75	250	6.00	16.0	10.0	16.60	.15	1	.67	6.06
Fayette	2.50	2.00	.10	.25			2.00	2.00	.55	.30	.90	1.00	.25	11.85	150	7.00	11.0	10.0	11.60	.25	1	.44	7.17
Franklin	2.00	4.00	.30	.25	2.00	.25	3.00	4.00	.70	.50	1.00	1.00		19.00	240	6.50	16.0	12.5	17.60	1.40	1	.56	7.08
Giles	2.15	3.75	.25	.25			1.50	2.40	.60	.50	.25	.25	1.50	13.40	200	6.00	10.0	8.0	12.80	.60	1	.40	6.30
Haywood	3.00	6.00	.25	.25			1.00	3.00	1.00	.30	.50	.15		15.45	200	6.00	11.0	8.0	12.88	2.57	1	.50	7.28
McNairy	1.50	3.00	.20	.20			1.50	2.80	.84	.80	.33			11.17	122	7.00	8.0	10.0	9.34	1.83	1	.76	8.50
Madison	3.25	3.80	.24	.20			1.26	3.12	1.00	.38	.85	.22	1.05	15.37	168	7.00	12.5	10.0	13.11	2.26	2	.62	8.40
Maury	2.00	6.75	.25	.25	3.00	.75	2.00	4.80	1.50	.75	2.25	.50		24.80	300	7.00	25.0	12.5	24.12	.68	1	.53	7.22
Shelby	2.00	4.50	.50	.40			2.00	1.50	.45	.30	.50	.10		12.25	100	8.00	6.0	15.0	8.90	3.35	1	.50	11.35

TEXAS.

																Cents.		Cents.					Cents.
Anderson	$2.17	$3.66	$0.17	$0.32			$1.17	$1.83	$0.60	$0.27	$0.67	$0.40	$0.02	$11.29	122	6.42	7.7	9.2	$8.56	$2.73	3	$0.50	8.67
Angelina	1.50	1.00	.10	.50			1.25	1.50	.40	.15	.50	.10	.50	7.50	100	6.50	6.0	10.0	7.10	.40	1	.50	6.90
Atascosa	2.00	2.00	.25	.25			1.00	2.00	.83	.42	.30			9.05	125	6.00	7.5	10.0	8.25	.80	1	.53	6.64
Austin	5.00	4.00	.25	.25			1.75	8.00	1.50	.75		.25		21.75	250	7.00	17.0	15.0	20.05	1.70	1	1.07	7.68
Bastrop	3.67	2.83	.27	.32			3.00	4.36	1.73	.52	1.22	.12	.13	18.17	208	6.83	14.7	12.5	15.98	2.19	3	.70	7.85
Bell	3.37	3.17	.17	.28		$0.08	.96	1.68	.57	.25	.13	.16	.02	10.92	116	6.67	7.5	11.0	8.53	2.39	6	.48	8.70
Bowie	2.50	7.00	.25	.15			1.00	2.00	.50	.25	.25	.10	.50	14.50	125	6.00	8.0	9.0	8.22	6.28	1	.53	11.02
Brazoria	4.00	5.00	.25	.50			1.00	2.65	.67	.33		.50		14.90	167	7.00	10.0	10.0	12.69	2.21	1	.53	8.32
Brazos	5.00	4.50	.25	.50			1.50	2.25	.60	.35	.15			15.10	150	7.25	10.0	12.5	12.12	2.98	1	.50	9.23
Brown	2.50	1.75	.08	.45			1.00	1.50	.90	.52	.40	.25	.30	9.65	112	6.75	7.0	10.0	8.33	1.32	2	.45	7.99
Burleson	3.00	2.00	.15	.25			.50	2.00	.40	.20	.50	.50		9.50	100	7.00	6.0	13.0	7.78	1.72	1	.67	8.72
Burnet	3.00	5.00	.25	.50			.50	3.00	1.00	.75	.50	.50		15.00	125	7.00	9.0	10.0	9.65	5.35	1	.80	11.28
Caldwell	3.00	3.00	.20	.50			1.50	2.50	.60	.35	.10	1.00		12.75	140	7.50	8.0	14.0	11.62	1.13	1	.60	8.31
Callahan	1.88	2.75	.05	.50			.75	1.68	.50	.25	.75	.25		9.36	112	6.50	7.0	9.6	7.93	1.43	2	.50	7.79
Camp	1.50	6.00	.25	.20			1.50	1.50	.25	.20	.10	.40		11.90	100	5.50	6.0	10.0	6.10	5.80	1	.50	11.30

TABLE 21.—*Average cost of producing an acre of cotton in 1896 on farms showing a* ***LOSS****, by counties*—Continued.

[Wherever a blank occurs in these tables it means that no expense was incurred.]

TEXAS—Continued.

County.	Rent.	Plowing.	Seed.	Planting seed.	Fertilizers.	Distributing fertilizers.	Chopping and hoeing.	Picking.	Ginning and pressing.	Bagging and ties.	Marketing.	Repairing implements.	Other expenses.	TOTAL COST.	Pounds of lint.	Price per pound.	Bushels of seed.	Price per bushel.	TOTAL RETURN.	LOSS.	Number of farms reporting.	Cost of picking per 100 pounds.	Cost of production per pound.
																Cents.		Cents.					Cents.
Cass	$2.06	$2.94	$0.15	$0.44	$0.81	$0.09	$1.69	$3.62	$1.12	$0.55	$0.61	$0.56	$0.06	$14.70	217	5.75	13.0	10.6	$13.52	$1.18	4	$0.56	6.09
Cherokee	2.50	4.50	.20	.50	......	......	1.50	3.00	.75	.30	.25	.50	.75	14.75	200	6.00	10.0	10.0	13.00	1.75	1	.50	6.88
Coleman	3.00	2.50	.15	.25	......	......	1.00	3.30	1.00	.35	1.00	1.00	.25	13.80	185	6.50	11.0	10.0	13.12	.68	1	.59	6.86
Colorado	4.00	2.67	.22	.33	......	......	1.42	2.13	.74	.23	.58	.33	......	12.65	131	7.17	8.3	11.7	10.28	2.37	3	.54	8.92
Comanche	2.00	1.80	.05	.35	......	......	.75	1.80	.85	.80	.20	.05	.20	8.85	120	6.50	7.0	11.0	8.57	.28	1	.50	6.73
Coryell	2.98	2.25	.10	.33	......	......	1.50	2.25	.70	.25	.50	.55	......	11.41	130	6.50	8.0	10.0	9.25	2.16	2	.58	8.16
Dallas	3.50	3.00	.10	.20	......	......	1.25	2.00	.50	.20	.15	.25	.50	11.65	125	7.00	7.5	10.0	9.50	2.15	1	.53	8.72
Denton	3.00	1.50	.25	.30	......	......	3.00	3.00	.80	.30	.50	.50	......	13.15	200	6.00	10.0	10.0	13.00	.15	1	.50	6.08
Eastland	2.50	2.75	.15	.50	......	......	.75	3.35	1.00	.50	.75	.50	......	12.75	133	6.00	11.0	12.5	9.36	3.39	1	.84	8.55
Ellis	3.50	1.25	.10	.45	......	......	1.00	4.50	.85	.42	.50	.50	.44	13.51	167	6.25	11.0	12.5	11.81	1.70	1	.90	7.27
Erath	3.00	3.00	.15	.60	......	......	1.00	3.00	.75	.25	.50	.50	.50	13.25	168	7.00	11.0	12.5	13.14	.11	1	.60	7.07
Falls	4.00	3.25	.16	.28	......	......	.87	4.75	1.60	.80	.90	.25	......	16.86	190	6.25	13.0	11.5	13.34	3.52	2	.83	8.08
Fannin	4.00	5.00	.15	.75	......	......	1.00	5.00	1.75	.85	.50	2.00	......	21.00	250	6.00	15.0	15.0	17.25	3.75	1	.67	7.50
Fayette	5.00	2.00	.20	.25	......	.75	1.50	2.00	.50	.25	.25	.25	.35	13.30	137	7.00	8.0	12.5	10.59	2.71	1	.49	8.98
Franklin	2.40	4.33	.13	.32	......	......	1.17	2.08	.60	.25	.22	.42	.08	12.00	137	6.67	10.0	10.0	10.17	1.83	3	.51	8.03
Freestone	2.58	3.83	.22	.32	......	......	.92	2.63	1.72	.48	.28	.67	.33	13.98	178	6.22	10.7	15.6	12.74	1.24	3	.49	6.92
Goliad	3.50	7.50	.50	.50	......	......	1.00	4.80	1.50	.75	1.00	1.00	2.00	24.05	300	6.00	20.0	20.0	22.00	2.05	1	.53	6.68
Gonzales	3.16	2.66	.17	.27	......	......	.75	3.00	1.00	.38	1.27	.37	.57	13.60	192	6.46	11.7	10.3	13.36	.24	3	.52	6.45
Grayson	2.50	3.00	.07	.20	......	......	1.00	2.50	.65	.20	.15	.25	......	10.52	133	7.00	8.0	12.5	10.31	.21	1	.63	7.16
Grimes	3.00	5.00	.15	.15	......	......	1.00	2.00	.50	.25	.50	.05	1.00	13.60	125	6.25	12.0	15.0	9.61	3.99	1	.53	9.44
Hamilton	2.06	3.50	.08	.27	......	......	.65	1.73	.77	.44	.40	.93	.50	11.33	132	6.67	8.3	10.7	9.55	1.78	3	.44	7.91
Harris	3.00	3.37	.36	.48	2.00	.62	1.00	3.00	.88	.45	.80	.25	......	16.21	174	7.50	10.0	12.5	14.31	1.90	2	.57	8.60
Harrison	1.69	3.25	.15	.22	.50	.12	1.06	2.44	.99	.41	.61	.38	.33	12.15	158	6.25	9.8	11.8	11.00	1.15	4	.51	6.96
Hays	3.00	4.00	.30	.50	......	......	2.50	3.75	1.22	.65	1.50	.25	1.00	18.67	250	6.50	16.0	15.0	18.65	.02	1	.50	6.51
Henderson	2.25	3.68	.15	.32	......	......	.88	1.42	.52	.18	.85	.30	.12	10.67	129	6.00	7.5	10.0	8.49	2.18	2	.37	7.69
Hill	3.50	2.87	.15	.38	......	......	.62	2.22	.54	.35	.60	.18	.08	11.49	149	6.90	9.5	10.0	11.27	.22	2	.50	7.07
Hood	4.00	.75	.10	.25	......	......	.38	.50	.48	.22	.20	.25	.30	7.43	100	6.00	6.0	20.0	7.20	.23	1	.17	6.23
Hopkins	2.75	4.25	.22	.12	.50	.50	2.00	2.18	.63	.28	.22	.65	.12	14.42	142	6.75	9.5	12.2	10.84	3.58	2	.51	9.34
Houston	2.50	2.75	.15	.18	1.50	.42	1.67	2.37	.68	.31	.75	.42	.58	14.28	158	6.50	10.0	9.3	11.11	3.17	3	.50	8.45
Jack	2.25	1.75	.10	.20	......	......	.62	1.25	.40	.19	.15	.42	.25	7.58	104	6.25	6.5	12.2	7.32	.26	2	.40	6.53
Johnson	3.25	2.50	.28	.25	......	......	1.37	3.62	.65	.27	.18	.25	......	12.62	162	6.50	10.5	11.5	11.78	.84	2	.74	7.04
Lamar	4.00	3.83	.27	.25	.33	.17	2.08	3.67	1.03	.75	1.42	.55	1.08	19.43	198	7.33	14.0	13.2	16.11	3.32	3	.62	8.88
Lavaca	4.00	7.50	.20	.50	......	......	.85	3.50	1.10	.40	1.00	.40	......	19.45	235	7.00	11.0	15.0	18.10	1.35	1	.50	7.57
Lee	3.00	3.00	.25	.30	......	......	.50	3.00	.50	.25	.25	.50	......	11.55	125	7.00	9.0	12.0	9.83	1.72	1	.80	8.38

Leon	2.29	3.22	.20	.23	.58	.13	1.64	2.47	1.02	.34	.73	.75	......	13.60	179	6.33	10.2	9.8	12.15	1.45	6	.46	7.04
Limestone	2.67	4.16	.30	.30	......	......	1.33	2.56	.76	.28	.58	.42	......	13.36	168	6.33	10.3	11.3	11.80	1.56	3	.51	7.26
McLennan	3.63	2.52	.12	.30	......	......	.82	1.78	.52	.22	.19	.38	.40	10.88	121	6.50	8.8	12.1	8.96	1.92	4	.49	8.12
Madison	3.00	3.25	.15	.33	......	......	1.67	2.42	.72	.37	.71	.12	.27	13.01	169	6.33	11.0	10.0	11.92	1.09	3	.48	7.05
Marion	1.50	4.00	.13	.25	......	......	1.50	1.25	.45	.25	.25	1.00	.40	10.98	100	6.50	6.0	13.5	7.31	3.67	1	.42	10.17
Mills	2.00	2.00	.10	.35	......	......	.50	2.00	.65	.25	.50	.25	1.00	9.60	125	6.50	4.0	10.0	8.52	1.08	1	.53	7.36
Montague	2.50	.87	.20	.28	......	......	1.25	2.25	.72	.28	.50	1.00	.50	10.35	116	6.50	8.0	12.5	8.44	1.91	2	.65	8.06
Montgomery	3.00	3.50	.50	.50	......	......	2.50	3.50	1.75	.75	3.00	.50	.50	20.00	250	6.50	18.0	8.0	17.69	2.31	1	.47	7.42
Nacogdoches	1.92	3.00	.15	.25	......	......	1.00	1.72	.55	.33	.25	.30	.35	9.82	144	6.00	9.0	10.0	9.51	.31	2	.40	6.19
Navarro	3.00	3.00	.15	.25	......	......	1.00	2.00	.50	.25	.20	.15	......	10.50	135	6.00	13.0	8.0	9.14	1.36	1	.49	7.01
Newton	3.00	5.25	.35	.50	3.00	.75	1.25	7.50	1.50	.90	3.60	2.00	......	29.60	395	6.88	20.0	15.0	23.98	5.62	1	.82	8.72
Palo Pinto	2.00	3.50	.10	.50	......	......	.75	2.25	.65	.25	.75	......	......	10.75	140	6.30	8.0	10.0	9.62	1.13	1	.54	7.11
Panola	1.62	3.45	.16	.18	......	......	1.38	2.10	.49	.20	.45	.30	.08	10.41	134	6.25	8.0	9.2	9.01	1.40	2	.52	7.22
Polk	3.25	5.00	.20	.18	1.00	.12	1.50	5.00	1.63	.82	.38	.75	.25	20.08	275	6.00	16.0	10.0	18.16	1.98	2	.61	6.72
Raines	2.32	1.00	.12	.17	......	......	1.75	2.18	.20	.11	.40	.20	.50	8.95	125	6.50	8.0	10.0	8.92	.03	1	.58	6.52
Red River	2.23	4.16	.17	.33	......	......	2.50	2.42	.82	.37	.50	.83	.33	14.66	153	7.00	7.3	10.0	11.42	3.24	3	.53	9.10
Robertson	3.12	5.00	.25	.38	......	......	.75	3.43	.96	.33	.55	.20	.12	15.09	200	6.75	11.0	9.5	14.47	.62	2	.57	7.02
Runnels	3.50	2.50	.10	.12	......	......	.95	3.00	.75	.35	.50	.25	......	12.02	166	6.50	10.0	10.0	11.79	.23	1	.60	6.64
Rusk	2.45	3.92	.17	.38	......	......	1.25	2.50	.83	.30	.30	.50	.30	12.90	175	6.08	10.0	9.0	11.59	1.31	3	.48	6.86
Sabine	3.50	3.75	.28	.58	......	......	1.50	3.50	1.07	.40	.62	1.00	......	16.20	182	6.25	11.0	11.0	12.58	3.62	2	.64	8.24
San Augustine	2.70	3.56	.17	.47	......	......	.92	2.67	.88	.40	.75	.17	.33	13.02	175	5.92	10.7	7.7	11.09	1.93	3	.51	6.97
San Saba	2.98	2.33	.07	.38	.17	.08	1.17	1.47	.83	.41	.68	.15	.43	11.15	122	6.50	8.3	11.7	8.78	2.37	3	.40	8.34
Shackelford	2.00	3.50	.15	.50	......	......	2.00	3.60	1.00	.35	.25	.50	......	13.85	200	6.00	11.0	11.5	13.26	.59	1	.60	6.30
Smith	2.34	3.00	.18	.25	......	......	1.33	1.87	.60	.29	.25	.35	.87	11.33	143	6.67	8.7	10.7	10.41	.92	3	.44	7.27
Somervell	3.00	1.25	.12	.23	......	......	.30	1.61	.45	.19	.56	.50	......	8.15	107	6.50	6.0	12.5	7.70	.45	1	.50	6.92
Tarrant	3.00	3.00	.10	.24	......	......	1.09	2.20	.89	.24	.29	.28	.10	11.43	139	6.83	9.3	12.5	10.63	.80	3	.53	7.39
Titus	3.00	2.94	.17	.24	......	......	2.25	2.75	.87	.32	.56	.59	.30	13.99	179	6.56	10.8	10.8	12.42	1.57	4	.51	7.16
Travis	3.00	1.50	.10	.25	......	......	.40	2.00	.90	.50	.50	1.00	2.00	12.15	150	7.00	12.0	10.0	11.70	.45	1	.44	7.30
Trinity	2.50	1.00	.25	.75	2.00	.75	1.00	2.00	.65	.40	.75	......	......	12.05	150	6.00	8.0	12.5	10.06	2.05	1	.44	7.37
Tyler	3.50	4.09	.20	.21	1.38	.31	1.44	4.25	1.12	.56	.34	.38	.56	18.34	225	6.31	13.5	13.8	16.17	2.17	4	.63	7.32
Van Zandt	1.96	4.65	.05	.25	.25	.33	1.25	2.62	.75	.27	.25	.75	......	13.38	175	6.50	15.0	10.0	12.88	.50	1	.50	6.79
Victoria	3.00	2.00	.15	1.50	4.00	2.00	1.50	4.00	1.06	.50	1.50	......	......	21.21	266	7.00	16.0	12.5	20.62	.59	1	.50	7.22
Walker	3.00	5.00	.10	.25	......	......	2.00	2.33	.73	.54	.75	1.00	......	15.70	160	6.25	10.7	10.8	11.18	4.52	2	.49	9.09
Waller	2.50	3.00	.30	.50	3.00	1.00	1.00	4.00	.90	.60	......	.50	......	17.30	250	6.00	15.0	10.0	16.50	.80	1	.53	6.32
Washington	4.00	2.50	.37	.18	1.00	.50	2.00	3.50	.92	.38	.16	.50	.25	16.26	208	6.75	13.5	13.5	15.93	.33	2	.56	6.91
Wilbarger	2.00	1.50	.12	.25	......	......	.75	4.50	.80	.45	1.00	1.00	.50	12.87	167	6.50	10.0	15.0	12.36	.51	1	.90	6.81
Williamson	4.50	1.50	.15	.15	......	......	.75	1.80	.60	.20	.25	.50	1.00	11.40	150	6.50	10.0	12.5	11.00	.40	1	.40	6.77
Wilson	2.50	3.00	.25	.50	.25	......	2.00	5.00	1.15	.60	1.50	1.00	1.00	18.75	250	6.00	16.7	15.0	17.50	1.25	1	.67	6.50
Wise	3.00	1.67	.11	.24	......	......	.65	2.10	.61	23	.16	.20	.92	9.89	117	6.75	7.5	13.2	8.83	1.06	3	.60	7.61
Wood	2.95	3.75	.16	.26	......	......	1.75	2.94	.92	41	.47	.51	1.13	15.25	194	6.56	11.1	10.0	13.71	1.54	4	.51	7.29

VIRGINIA.

															Cents.		Cents.					Cents.
Greenesville	$2.00	$4.50	$0.30	$0.25	$1.00	$0.17	$1.00	$0.90	$0.40	$0.16	$0.50	$0.10	$0.10	$11.38	100	7.00	6.0	10.0	$7.60	$3.78	1	$0.30	10.80
Mecklenburg	2.25	4.00	.35	50	2.12	.50	.62	2.75	1.48	.75	.38	.12	.15	15.97	164	7.00	11.0	11.8	12.74	3.23	2	.56	8.95
Southampton	5.00	5.00	.25	25	6.00	.20	3.00	3.60	1.00	.70	......	.25	......	25.25	300	7.00	20.0	12.5	23.50	1.75	1	.40	7.58

O

www.ingramcontent.com/pod-product-compliance
Lightning Source LLC
Chambersburg PA
CBHW021949160426
43195CB00011B/1297

* 9 7 8 3 3 3 7 7 7 5 3 1 5 *